GW01606023

The Covenant Chain

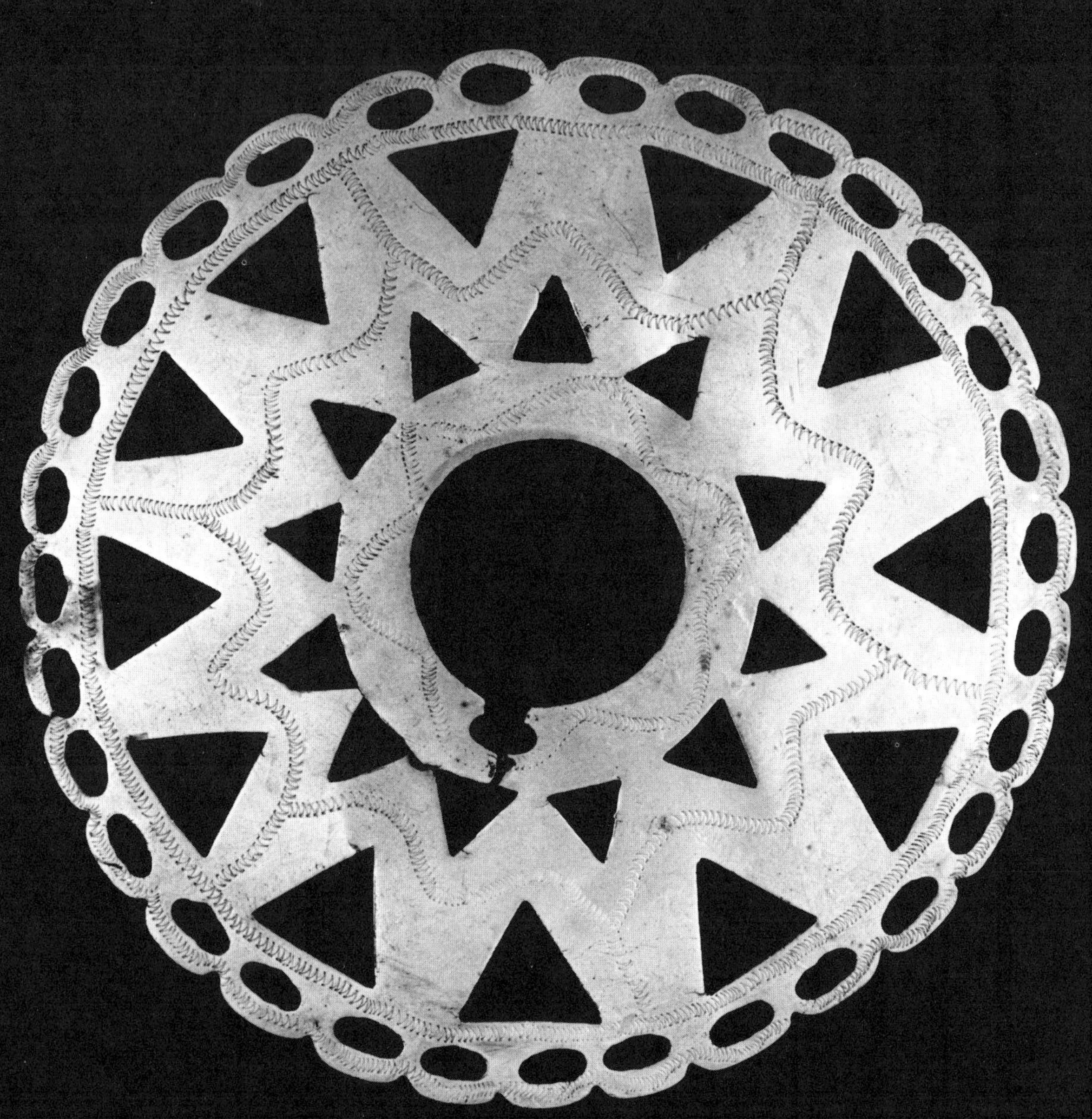

The Covenant Chain

INDIAN CEREMONIAL AND TRADE SILVER

THE COVENANT CHAIN BY N. JAYE FREDRICKSON

CATALOGUE OF THE EXHIBITION BY SANDRA GIBB

A TRAVELLING EXHIBITION OF THE NATIONAL MUSEUM OF MAN

NATIONAL MUSEUMS OF CANADA / OTTAWA

PUBLISHED BY
the National Museum of Man
National Museums of Canada
Ottawa, Canada K1A 0M8

CATALOGUE NO.: NM92-73/1980E

DISTRIBUTED IN
THE UNITED STATES,
CENTRAL AND SOUTH AMERICA,
AUSTRALIA, NEW ZEALAND
AND SOUTHEAST ASIA BY:
The University of Chicago Press
5801 South Ellis Avenue
Chicago, Illinois 60637

HARD COVER: ISBN 0-660-10347-8
SOFT COVER: ISBN 0-660-10348-6

ÉDITION FRANÇAISE
La chaîne d'alliance:
l'orfèvrerie de traite et
de cérémonie chez les Indiens
RELIÉ: ISBN 0-660-90261-3
BROCHÉ: ISBN 0-660-90262-1

PRINTED IN CANADA

STAFF EDITOR
Viviane Appleton

PHOTOGRAPHS OF ARTIFACTS
Richard Garner

TYPESETTING
Mono Lino Typesetting Co. Ltd.

PRINTING
Thorn Press Ltd.

DESIGN
Frank Newfeld

FRONTISPIECE
126 Silver Brooch

CONTENTS

FOREWORD

CONTRARY TO THE WIDELY HELD BELIEF, silversmithing in Canada in the late eighteenth century depended more on the requirements of the fur trade than on those of the Church. The high visibility of surviving ecclesiastical silver leaves the impression that without Church patronage the Canadian silver craft might not have survived New France's transition to British control after 1763. The importance of Church patronage is not to be minimized, but what really held the silver craft together was the sizeable orders for Indian trade silver that the North West Company and independent fur traders placed with Montreal and Quebec silversmiths. While this knowledge is not new, it is only in recent years that the extent and importance of the work done by colonial silversmiths for the fur trade have been properly evaluated. This catalogue demonstrates the diversity and quantity of the silver ornaments made for the fur trade. It also describes the key role silver played in Indian–white relations during the period of exploration.

In the period 1750–1830, individual orders placed with the Montreal and Quebec silversmiths by the fur traders ranged in value from a few hundred Pounds to several thousand Pounds Sterling, and the pieces made numbered in the tens of thousands. Gorgets, armbands, spoon lockets, Luckenbooth-type brooches, ear-bobs, ear-wheels, small and large crosses, wristbands and many other items were made to please the Indians. The quantity that was produced is astounding. For example, Robert Cruickshank, a Montreal silversmith, had as many as five apprentices devoting much of their time to fashioning trade silver.

In volume and value, trade silver was essential to the survival of the silversmiths. Nevertheless, most of them were forced to run other businesses as well to eke out a livelihood. Cruickshank operated a large hardware business in Montreal, and others worked as watch-makers or clock-makers, gunsmiths or merchants, and even wigmakers.

The quantity of material produced by the silversmiths indicates how important the silver ornaments were in the Indian culture, as furs could just as easily have been traded for blankets, muskets or clothing. Not only did the market for trade silver bolster a faltering craft in Quebec in the late eighteenth century, it introduced a new element in the rich material culture of the eastern North American Indians.

This exhibition and its catalogue shed new light on a previously unexplored aspect of the fur trade in North America. In presenting a different perspective on eighteenth-century Canadian silversmiths, we can see the far-reaching implications of the fur trade. Also revealed are the close links between the sophisticated colonial craft of silversmithing and the evolving material culture of the North American Indian.

ACKNOWLEDGEMENTS

INDIAN TRADE SILVER is part of our cultural heritage—a fascinating product of the interaction between two profoundly different cultures. But only a few scholars and collectors have known much about it. The exhibition and this book are intended to introduce many more people to this unique art form. We hope that it will capture their imagination as it has captured ours.

The idea for an exhibition of Indian trade silver was proposed by Barbara Tyler, then of the National Museum of Man, whose encouragement was instrumental in the mounting of a major exhibition and in adding significantly to our knowledge of native material culture.

Although exhibitions are normally the product of longstanding research projects, this one generated a burst of research in an area of material culture that had been investigated only sporadically since the 1920s. Among the early scholars who studied trade silver were the late Marius Barbeau, of the National Museum of Canada, and the American anthropologist Arthur Woodward. By using their unpublished research notes, we were able to compile information on the silver and locate collections of it in various institutions. We owe these pioneers a great deal.

The History Division of the National Museum of Man, and in particular Jean Friesen, gave valuable guidance in the early stages of research. Archives and museums across North America opened their collections to us as we pieced together the unusual story of trade silver. Considerable advice and assistance on the ethnographic content came from the staff of the Canadian Ethnology Service of the National Museum of Man, particularly Ted. J. Brasser.

For the preparation of the catalogue, we are particularly indebted to Viviane Appleton for her skilful editing of the manuscript and to Louise L. Trahan for her work on the French edition. Through their efforts, the exhibition will have a permanent record. That record has been enhanced by the painstaking work of Richard Garner in photographing the silver. For the presentation, we are indebted to the talents of book designer Frank Newfeld.

The task of preparing for display the artifacts that came to us from numerous lending institutions fell on the Canadian Conservation Institute. We are especially indebted to Valerie Free for her conscientious and careful work. Every care has been taken to ensure that the silver will be shown in a way that is pleasing to the visitor and safe for the objects. For that we must thank the designer of the exhibition, Luc Matter, and the conservators at the Canadian Conservation Institute, especially John H. Grant and Charles E. S. Hett.

It took a lot of people to put together an exhibition of this size and complexity. They have all earned our heartfelt thanks for generously sharing their skills and expertise with us.

N. Jaye Fredrickson
Winnipeg

Sandra Gibb
National Museum of Man
Ottawa

THE COVENANT CHAIN

THE COVENANT CHAIN is the symbol of a pledge of friendship. Historically, it represented Indian–European alliances in seventeenth- and eighteenth-century New England and New York. Symbolically, it has come to mean much more.

The tradition of the Covenant Chain originated in the early contacts between Dutch colonists and the River Indians of the Hudson River region. As early as 1618, they formed an alliance, described symbolically as a Dutch ship tied to a tree, first with a rope and later with an iron chain. The rope represented an alliance of equals; iron underscored its strength. Although the Mohawks superseded the River Indians and the British displaced the Dutch, the Covenant Chain remained the symbol of political alliance in the region. The iron chain was further refined in ceremonial discourse, and by the early eighteenth century had become a silver chain. Silver is more durable and more beautiful than iron, and thus enhances the significance of the covenant.

Periodic renewal of the covenant was necessary. Formal meetings were held between partners to discuss the details of military support, trade arrangements and land use as Indian and European struggled to control the region. Gifts of wampum, silver, weapons, furs and tools were exchanged as tokens of good will. This became known, in the days of the British–Iroquois covenant as "brightening the Covenant Chain".

The Covenant Chain alliances ended with the imposition of European colonial government in Indian territories and subjugation of the Indians to colonial rule. There could be no covenant where there was no equality.

But the Covenant Chain continues to symbolize elements of this early cultural exchange that are often lost in modern interpretation. Indians and Europeans met and bargained as equals, pledged friendship, and exchanged not only trinkets but knowledge, skills and tools that were useful to life in North America. They adopted some of each other's way of life. They evolved a commerce, neither wholly Indian nor wholly European, that profoundly influenced the future development of North America.

I / THE FUR TRADE: ITS CULTURAL SIGNIFICANCE

IN NORTH AMERICA, a pledge of friendship between Indians and Europeans was a solemn event, and gifts were exchanged to express good will. The Indians offered beaver and other furs to the first explorers, as they had to the fishermen that preceded them, receiving clothing and jewellery in return. As the materials of each culture became valued by the other through incorporation into existing cultural patterns, the encounters multiplied. From these early diplomatic exchanges between white and Indian peoples grew the fur trade that so profoundly affected North American native life.

The fur trade was crucial to the exploration and settlement of the entire continent. Traders, in their quest for the furs that were proving so popular in Europe during the seventeenth and eighteenth centuries, were drawn farther and farther inland. Early settlement, dependent upon the communications established by the fur trade, followed its routes. In the seventeenth century, the importance of river transportation in bringing trade goods inland and furs out determined that Canadian development would be most intense along the banks of its main waterway, the St. Lawrence River system. As furs grew scarce in eastern Canada towards the end of the eighteenth century, traders expanded west and north, establishing a network of forts along other major waterways. Into these areas, settlement soon followed.

Cultural contact brought great change to the Indians who inhabited the New World. The pre-contact subsistence economies based on various combinations of hunting, fishing and agriculture were disrupted by the growing trade with Europeans. As it became easier to obtain implements, clothing and other items in exchange for furs than to produce these things themselves, the Indians devoted more and more time to procuring furs. Not only was the technology and material culture of the North American Indian markedly altered, but social organization was modified to meet the new needs of trade, and cultural values were adjusted to accommodate the new situation. Certainly, the effects of contact with Europeans were profound.

In considering the impact of the fur trade on the Indians and on North

American history, however, an important aspect is often neglected. The fur trade as we understand it today developed from mutual exchanges between two different and well-developed cultural systems. It was therefore shaped by both contributing cultures. The essential creativity of acculturation produced a system neither wholly European nor wholly Indian but an integration of the two. While the European contribution to this process has been recognized, the Indian contribution has received less attention. Yet, elements of Indian culture significantly influenced both the conduct of the North American fur trade and the kinds of goods bartered. Trade silver is a product of these influences.

The Indians' contribution to the form of the fur trade stemmed from their highly developed system of gift exchange. In the sixteenth century, the peoples of the East Coast and the Great Lakes region considered the exchange of gifts a significant part of social and political relations. Leaders bestowed gifts on their followers to confirm allegiance. Parents received gifts during the naming ceremony of their child. Marriages and deaths were occasions of generous gift-giving. In each case the presents carried messages of more import than any verbal exchange.

The most important exchange of gifts occurred in relations between tribes or confederacies. Perpetual intertribal warfare and the consequent preoccupation with security had led the Indians to develop elaborate procedures for forming alliances and sealing agreements. The beaver pelt, wampum belt, calumet and hatchet used in alliance ceremonies contained messages beyond their material utility. Wampum belts bore designs of war or peace. The hatchet was a symbol of war, which when buried signified the end of conflict. When a treaty was made, the exchange of beaver and wampum was in itself stronger than the words spoken.

Europeans in early contact with aborigines all along the eastern coast of North America found it necessary to comply with this custom. Although somewhat surprised at the Indians' insistence on receiving something in return for their gifts, newcomers must soon have learned the consequences of withholding a reciprocal offering. By exchanging gifts with various tribes to cement alliances, the Spanish, Dutch, French and English became involved in the many conflicts of the Indian wars, and at the same time acquired allies in their own struggles for the control of North America. One of the strongest and most enduring alliances in this many-faceted power struggle was that negotiated between Britain and the Iroquois, or the Five (later Six) Nation Confederacy. A powerful ally of the Dutch in their war against the French, the Iroquois had effectively fought the Huron Indians – their traditional enemy and ally of the French. The Iroquois' subsequent military alliance with the British was also an important factor in the British–French conflict. Only recently have historians begun to assess to what extent alliances with the Indians affected the outcome of European rivalries in North America.

The Covenant Chain is a significant element of this network of alliances. Originating in agreements between the Dutch and their Indian allies in North America, it later became an important symbol of the British–Iroquois alliance during the eighteenth century. On 24 June 1755, Sir William Johnson, British superintendent of Indian affairs in colonial New York, assured the confederate council of the Six Nations at Mount Johnson, New York, of the strength of the Covenant Chain.

> You well know and these Books testifie that it is now almost 100 years since your Forefathers and ours became known to each other. That upon our first acquaintance we shook hands and finding we should be useful to one another, entered into a covenant of Brotherly love and mutual friendship. And tho' we were at first only tied together by a Rope, yet lest this Rope should grow Rotten and break, we tied ourselves together by an iron Chain – lest time and accident might rust and destroy this Chain of iron, we afterwards made one of Silver; the strength and brightness of which would be subject to no decay. The ends of this Silver chain we fixt to the immoveable mountains, and this in so firm a manner, that the hands of no mortal Enemy might be able to remove it. All this my Bretheren you know to be Truth; you know also that this Covenant Chain of love and friendship was the dread and envy of all your Enemies and ours, that by keeping it bright and unbroken, we have never spilt in anger one drop of each other's blood to this day. You well know also that from the beginning to this time we have almost every year strengthened and brightened this Covenant Chain in the most publick & solemn manner.*

***Documents Relative to the Colonial History of the State of New York* (Albany, N.Y.: Weed, Parsons, Printers, 1855), vol. 6, pp. 969–70.

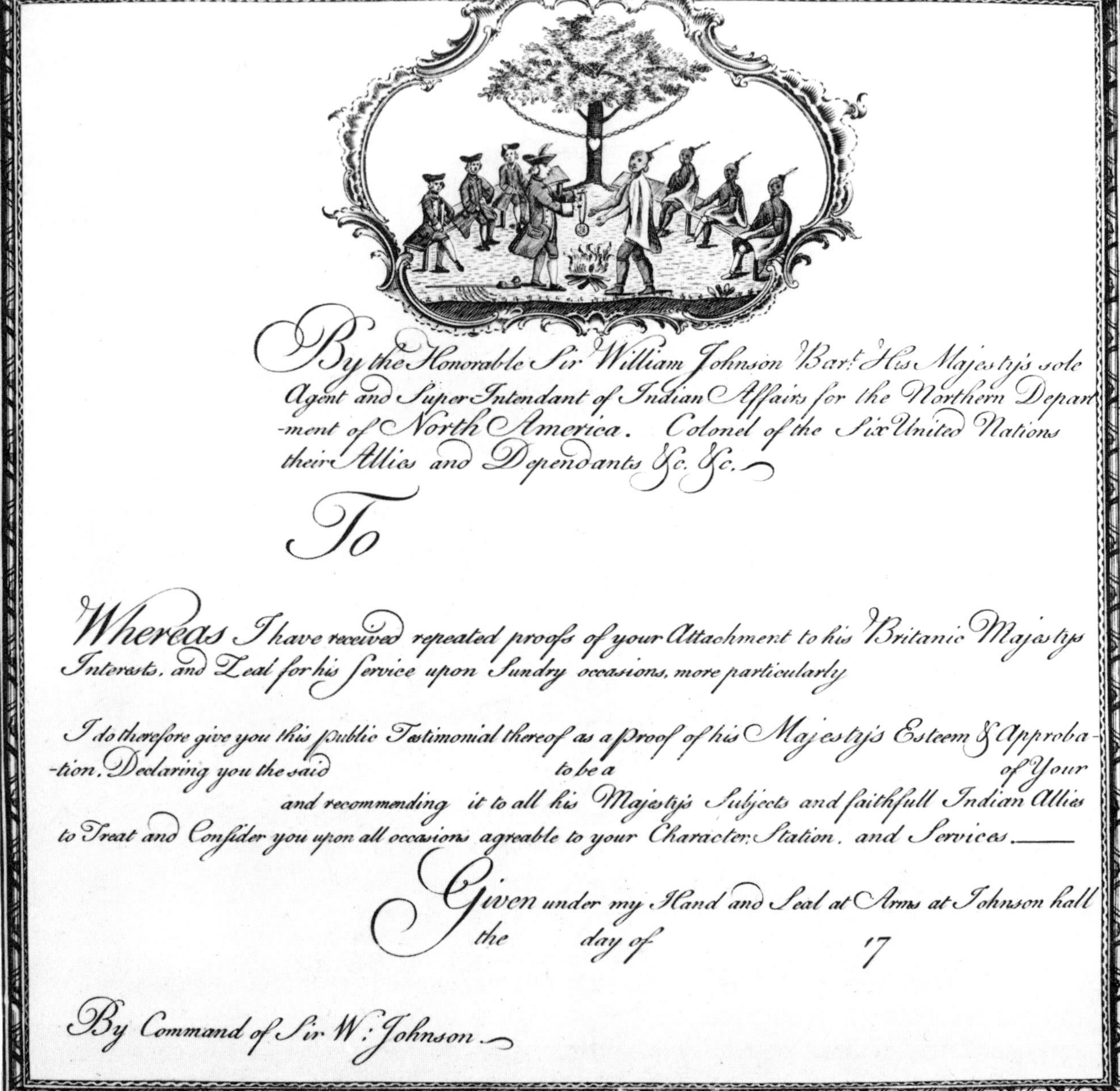

By the Honorable Sir William Johnson Bar.t His Majesty's sole Agent and Super Intendant of Indian Affairs for the Northern Depart-ment of North America. Colonel of the Six United Nations their Allies and Dependants &c. &c.

To

Whereas I have received repeated proofs of your Attachment to his Britanic Majestys Interests, and Zeal for his Service upon Sundry occasions, more particularly

I do therefore give you this publick Testimonial thereof as a proof of his Majesty's Esteem & Approba-tion, Declaring you the said to be a of Your and recommending it to all his Majesty's Subjects and faithfull Indian Allies to Treat and Consider you upon all occasions agreable to your Character, Station, and Services.

Given under my Hand and Seal at Arms at Johnson hall the day of 17

By Command of Sir W: Johnson.

It was in this context of brightening the Covenant Chain that the Iroquois and the British conducted their early transactions. To the British, the fur trade was a commercial venture, but, to the Indians, trade was carried out within the context of political relations. As one Iroquois spokesman is reported to have explained it in 1735, "Trade and Peace we take to be one thing."* Economic life was an integral part of social relations.

Diplomatic ceremony continued to characterize the fur trade even after the economic significance of the trade surpassed its symbolic value in the eyes of the European participants. A typical eighteenth-century trading ceremony at a Hudson's Bay Company fort contained all the elements of the earlier diplomatic negotiations. Upon arrival at the fort, the Indians exchanged salutatory gunshots with the English. Factor and chief exchanged greetings and assured one another of their good will and readiness to trade. Then the factor outfitted the chief in elaborate European clothing, and gave his lieutenant another less fancy costume. Food, tobacco, brandy and rum were distributed, and two or three days of revelry ensued. At the close of this merriment, the league of friendship was renewed when Englishman joined Indian in the smoking of the calumet. Having affirmed peace, friendship and brotherly love, they moved on to the trade of "good goods", quality being considered another sign of affection between the two groups. Elements of

*Quoted in Abraham Rotstein, "Trade and Politics: an Institutional Approach", *Western Canadian Journal of Anthropology*, vol. 3, no. 1 (1972), p. 14.

1

Documents of commission like this one were issued by Sir William Johnson, British superintendent of northern Indians for colonial New York in the second half of the eighteenth century. They were presented to influential Indian leaders, making them "gorget captains" or "great medal chiefs". Many of the recipients had already served in the British army with the rank of captain, and when he issued their commissions. Johnson was trying to obtain back-pay for his Indian officers.

The engraving at the top of the commission pictures an Indian and an Englishman standing under a European depiction of the Iroquois Tree of Peace. From the tree hangs the Silver Chain of Friendship – the Covenant Chain. Across the council fire, the Englishman presents a medal to the Indian.

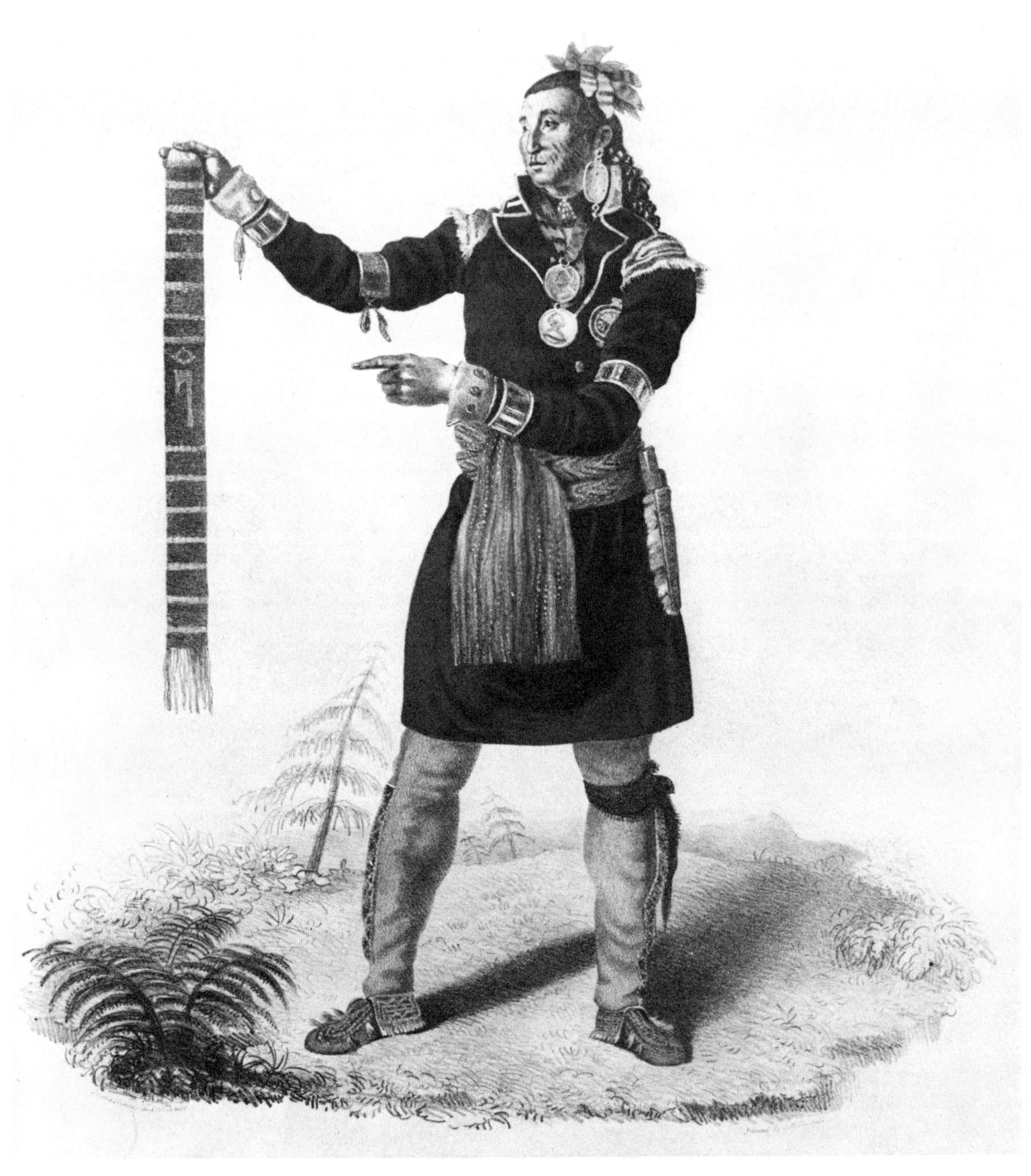

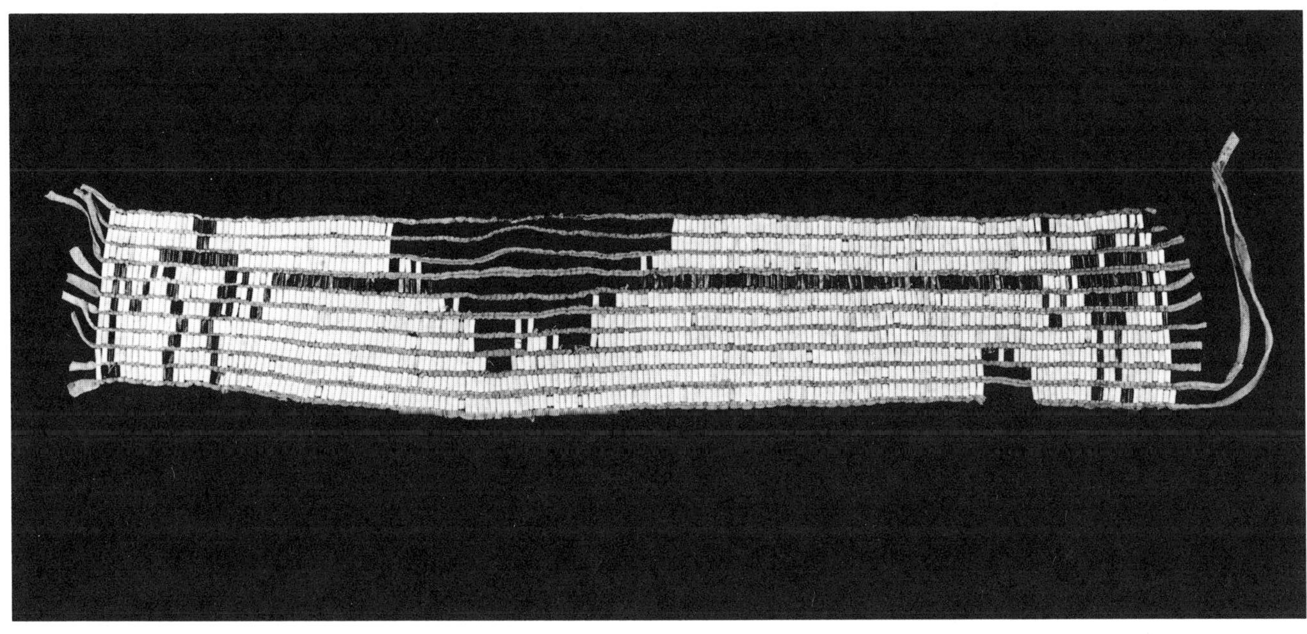

2

Nicholas Vincent Isawanhonhi,
a Huron Chief

Wampum belts such as the one held by Isawanhonhi in this portrait were an important diplomatic symbol in the culture of the Woodland Indians long before the coming of Europeans. Messages were woven into the pattern formed by the coloured shell beads. Not only war and peace, but birth, marriage and death were recorded in this way, and the belts presented to mark the occasion.

3

In this wampum belt, the silver chain of friendship, as the Covenant Chain was sometimes called, links the Indian on the right and the white man on the left. The belt's exact history is not known, but it was probably used to renew the traditional alliance between the Iroquois and the British.

diplomatic ceremony in the conduct of the fur trade continued into the nineteenth century.

Indian cultural preferences also influenced the kinds of goods Europeans offered in exchange for furs, especially during the highly competitive period up to 1821. Europeans could discern no need for the beads, bells and other trinkets favoured by the Indians; perhaps they were valued for their "decorative, aesthetic, magical, curiosity, or amusement 'value'."* Close attention was paid to the Indians' preferences in colour, design and texture, as well as utility, although the significance of their preferences was not understood. If an Indian wanted stripes and stars on his blankets, the strouds would be duly made in that pattern.

At the same time, European economic necessity dictated the terms of trade to some degree. The cost of the item and the need to make a profit militated against impractical choices. For example, in 1794 the director of the Company of Explorers of the Upper Missouri wrote to Jean-Baptiste Truteau, who was to expand trade upriver to the Mandan villages:

> When he has the opportunity he shall take note of the articles most desired by each nation, this is, bagatelles and things of little value, since it is not desirable to cause them to wish for goods that are dear, and which transportation a long distance will make still more dear.**

In the years from the initial trading contacts between Europeans and Indians in the sixteenth century up to the mid-nineteenth century, many articles of trade met the requirements of both parties. Foodstuffs, such as sugar, tea and flour, and domestic articles, such as brass kettles, iron pots, spoons, scissors, knives and needles, were very popular. New weapons and implements in the form of guns, axes, fishhooks and beaver traps greatly increased the number of animals that could be harvested by a single Indian band. The gun and, for some groups, the horse were responsible for an increase

*Quoted in Wilcomb E. Washburn, "Symbol, Utility and Aesthetics in the Indian Fur Trade", in *Aspects of the Fur Trade: Selected Papers of the 1965 North American Fur Trade Conference* (St. Paul: Minnesota Historical Society, 1967), p. 50.

**Quoted in John Ewers, "The Influence of the Fur Trade upon the Indians of the Northern Plains", in *People and Pelts: Selected Papers of the Second North American Fur Trade Conference,* ed. by Malvina Bolus (Winnipeg: Peguis Publishers, 1972), p. 9.

in the deadliness of intertribal warfare. In addition, ornamentation among the eastern Indians became more elaborate with the introduction of new decorative materials – glass beads, bells, and metal ornaments. Many of these items were readily incorporated into the existing Indian culture.

Thus, to say that the Indian was the victim of a destructive cultural onslaught is an oversimplification, and ignores his role in a two-way encounter. The items the Indians acquired in trade were to some extent determined by their own preferences, and evidence indicates that they were good judges of quality. More importantly, Indians attributed to some articles a significance and utility unforeseen by Europeans. For example, the small mirrors favoured in trade were worn in various ways for personal adornment. On occasion, Indians were even known to fashion ornaments from valued utensils, such as brass kettles, rather than use them for their intended purpose. In this way, trade items, while European in manufacture, might acquire uniquely Indian characteristics. An object removed from one cultural context and successfully incorporated into another demonstrates the creative force of acculturation.

An excellent example of the unique combination of European and Indian influences on the selection of trade goods is the variety of silver ornaments distributed in America. Initially introduced in the form of diplomatic gifts, silver later became a popular item in the commercial trade of the eighteenth and nineteenth centuries. Silver jewellery designed specifically for the fur trade frequently imitated traditional Indian ornaments fashioned in other materials, such as stone, shell and leather. Sometimes jewellery was worn in the European manner, but it was often adapted to the Indians' own distinctive uses. As native demand for silver grew, the Indians learned to fashion articles from the metal themselves. Thus, silversmithing took its place among the arts developed by the mingling of these two cultures.

II / INTRODUCTION OF SILVER TO THE INDIANS

SILVER WAS INTRODUCED to North American Indians in the form of medals. Their first recorded use in European–Indian diplomatic negotiations was the 1661 presentation of silver medals to "friendly Indians" by the colony of Virginia. Medals of silver, brass, copper and pewter were soon widely used to honour an Indian chief or to secure friendly relations with Indian tribes.

Initially, all European powers in North America bestowed upon Indian allies the official medals of their countries. These were struck to commemorate an important event in the life of the monarch or the history of the nation. They bore the head of the reigning monarch on one side and the official coat of arms on the reverse. Charles II medals were issued as early as 1670 to Indians close to the English colonies, and by 1693 the French government was distributing Louis XIV medals in New France. The small number of Spanish medals that have been found among the southern Indians suggests that the Spanish government may have bestowed them less frequently. The earliest-known Spanish medal in North America is a Philip V medal of 1701. It is interesting to note that Russian explorers and traders were also offering silver medals to the Indians of the West Coast. Records indicate that Russian medals were distributed in the eighteenth century, but the earliest surviving medal was issued by Alexander I, who reigned from 1801 to 1825.

Medals bearing the insignia of European nations had great political significance for their Indian owners, and were worn as badges of friendship, not merely as ornaments. Upon deciding to switch support from the English to the French in December 1756, a group made up of Iroquois, Nipissings, Algonquins, Ottawas, Potawatomi and one Oneida chief surrendered their English medals to Vaudreuil. The French leader was quick to replace the English decorations with French medals, thereby confirming acceptance of the new allies. The Spanish, in welcoming former French allies, similarly realized the importance of replacing the tokens of France. When a new monarch came to the throne, Indians were expected to give up their old

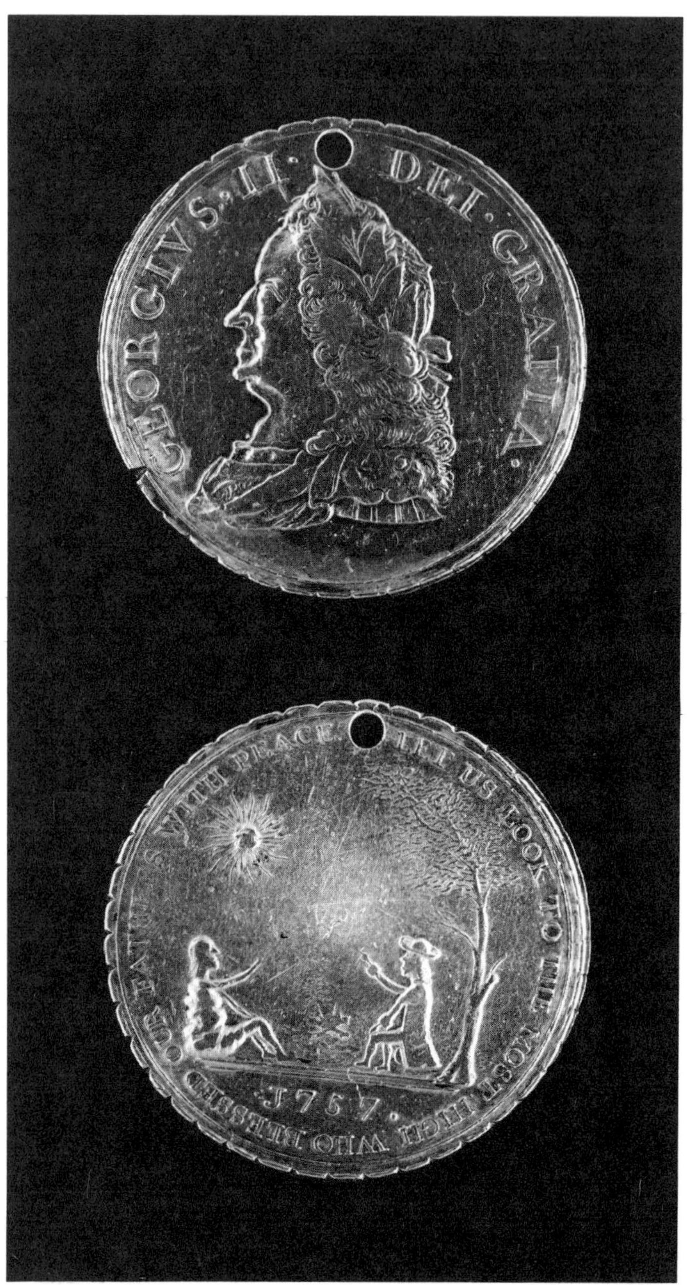

4

In 1757, a Quaker group in Philadelphia requested a special medal be struck for presentation to Indian allies. This group was known as the Friendly Association for Regaining and Preserving Peace with Indians by Pacific Means, and the medal was designed to help them in their cause. It bears the head of George II *of Great Britain.*

Edward Duffield engraved the die, and the Philadelphia silversmith, Joseph Richardson, who was a member of the Society of Friends (Quakers), struck the medals. This popular medal has been found in copper and pewter as well as silver.

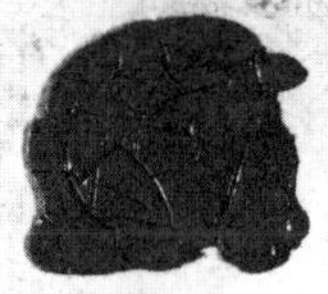

FREDERICK HALDIMAND, *Captain-General and Governor in Chief of the Province of Quebec, &c.&c.&c. General and Commander in Chief of his Majesty's Forces in said Province, and Frontiers, &c.&c.&c.*

To Chawanon Grand Chief of the Folles Avoines

IN consideration of the Fidelity, zeal and attachment, testified by Chawanon Grand Chief of the Folles Avoines to the Kings Government, and by virtue of the power and authority in me vested, I do hereby confirm the said Chawanon Grand Chief of the Folles Avoines aforesaid having bestowed upon him the Great Medal, willing all and singular the Indians, Inhabitants thereof, to obey him as Grand Chief, and all Officers and others in his Majesty's Service to treat him accordingly. GIVEN under my hand and Seal at Arms, at Montreal this Seventeenth Day of August One thousand seven hundred and seventy eight in the Eighteenth Year of the Reign of our Sovereign Lord George the Third, by the Grace of God of Great Britain, France and Ireland King, Defender of the Faith and so Forth

SUR les bons témoignages qui nous ont été rendus de la fidélité, le zèle & l'attachement de Chawanon Grand Chef des Folles Avoines au Gouvernement du Roi ; & en vertu du pouvoir à nous donné, nous l'avons confirmé Grand Chef des Folles Avoines susdit, lui ayant donné la Grande Médaille, Ordonnons à tous Sauvages & autres dudit Village, de l'obéir comme Grand Chef, & à tous nos Officiers & autres au Service de Sa Majesté, d'avoir pour lui les égards dûs à sa qualité de Grand Chef & a la Grande Médaille : en foi de quoi nous avons signé la Présente, à icelle fait apposer le Cachet de nos Armes, & contre-signé par l'un de nos Sécrétaires, à Montréal, ce Dix Septième jour d'Aoust l'année mil sept cent soixante & dix huit

Fred: Haldimand

BY HIS EXCELLENCY'S COMMAND.

E Foy

5

Frederick Haldimand, Captain-General and Governor in Chief of the Province of Quebec, issued certificates of recognition as well as medals to favoured Indians. Most medals were struck in at least three sizes, and the size awarded indicated the recipient's status in European eyes. In the certificate reproduced here, Chawanon, chief of the Folles Avoines (Menomini), was declared a "Grand Chief", and probably received the largest size of George III presentation medal.

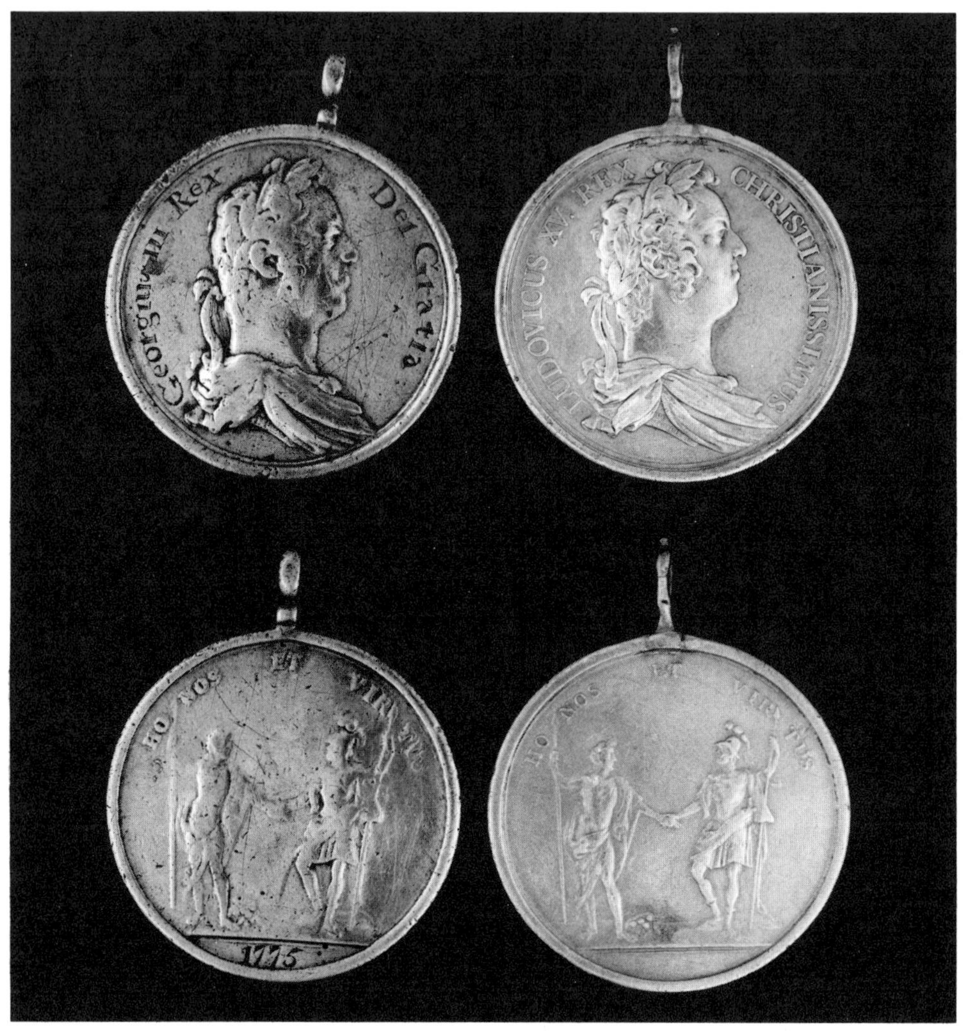

6 *The medal on the right is a standard French medal bearing the head of Louis* XV. *Originally similar, the altered medal on the left was probably presented to an Indian ally by the French prior to the cession of Canada to the British in 1763. At some point during or after the war, the owner of this medal, like many other Indians, switched his support to the British. His French medal was altered by engraving the name of George* III *over that of the French monarch to signify the new alliance.*

medals in exchange for new ones, although quite often they did not. Rather than surrender official medals upon changing an alliance or acknowledging a new monarch, the Indians frequently obliterated insignias, preferring to keep the medal for adornment while destroying its political significance.

As medals became increasingly popular among North American Indians, special medals were struck for presentation exclusively to them. The earliest known was struck in Virginia in 1670 to allow the friendly Indians who received it access to the white settlements. Special Indian medals were soon produced in Europe as well as in the American colonies, although few, if any, appear to have been made in Canada. The medals might or might not bear an official insignia, but always carried some indication of their intended use. One of the best known of these "peace medals" was produced by Joseph Richardson, a Philadelphia silversmith, at the request of the Friendly Association for Preserving Peace with the Indians of Pennsylvania. Struck in 1757, it bears on the obverse the bust of George II, and on the reverse an illustration of a Quaker and an Indian smoking a peace pipe, encircled by the inscription "Let us look to the Most High Who blessed our fathers with peace". The special medals were usually struck in a variety of metals and sizes, the larger silver medals being intended for presentation to greater chiefs and the smaller, less expensive medals to persons of lower rank.

With the growing hostility between the European powers in North America, particularly the French and the British, the role of Indian allies took on added importance, and the amounts and kinds of silver articles presented in alliance ceremonies increased. The silver gorgets worn by British and French officers as decorative vestiges of armour were given to Indian war chiefs. These official gorgets were crescent-shaped and bore the insignia of the monarch. Accompanied by armbands, they were valued by the Indians as a mark of rank and prestige. War leaders thus decorated were given an officer's commission with the rank of captain as well as captain's pay. The commission entitled the officer to military courtesy when in the field with the regular troops and to an honour guard and running fire when he visited a fort. Captain Joseph Brant, whose Mohawk name was Thayendanegea, was a prominent gorget captain in the British army.

In their efforts to win tribal alliances, European governments also gave out quantities of smaller silver items. Brooches, earrings, nose-bobs, armbands, crosses, finger-rings, and circular gorgets, or moons, were distributed as diplomatic largesse.

In the covenants between British and Iroquois, French and Micmac, alliance was always pledged between sovereigns. In accordance with the wishes of the Indians, king always negotiated with king, as happened in 1710, when four Iroquois chiefs, three of them Mohawk, were presented at the English court of Queen Anne by a Dutch American named Schuyler. The English had come to rely quite heavily on their Mohawk allies, who controlled the Richelieu River–Lake Champlain waterway linking the St. Lawrence River with New England. In conflicts with the French on Hudson Bay and along the St. Lawrence, the English had realized the importance not only of the Iroquois' control of the communications network but of their active military aid. In order to bolster Iroquois friendship and solicit increased support in the war, Queen Anne had invited their sachems to England.* The Hudson's Bay Company, indirectly interested in the Mohawk alliance, also entertained the chiefs during their visit.

There was an exchange of gifts to confirm the pledges made at this meeting. The chiefs offered wampum to Queen Anne. In return, she presented a set of Communion silver and furnishings for the chapel that she had ordered built for the Iroquois at Fort Hunter, New York, in 1712. Thus confirmed, the British–Iroquois alliance had considerable impact on subsequent developments in Iroquois history. After the American Revolution, the Iroquois allies left their New York territory to settle on the 768,000 acres along the Grand River provided by the Haldimand treaty of 1784 as compensation for their losses. There they rebuilt Her Majesty's Chapel of the Mohawks. Another group of the Six Nations moved to the Bay of Quinte, settling at Deseronto. The Communion silver, which had been buried during

* Portraits of the four chiefs painted at the time of their visit to Queen Anne's court are in the collection of the Public Archives of Canada, Ottawa.

7 *This engraving of Hendrik, a leading Mohawk sachem of the eighteenth century, illustrates the crescent-shaped military gorget and the ear ornaments worn by Iroquois leaders, who usually also wore silver armbands and legbands. Hendrik carries a pipe-tomahawk, a symbol of peace and alliance like the silver presentation ornaments. In later years the pipe-tomahawk became a popular trade item, manufactured by whites specifically for the fur trade.*

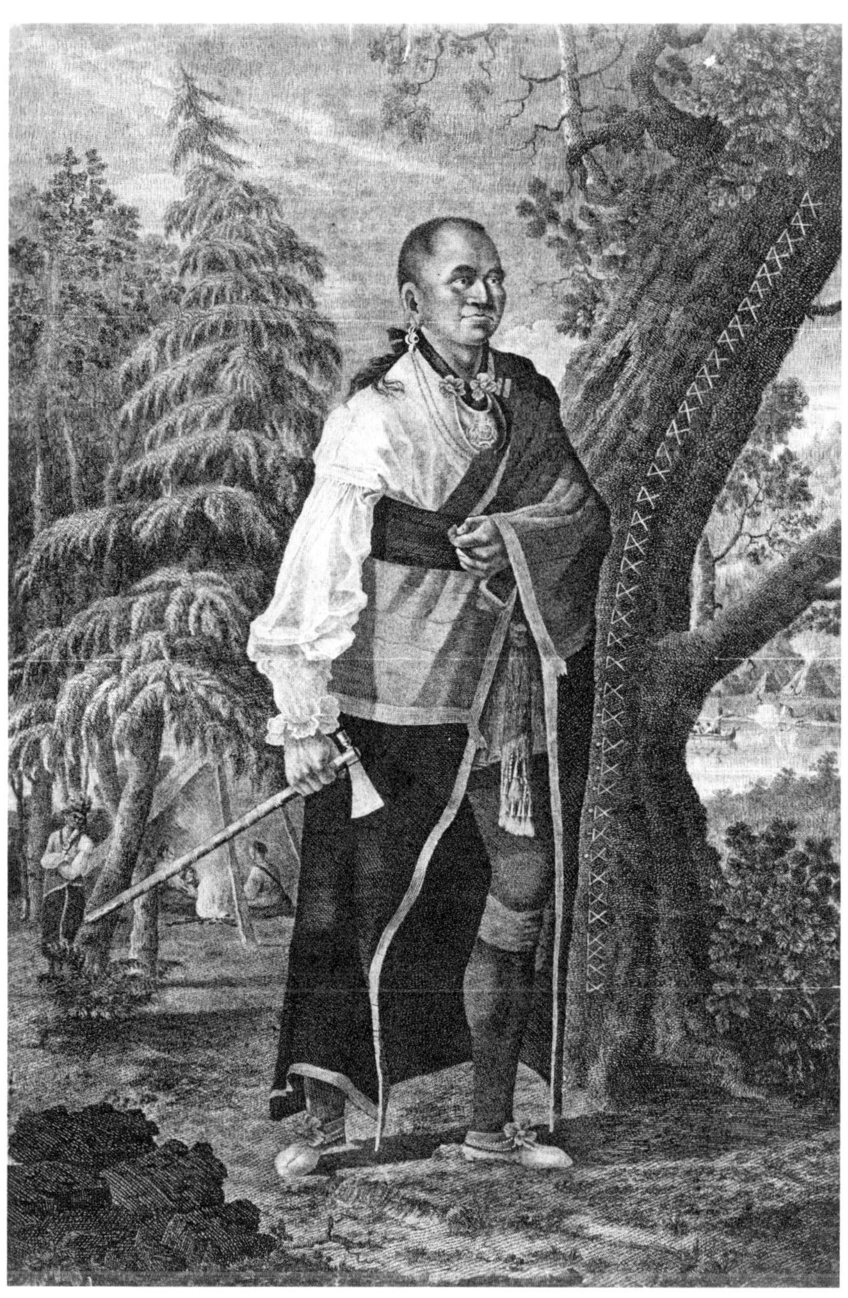

29

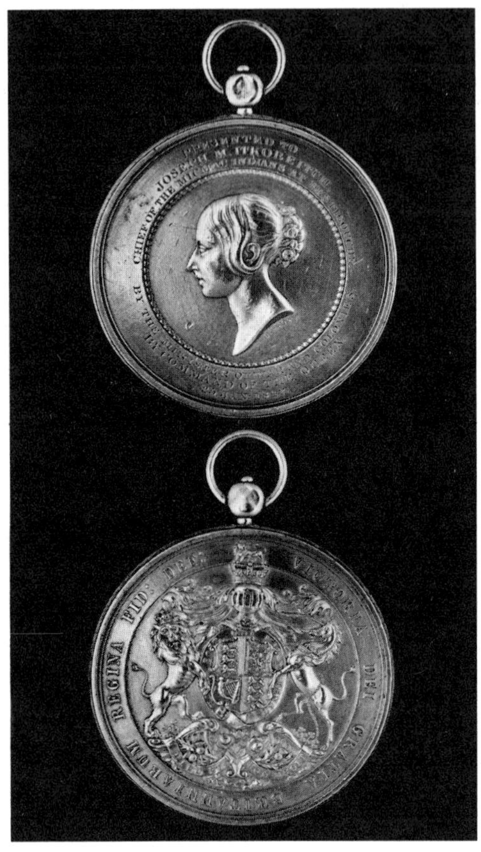

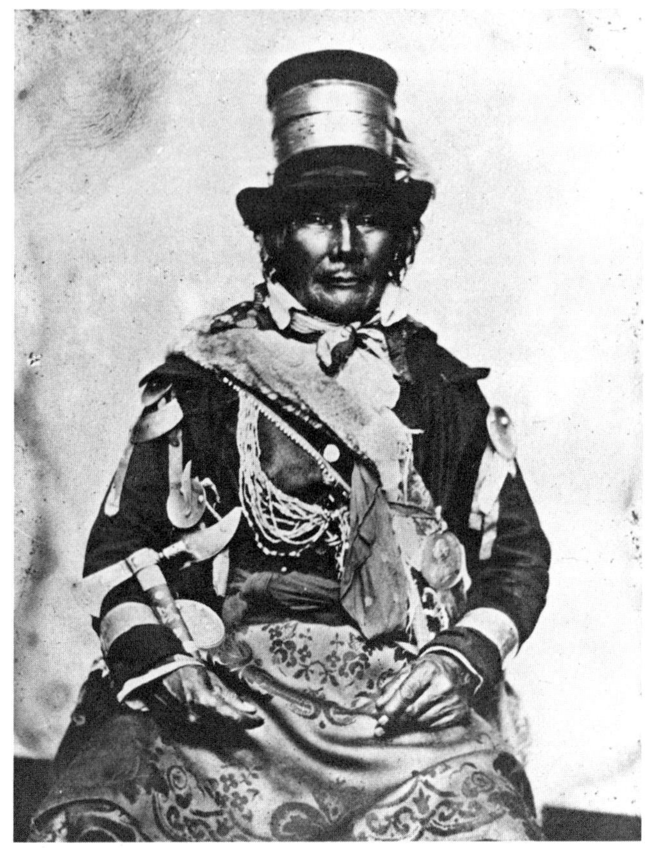

8

In 1842, several Micmac chiefs travelled to England to see Queen Victoria. They were refused an audience, but this medal was struck and presented to them later that year. The inscription reads: "Presented to Joseph M. Itkobeitch, Chief of the Micmac Indians at Restigouche, by the Minister of War and Colonies, by command of the Queen. 25, Jan: 1842."

9

Oshawana was Tecumseh's chief warrior at the Battle of the River Thames during the War of 1812. His European suit is decorated with a variety of silver ornaments, and silver headbands encircle the crown of his top hat. Circular and crescent gorgets are attached to his sleeves. He wears wampum beads as well as silver wristbands, medals and brooches, and carries a presentation pipe-tomahawk.

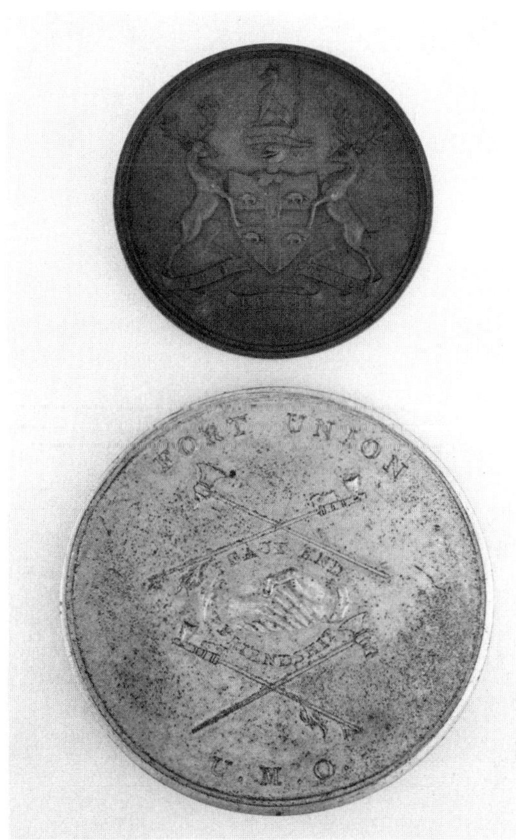

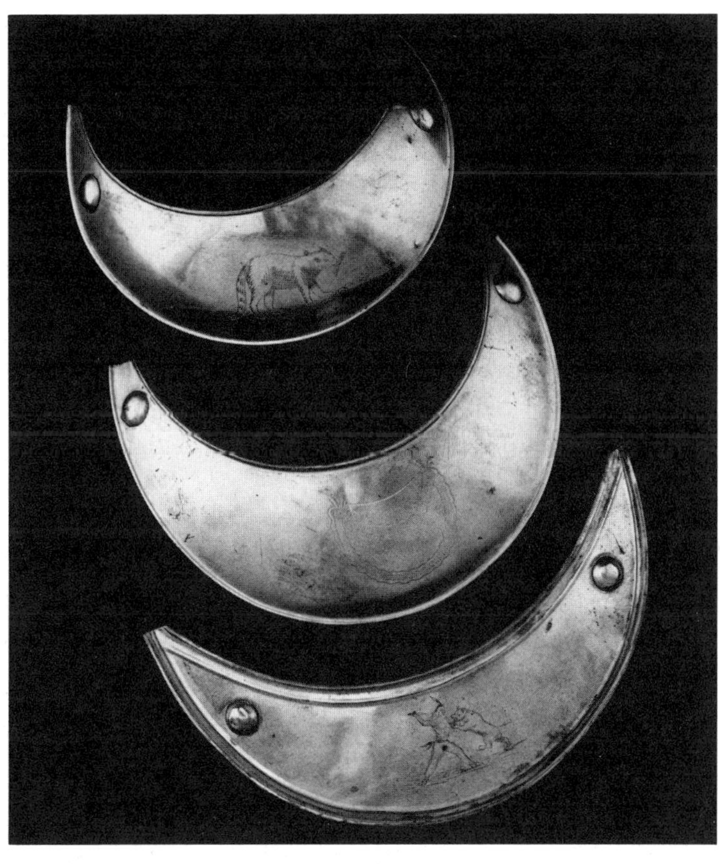

10

The prestige the Indians attached to official European medals led to the introduction of medals made especially for the fur trade. The Hudson's Bay Company produced the medal on top, bearing its coat of arms on one side and the bust of George III on the other, for presentation to Indians who traded at Company posts. Similarly, the American Fur Company produced the other medal for Indians trading at Fort Union. The two medals not only looked like official medals, they served very much the same purpose – to promote peaceful and profitable relations with the Indians.

11

These crescent-shaped chest ornaments closely resemble the military gorget worn on officers' uniforms in the eighteenth century. In design, most trade gorgets seem to have developed from the rather flat, elongated French military gorget, instead of the deeply crescentic British gorget. The engravings on the pieces are varied, and include animals, scenic tableaux, and geometric patterns.

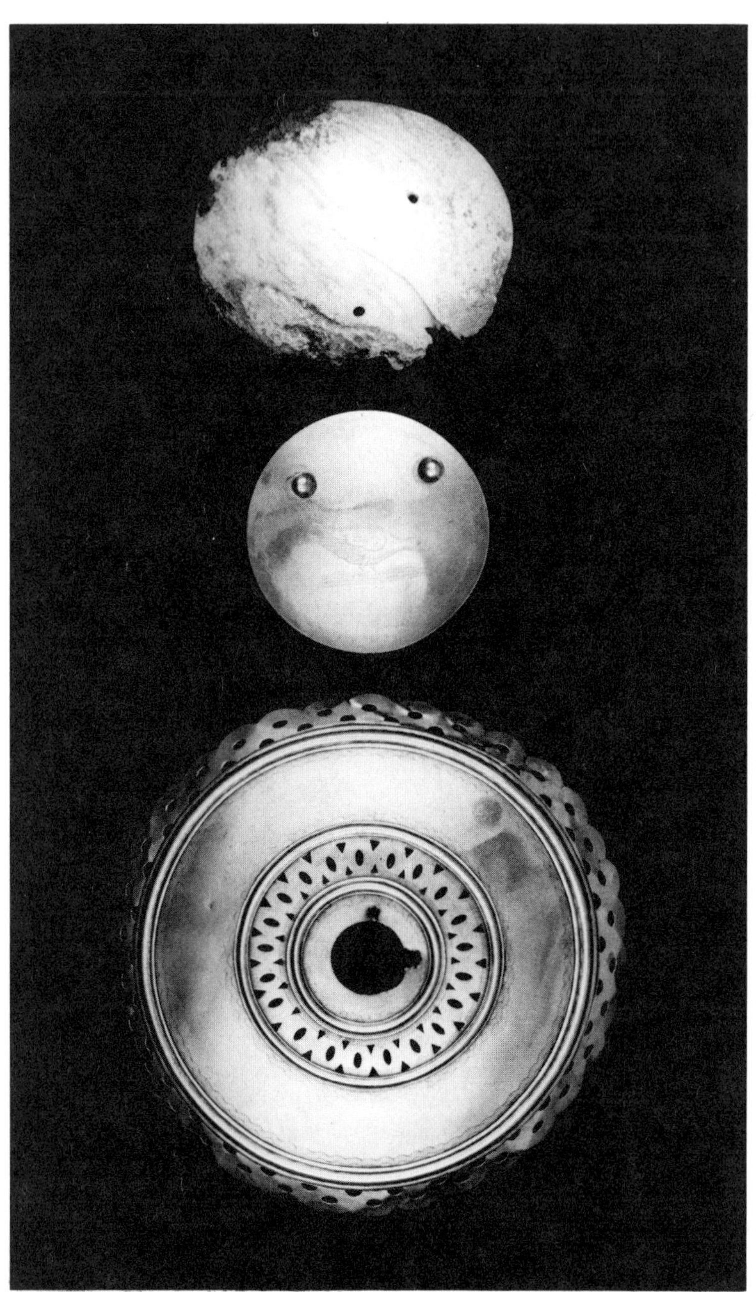

12

The round gorget, or breastplate, was popular with the Indians. Concave gorgets resembled the aboriginal shell ornaments that were hung from the neck, such as the one illustrated here. Sometimes large round brooches were also called gorgets because of their size, but they followed the European style of presenting their convex surface to the viewer.

the Revolution, was dug up in 1785 and brought to Canada, where the two groups divided it. It has remained in ceremonial use among the Brantford and Bay of Quinte Indians to the present day, a visible symbol of enduring Iroquois loyalty to the British Crown.

For the Indians these diplomatic observances also pervaded all trade negotiations. Although Europeans tended to view trading as a strictly commercial enterprise, both English and French traders saw the necessity for acceding to the Indians' insistence on ceremony. In 1616, Peter Biard called these elaborate trade formalities impertinent, "since the Indians wished nothing less than to ally themselves with the mighty King of France."* Nevertheless, silver became a very popular article of trade during the eighteenth century. The Europeans, anxious not only for profit but for the diplomatic alliances that accompanied trade, became conscious of the need to include silver in their trading outfits. Not only did the Indians want silver for their furs, but they would "take nothing but Silver Ware for their Services, as Expresses or Parties to escort Men, or Presents, should such Services be wanted."**

With this increase in the demand for trade silver, it became difficult to supply all the requirements from Europe, and silversmiths in the colonies were called upon to augment the supply of imported silver. By the mid-eighteenth century, silver articles were being produced in North America specifically for the Indian trade. Philadelphia and Quebec evolved as centres of production, the main source of their metal being the Spanish silver piastres circulating in North America and commonly referred to as "pieces of eight".

When piastres were in short supply, orders still went to Europe after 1760, but high production costs and strict regulations on the purity of silver jewellery in France and England made this an increasingly expensive alternative. These factors led to the introduction in North America of "German silver", a mixture of silver and base metals that could legally be produced in Germany. The traders soon found, however, that the Indians did not value jewellery made of German silver as highly as that made of pure silver.

---

*Rotstein, p. 14.

**George Croghan to Sir William Johnson, 18 February 1765, *The Papers of Sir William Johnson* (Albany: University of the State of New York, 1927), vol. 9, pp. 576–7.

III / PRODUCTION OF SILVER IN NORTH AMERICA

SILVER, LIKE GOLD, is a rare and costly metal that, from early times, has been held in particular esteem. Prized for its lustre, weight, permanence and malleability, it was widely used in fabricating important ceremonial objects. In seventeenth- and eighteenth-century Europe, it was also considered an investment: "In times of prosperity the family plate was displayed upon the sideboard to the admiration of friends and visitors; in case of need it could quickly be turned into money." * Moreover, canon law had decreed that ecclesiastical vessels be made of the noble metal. Silver, and the silversmith, were important in European culture.

Thus, it is not surprising to find three silversmiths working in New France before 1700. The earliest silversmiths were born and trained in France, but once established in Canada began training their own apprentices. In fact, they were the first craftsmen to introduce the European apprenticeship system into Canada. As in Europe, the young worker was bound to the craftsman for several years, during which time he was provided with shelter, food and clothing. In return for his services, the apprentice was taught the silversmith's craft. By the early 1700s, native-born smiths were practising in New France. Three of the most noted were François Ranvoyzé, who was born in Quebec City in 1739 and died there in 1819; Pierre Huguet *dit* Latour, Sr., who was born in Quebec in 1749 and worked in Montreal, where he died in 1817; and his son Pierre Huguet *dit* Latour, Jr., 1771–1829, who also worked in Montreal. **

In the eighteenth century, silversmiths of many different origins came to the colonies of Canada. The predominantly French character of the Quebec silversmiths changed after 1763 with the influx of craftsmen from England,

---

*Ramsay Traquair, *The Old Silver of Quebec,* published under the auspices of the Art Association of Montreal (Toronto: Macmillan, 1940), p. 1.

**John E. Langdon, *Canadian Silversmiths 1700–1900* (Toronto: Stinehour Press, 1966), p. 94.

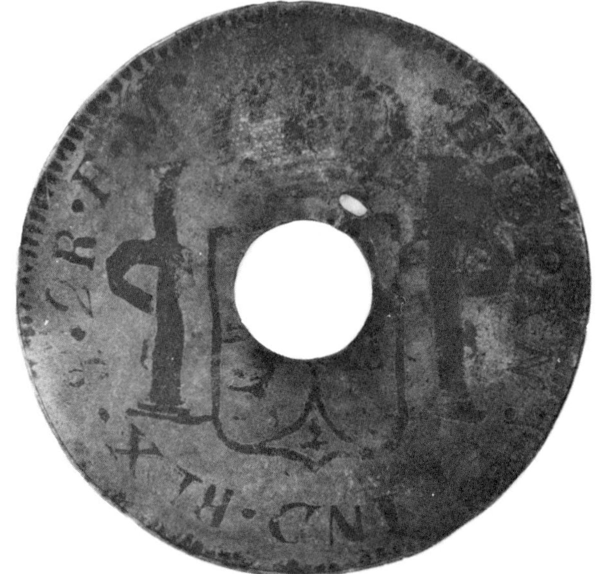

13

Coins were the main source of silver in eighteenth-century North America, where the currencies of many European countries circulated. Silversmiths converted the coins into pieces of ecclesiastical, domestic and trade silver. Although the coins were usually melted and reshaped, certain trade ornaments could be quickly produced by hammering a coin into a thin disc, and then cutting a brooch pattern in it. This unusual round brooch still bears traces of the original coin it was made from.

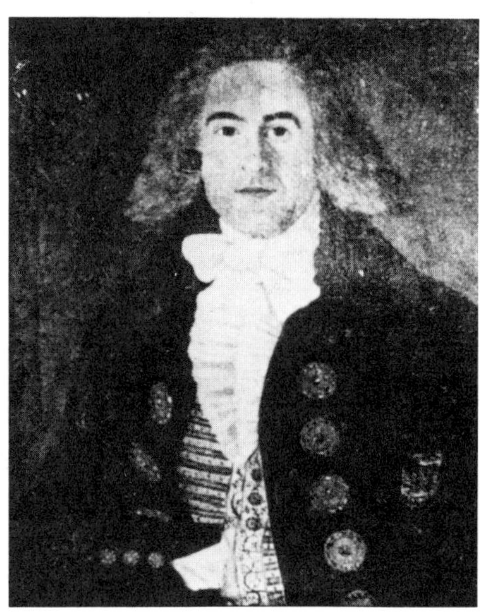

14

Robert Cruickshank was one of the major suppliers of trade silver to the Montreal-based fur traders. Born in England, he emigrated to Boston in 1767 and then moved to Montreal in 1773. In his shop on rue Notre-Dame in Montreal, he carried on a general hardware business as well as a large silver manufacturing operation. Many pieces of church and domestic silver and much of the Indian silver known today bear the familiar mark "RC" or "RC MONTREAL". Because he trained several apprentices before his death in 1809, it is possible that some of the items bearing his mark were made by them in his shop.

Scotland and Ireland. Outstanding among them were Robert Cruickshank of Montreal and James Hanna of Quebec City. Halifax, by this time, also contained a flourishing group of British silversmiths. The American Revolution produced a migration of loyalist craftsmen from New England, men who brought with them British, German and American training. Forty of these silversmiths settled in the Maritime colonies and in the Canadas. Among them were Benjamin Etter, born in Massachusetts, who settled in Halifax, and Ebenezer Whiting, born in Connecticut, who opened a shop in Newark (now Niagara-on-the-Lake, Ontario).

The silversmith, a craftsman of consequence, frequently performed other functions in the community. He participated in public affairs, church offices, and sometimes, under the French regime, militia duty. He often supplemented his income with work in another trade, such as jeweller, watchmaker, gunsmith or merchant. Robert Cruickshank, for example, conducted a large hardware business in Montreal during the eighteenth century.

The major role of the silversmith during the French regime was to supply the many churches with ecclesiastical silver. The chalice, monstrance and processional cross, as well as many smaller items used in the Roman Catholic Church, were made by local silversmiths. In design, these pieces resembled the church silver previously brought from France. In the Maritime colonies, as well as in the American colonies, domestic silver was produced locally, but ecclesiastical silver was imported from Britain.

Domestic silver increased in importance throughout the French and British colonies as population expanded and aspirations rose. Tableware such as cutlery, goblets, tureens, teapots and cups as well as personal articles such as jewellery were listed among the possessions of high-ranking colonial officials. As with ecclesiastical silver, the domestic silver in use at any one time was a combination of European and colonial-made pieces.

Documentary evidence indicates that by the mid-eighteenth century colonial silversmiths were participating in a new silver market, producing articles that were neither so ornate nor so well crafted as their customary work. Large quantities of silver "trinkets", or "toys", were in demand for the Indian trade. In 1759 a Detroit trader, Duperon Baby, wrote to his brother, François Baby, in Quebec, asking him to place an order for silver ornaments for the fur trade. The order was given to Jonas Schindler, a well-known

Quebec silversmith of German origin, for "one-hundred pairs of small ear-bobs and twenty-four ear-wheels", with the admonition that the silver "should be thin and well polished yet able to stand engraving."*

Coins were the primary source of silver in North America at that time. Coins of many European countries were in circulation – French, British, Dutch, Spanish and German predominating. The most popular for silver-smithing were the Spanish piastres. The silversmith had two methods of transforming coins into trade trinkets. By one method he simply hammered them into thin discs, producing ornaments that often retained traces of the coins' markings. By the other method, he placed the specified weight of silver coin into boiling-pans, which were put on the hearth of a refining furnace. Once the coins had melted, the impurities would be removed and the silver cooled for testing. Then the silver would be remelted and alloyed with a small percentage of copper to improve durability.** Finally, it was pounded or pressed into thin sheets.

Since almost all trade silver was fashioned from these thin sheets, little metal was required for each item and large-scale production was relatively inexpensive. The sheets were cut into different shapes to make gorgets, armbands, hair-pipes, wristbands, ear-rings, headbands, breast-buckles, finger-rings and brooches. Each piece was then fashioned into the desired form and decorated with engraved or pierced designs.

The craftsman who made a particular piece of trade silver can sometimes be identified by his distinctive mark. Each silversmith had his own mark, which he imprinted on his work with a punch, much as an author signs his name to a written work. In New France, silversmiths' marks resembled those used in France; the maker's initials were surmounted by a crown or fleur-de-lis and supported by a star or crescent, the whole being enclosed in a cartouche. After the conquest of New France, British influence and the influx of immigrants brought about a change in Canadian marks. The maker's initials in script or block type were enclosed in a rectangle, square, double circle or cartouche. By 1775, this had come to be the most common mark.

---

*Quoted in Langdon, p. 18.

**English coins contained the sterling ratio of 92.5 per cent silver to 7.5 per cent copper; this was known as the "true standard".

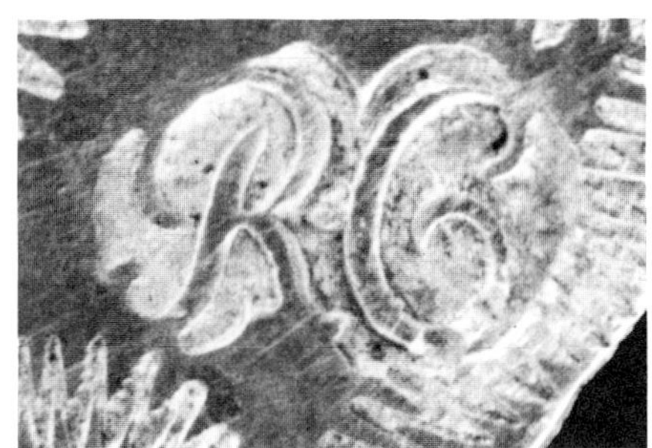

Robert Cruickshank
Boston, immigrated 1767–73
Montreal 1773–d. 1809

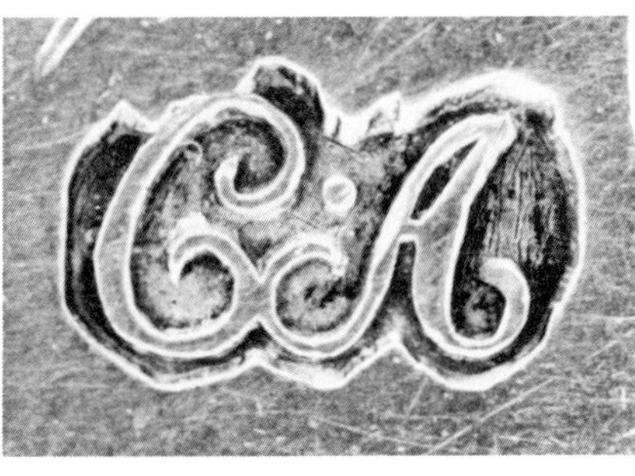

Charles Arnoldi
Montreal, b. 1779–d. 1817

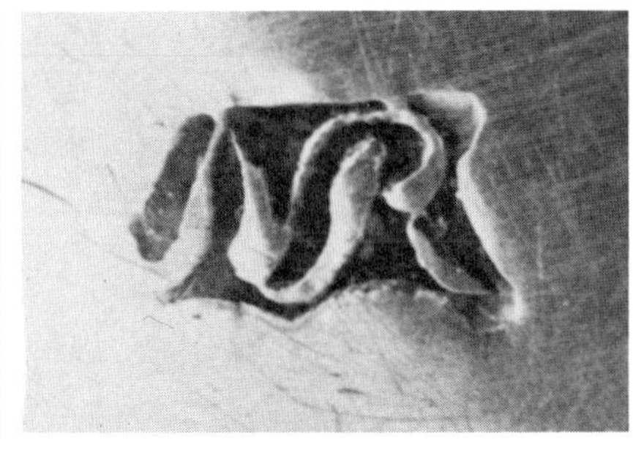

Narcisse Roy
Montreal 1765–1819

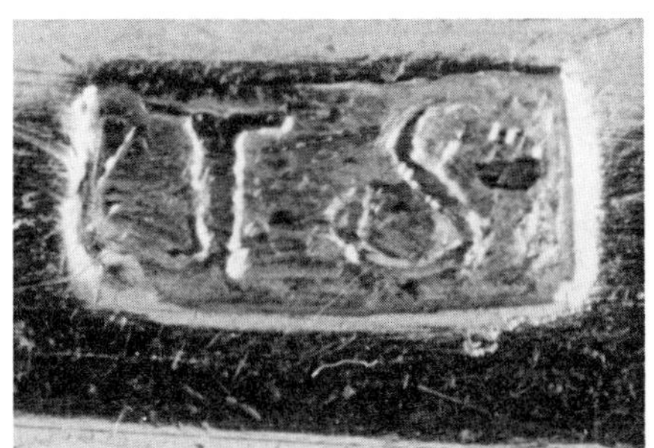

Jonas Schindler
Quebec City 1760–d. 1786
Widow Schindler
Montreal, started work 1786–d. 1823

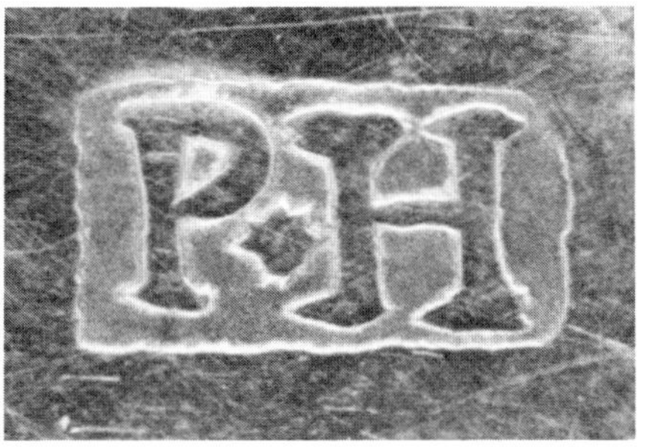

Pierre Huguet dit *Latour, Sr. and Jr.*
Montreal 1771–1829

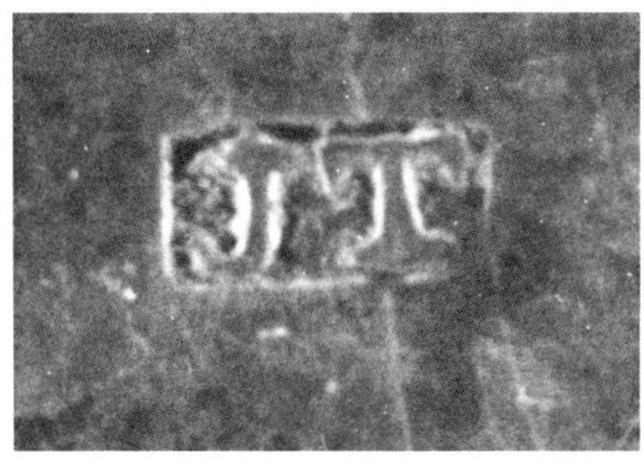

Jonathan Tyler
Montreal 1817–28

15

Many pieces of trade silver bear the marks of the craftsmen who fashioned them. These are some of the most common marks. The dates, when not otherwise explained, represent the earliest and latest known references to the silversmiths.

Unfortunately many of the smaller pieces, such as brooches, bear no markings. They may have been too small to accommodate a mark, or perhaps they were made by apprentices. Another possibility is that the makers of the unmarked pieces considered them too crude to be acknowledged.

f.° 16 Dt. Mons.r cruickshank & arnoldy:

200 Epinglette d'argent — 25.4s ... 50.8s
6 Brasselets a poignett — 4.16 ... 28.16
6 d.o ... 3 ... 18
12 Epinglette ... 4.16 ... 57.12
12 d.o ... 3.12s ... 43.4
12 Reliquaire ... 6 ... 72
12 pr. fois & Jone ... 1.10s — 18 } — 288...

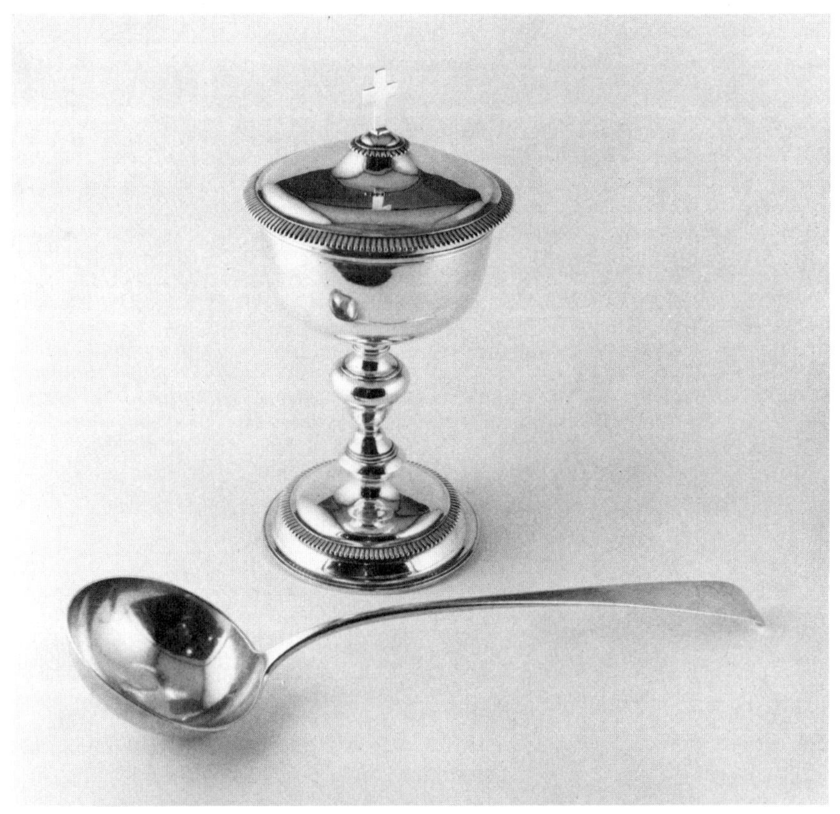

Occasional variations, such as the use of a full surname or the addition of a place name, occurred.

Makers' marks have made it possible to trace the origins of some of the silver items found at Indian archaeological sites. Unfortunately, not all trade silver was marked, possibly because, in spite of their economic importance, the craftsmen did not consider them significant works. Many of the small trinkets were probably produced by apprentices in a master silversmith's shop. They might use the master's mark to indicate the shop where the trinkets were produced, or might leave the pieces unmarked.

Unmarked trade silver must always be subjected to careful scrutiny. The recent appearance of unmarked forgeries has led many collectors to re-examine their silver artifacts by means of spectroscopy, which will provide a more accurate analysis of metallic composition, from which the age of the piece can be inferred.

Even marked silver should not be accepted at face value if the maker's mark cannot be documented. While established marks are difficult to duplicate, new ones can readily be created. Thus, anyone contemplating the purchase of a piece of trade silver should make every effort to determine its authenticity.

16

This entry from the account book of J.B. Blondeau, a Montreal merchant in the late eighteenth century, shows that he paid the silversmith partnership of Robert Cruickshank and Michael Arnoldi £288 for various pieces of trade silver, including brooches, bracelets and crosses. Recent research by Robert Derome, of the Université du Québec à Montréal, indicates that the "CA" maker's mark, previously attributed to Charles Arnoldi, may in fact represent the Cruickshank–Arnoldi partnership.

17

This ladle, made in Montreal by Narcisse Roy during the late eighteenth or early nineteenth century, is typical of the domestic silver produced at that time. An example of the ecclesiastical silver made by Quebec silversmiths is this ciborium by Robert Cruickshank, dating from the same period.

Trade silver, although fashioned more crudely than ecclesiastical and domestic silver, was probably more financially rewarding to the late eighteenth-century silversmiths of Quebec, because it required less silver and could be produced faster and more cheaply.

IV / INDIAN TRADE SILVER: THE HEIGHT OF ITS POPULARITY

PRESENTATION SILVER PLAYED A PART in Indian–white relations in North America for several centuries, but silver was actively traded only from about 1760 to 1821. By the mid-eighteenth century, silver "trinkets" were being produced in several centres in the New England colonies. In Canada, fur traders were buying trade silver from Montreal and Quebec silversmiths, particularly Robert Cruickshank, Jonas Schindler, the Arnoldi family, Pierre Huguet *dit* Latour, Sr. and Jr., and Narcisse Roy. Starting in about 1790, the Hudson's Bay Company imported silver goods from London for its trading posts. These were the major sources of the silver that became such a popular item in the fur trade.

During this period, the trading of silver for furs was primarily concentrated in the Great Lakes, East Coast and upper Mississippi regions. The Woodland peoples of the Great Lakes included the Ojibwa and Algonquin to the north and the Five Nations of the Iroquois league (Mohawk, Oneida, Onondaga, Cayuga and Seneca) to the south and east. Along the East Coast, the Abenaki, Delaware, Malecite and Micmac are known to have received silver in trade. On the upper Mississippi, the Fox, Sauk, Menomini, Winnebago and Kickapoo also obtained trade silver from Canadian and New England traders.

Other groups, whether by their own choice or that of the fur traders, received less silver. The Plains Indians of Canada, such as the Cree, Assiniboine and Blackfoot, added almost no silver to their highly decorated dress, with the exception of official medals and, in some instances, silver hair-pipes. Their counterparts to the south, especially the Sioux, Comanche, Kiowa and Cheyenne, wore elaborate silver hair-plates of twenty or more silver discs fastened to a plait of their fashionable ground-length hair. In general, the appearance of silver on the southern plains was a later development, with silver ornaments becoming more plentiful after 1850, when German silver also became commoner. Northern Indians also received less trade silver. The Ojibwa and Cree trading along James Bay at Fort Albany, Moose Factory and Eastmain began receiving silver after 1790, but not until

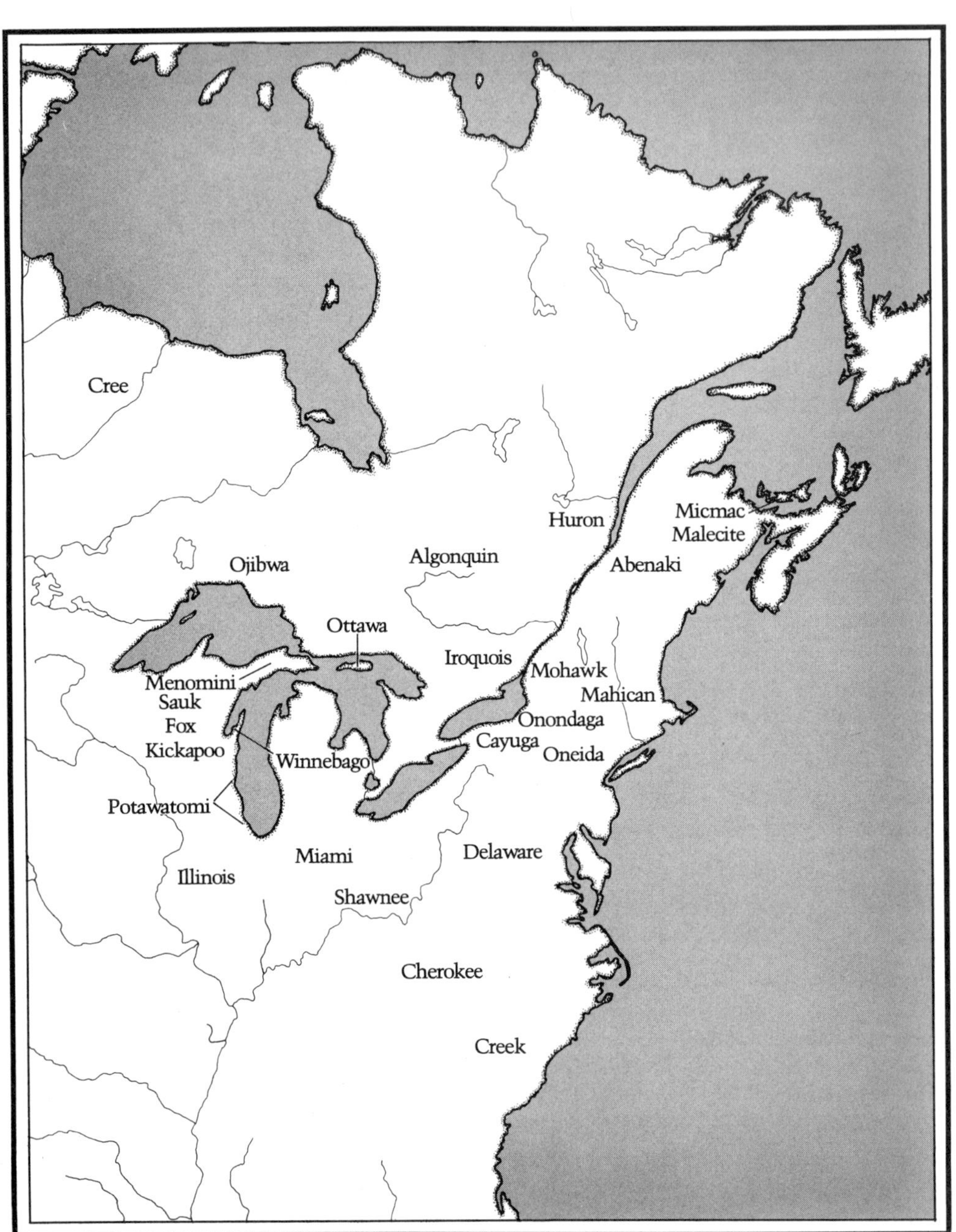

18

Indian Tribes That Traded for Silver, 1760–1821

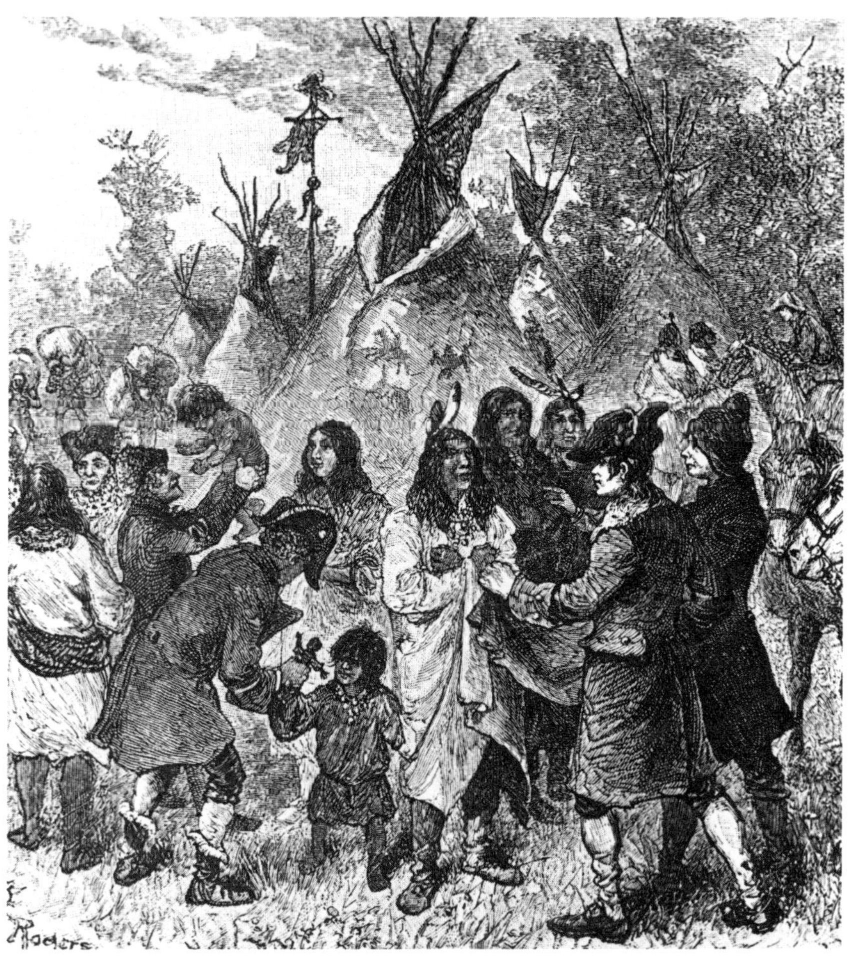

19

This sketch portrays rival companies soliciting trade in an Indian camp. At the height of the fur trade, between 1760 and 1821, competition was vigorous between the Hudson's Bay Company and the Montreal-based traders who eventually amalgamated as the North West Company. Independent traders were also very active on the Albany and Mississippi river systems. Silver was one of the most important trade goods during this period, but was dropped soon after 1821, when the Hudson's Bay Company acquired its rival and gained effective control of the fur trade.

Equivalents for barter of goods and skins

A Strowd of 2 yards long to be sold at 2 large Bevers or 3 dressed bucks

Strowd Stockings to be sold for a Buck Skin

Womens Worsted Stockings per pair a good Buck Skin

Men or Womens large white Blankets 1 large & 1 small Bever or 2 large Bucks

Mens Penniston Coats wth Gimps 3 Bucks, or 2 Bever

Mens Ruffled Shirts 2 Bucks or 2 middle-ing ditto or 2 otters, or 7 Racoons

Black Wampum per 100 weight if good 1 small Bever 1^{lb} 1/4

white Wampum per 100 weight 2 large Racoons, or 1 Martin Skin

Cutteau large knives – 1 large Raccoon, or 3 Musquash

Small knives for Women 1 Small Racoon or 2 Musquash

1 piece of best Roll Gartering 1 Bever, or 2 Doe Skins, or 6 Racoons

2 fathom of Ribbond – 1 Buck, or Middle Sized Bever

1 pound of Virmillion – 2 Bevers, or 3 Bucks, –

1 fathom Calicoe – 1 Bever, or 3 Doe Skins

1 ditto of Calimancoe – 1 middleing Bever, or 2 Doe Skins

Large Silk Handkercheifs – 1 Bever, or 2 good Doe Skins

Brass Kettles as they Weigh at the rate of 1^{lb} Bever per pound

Tin or Camp Kettles of a Gallon 1 Bever, or 1 Buck & Doe

Silver Arm Band well made, 4 Bucks, or 3 Bevers

Rist band Silver ditto 2 Bucks or 2 small Bevers

Broches of Silver – 1 Racoon Musquash

1 p^{r} Silver Ear Bobs – 1 good Doe Skin, or small Bever

large Silver Cross – 1 buck, or middleing Bever

Womens Silver Hair plate large 4 bucks, or 3 Bevers large

Gun powder 1^{lb} one small Bever, or 1 middle sized buck

12 Flints – 1 Small Racoon, or 2 Musquash

Looking Glass middle sized 2 Racoons, or 6 Musquash

Jews Harps 6 for a large Racoon

Bever Traps, 2 Bevers middle Sized, or 2 Bucks

3 Gallon Cag of Rum, 3 large Bevers – or 4 large Bucks

10 quart Cag of Rum – 2 large & 1 Small Bever, or 3 bucks & a Doe

20

These "Equivalents for Barter of Goods and Skins", taken from the papers of Sir William Johnson, identify the rates of exchange for most trading items in the British Indian Territory in 1765. Note that a silver armband would fetch four buckskins or three beaver pelts. Considering these low prices for furs, the volume of silver traded each year is remarkable. For example, in 1782 about 18,600 pieces of silver were requested for the Indian trade by a single post, Detroit.

1819 were the Chipewyan and Cree of the Churchill River and Lake Athabasca regions introduced to these "trinkets". In northern regions only small amounts were traded, and silver never became a popular ornament.

It is difficult to understand what factors might have determined the trading patterns of silver. The Plains Indians, much more independent of the fur trade than eastern Indians, received fewer trade goods of all kinds. The Indians of the boreal forest, with their less elaborate material cultures, were perhaps not attracted to silver ornaments. Probably the most significant factor in the distribution of silver was the intense competition between the Hudson's Bay Company and the Montreal-based traders. Certainly this would explain the Company's introduction of trade silver into its southerly regions in 1790, when the Montreal traders were consolidating their efforts into more effective competition. It is also significant that the 1819 introduction of silver into the Lake Athabasca and Churchill River regions occurred during the period of the most intense hostility and competition between the Hudson's Bay Company and the Nor'Westers in those areas. For the most part, however, the more heavily populated regions – the East Coast, the Great Lakes area and the upper Mississippi – were the centres of keenest competition, and it is in these regions that trade silver enjoyed its greatest circulation.

Silver also moved into new areas during the Indian migrations of the late eighteenth century. When the Woodland Ojibwa moved westwards to the margin of the plains, they carried with them their prized ornaments. They evidently also introduced a demand for silver at the new trading posts around Lake Winnipeg and along the North Saskatchewan River. This coincided with the introduction of silver in the trade inventories of the North West Company posts in that region. Silver trinkets found on the sites of these posts all appear to have come from Montreal silversmiths. Like the competitive phase in the interior, the flourish of silver in this area was brief, and virtually ceased after the 1821 consolidation of the Hudson's Bay and North West companies.

The recent discovery of an Ojibwa burial site on the Red Deer River in Manitoba, near the Saskatchewan border, has provided important evidence of the penetration of silver into the interior. High-water erosion of the riverbank exposed the site, which has been examined by archaeologists from the University of Saskatchewan. According to their findings, a male Ojibwa probably less than twenty years of age, had been buried wearing hair ornaments, headbands, brooches, armbands, gorgets, crosses and ear-wheels of silver, along with a variety of wampum and other shell ornaments. Common trade items, such as a knife, mirror, comb, bells and lead shot, were also found in the grave.

Some of the silver ornaments are imprinted with several readily identifiable makers' marks. The armbands, which had been cut up to make several narrower bands, bear the well-known "RC" of Robert Cruickshank of Montreal. A crescent gorget decorated with the engraving of a leaping bear carries the mark of Narcisse Roy.

The arrangement of these artifacts on the body has shed new light on the ways the Ojibwa wore their ornaments in the late eighteenth century.

V / THE USES AND SIGNIFICANCE OF SILVER IN INDIAN CULTURE

DESPITE THEIR EUROPEAN ORIGINS, the silver ornaments dispersed by trade through the New World were uniquely Indian in their cultural significance. Made exclusively for Indians and used exclusively by them, trade silver must be interpreted in those terms. This can be done but imperfectly from the archaeological and written records of the period, and many of the suggestions offered here are only tentative.

In general, it would appear from the portraits and graves of tribal leaders that possession of silver was a sign of rank. Certainly the ornaments were given in that spirit, and appear to have been received accordingly. The size of the medals varied, but corresponded with the importance of the recipient. Silver medals, even small ones, were more valuable gifts than the bronze ones often produced from the same die. Silver gorgets and armbands were worn after the fashion of the military, as a mark of rank. Quantity was an important element in the ceremonial dress of the tribal leader, and it was not uncommon for a chief to wear several crescent and circular gorgets as well as wristbands, armbands, legbands, a multitude of brooches, and several silver headbands on his Indian headdress or European hat.

Clearly, silver was preferred to the baser metals that many early ornamental trade goods were made of. An American observer of the early nineteenth century reported an incident that emphasizes this point. Taking a brass bracelet from one of the Indian women, he rubbed it with quicksilver, making it as bright and glittering as polished silver. When news of this travelled through the village, many women brought him their brass bracelets and rings to convert into silver. (There is no record of how the women reacted when, a few days later, the mercury wore off.)

The uses and significance of silver may be further understood by considering the kinds of jewellery worn. The most numerous was the simple brooch. Also known as a breast or shirt buckle, the brooch was a plain metal ring with an attached pin, varying in diameter from 1.5 to 3 centimetres or more. These were fastened in large numbers in every imaginable place – not only on jacket

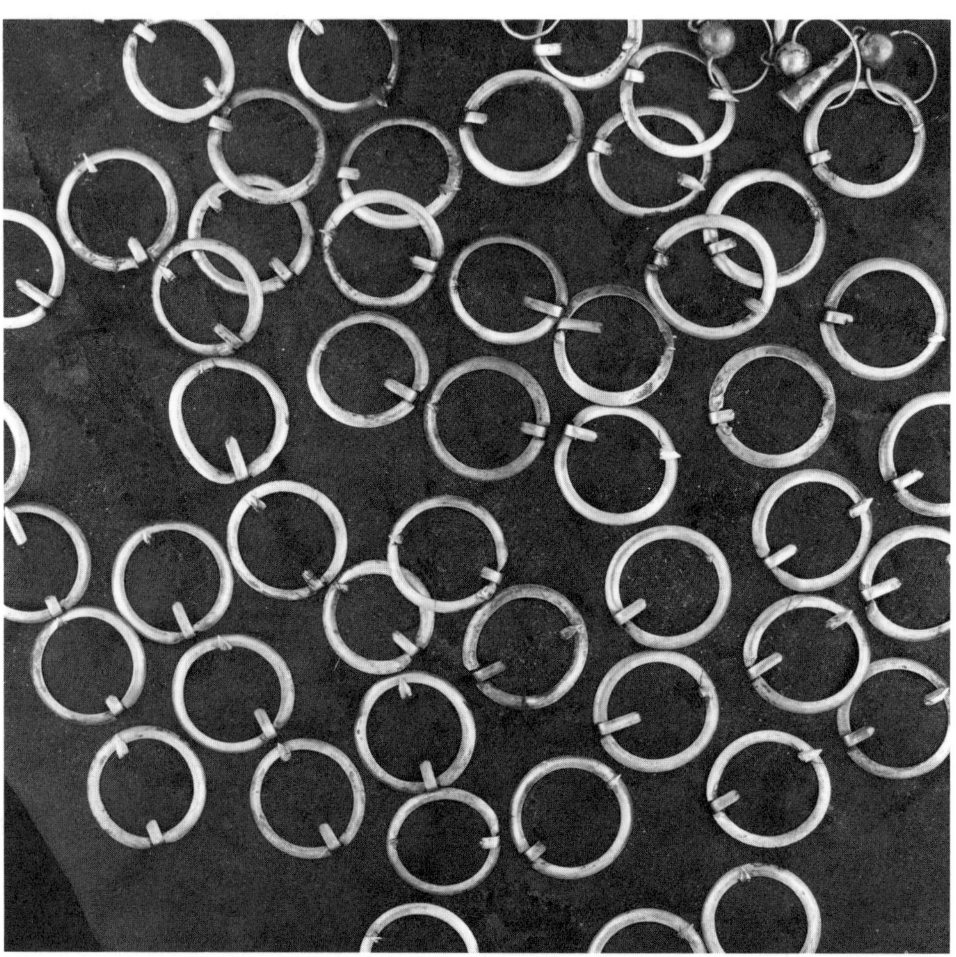

21

The simplest and most common brooch was the circular, or "ring", brooch. These were open in the centre, and had a fastener on the front. The brooch was attached to a garment by pushing the fabric up through the centre and piercing it with the pin.

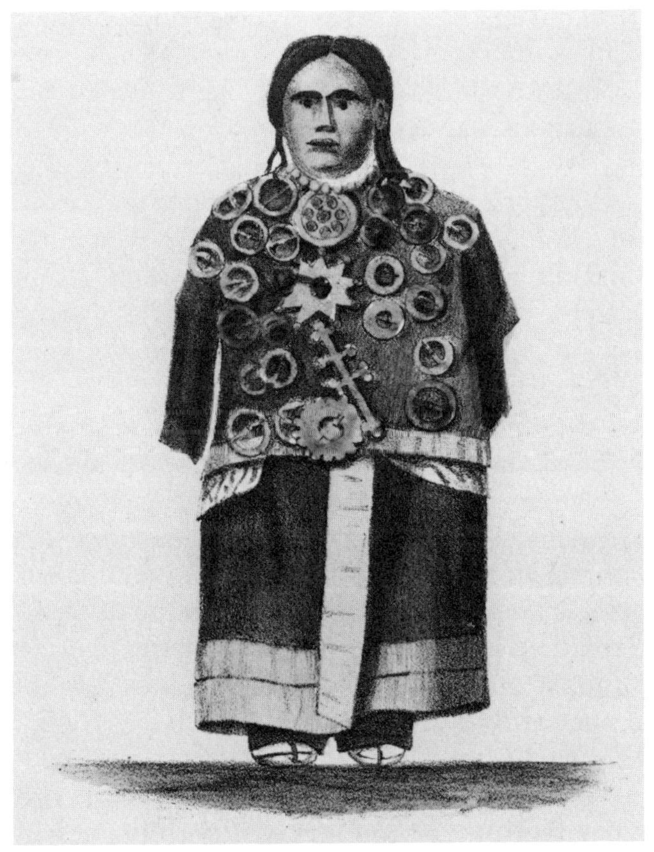

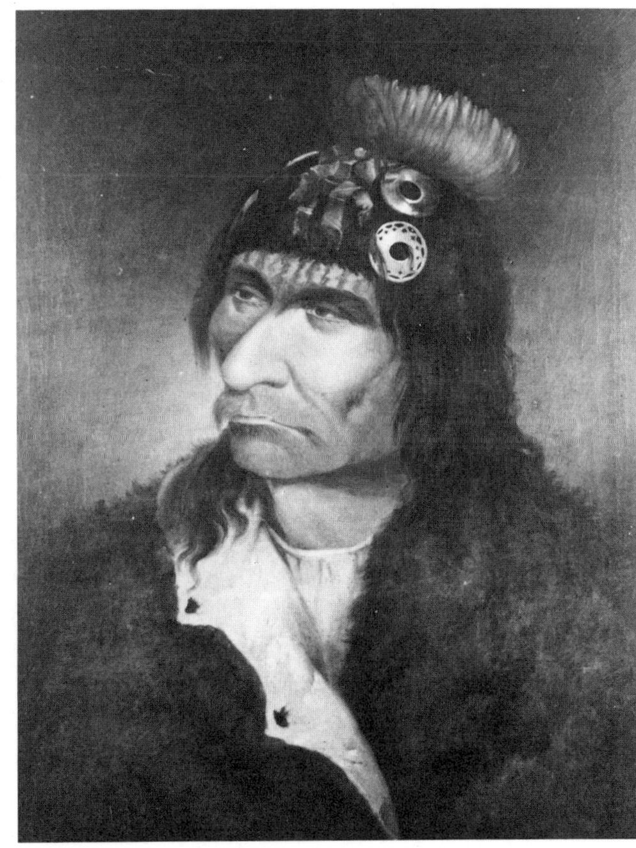

22

Nahneetis, the Guardian of Health

This sketch of an Ojibwa woman shows the most popular way of wearing brooches. Here they include the simple ring brooch, star brooch and cross.

23

Muck-A-Ta

Hair ornaments were popular in many Indian tribes. This portrait by Paul Kane shows that the simple round brooch was worn in the hair as well as on clothing.

or dress, but on hair, headdress, sash, and infant's swaddling bands. Iroquois women, in particular, wore large numbers of brooches in rows across the front and back of the bodice, a style perhaps derived from the German colonists, who had adopted a similar though more restrained mode.

Among the Ojibwa men, brooches were a popular hair ornament; they might be attached down the length of a plait of hair, or fastened to the narrow band that formed the base of a headdress. A third popular adornment in the nineteenth century was a necklace fashioned of brooches loosely strung together on a thread. The quantity of these simple circular brooches worn at one time is surprising, but before their introduction most of the Woodland Indians wore similarly large quantities of shell and bone ornaments.

Several shapes other than the simple circular brooch were popular. The heart, either single or double, often surmounted by a crown, has been referred to as the "national badge" of the Iroquois because of its prevalence among them. Few are to be found beyond the traditional Iroquois territory. The design is thought to have originated in Scotland. Known as the "Luckenbooth" brooch, it was a popular Scottish love token in the seventeenth century. It may have been introduced into the Thirteen Colonies by Scottish settlers and into Canada by the Scottish traders of Montreal. Possibly the British-trained silversmiths, such as Robert Cruickshank and James Hanna, introduced the Luckenbooth themselves.

Another form peculiar to the Iroquois was the Masonic brooch. It may have been introduced by the Mohawk-Iroquois war chief, Joseph Brant, who in 1775 became a member of the Masonic Order in London. In general, the Iroquois Indians attached no Masonic significance to the brooch, although they may have sensed the esteem it was held in by some Europeans.

The star brooch, with from eight to fourteen points, has no obvious tribal identification; it appears to have been popular throughout the region where silver was traded. Each point of the star was capped with an embossed circular knob, and the entire brooch was decorated with simple engraving. Combination designs, such as a star within a circle, were also popular in the larger brooches.

Rings for ear, nose and fingers were popular among many Indian peoples. Of the earrings, or ear-bobs, the simplest is the conical bangle, about 2.5 centimetres long and made of shaped sheet-silver; these are found among the

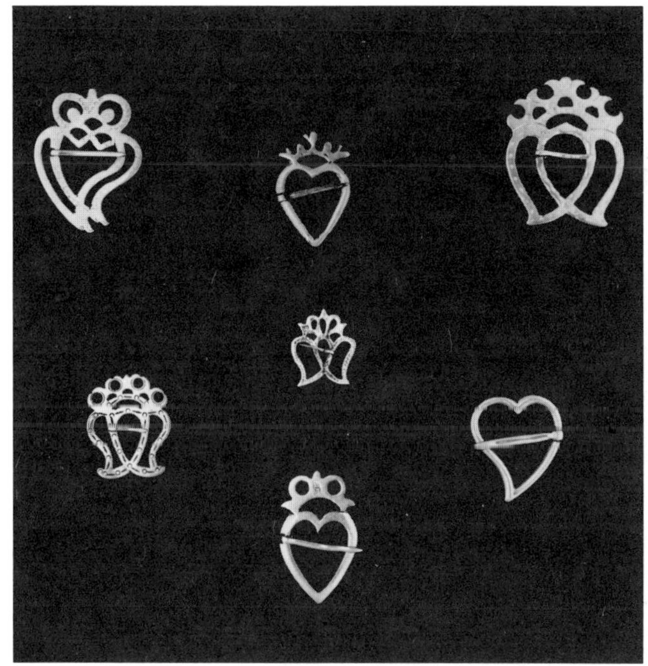

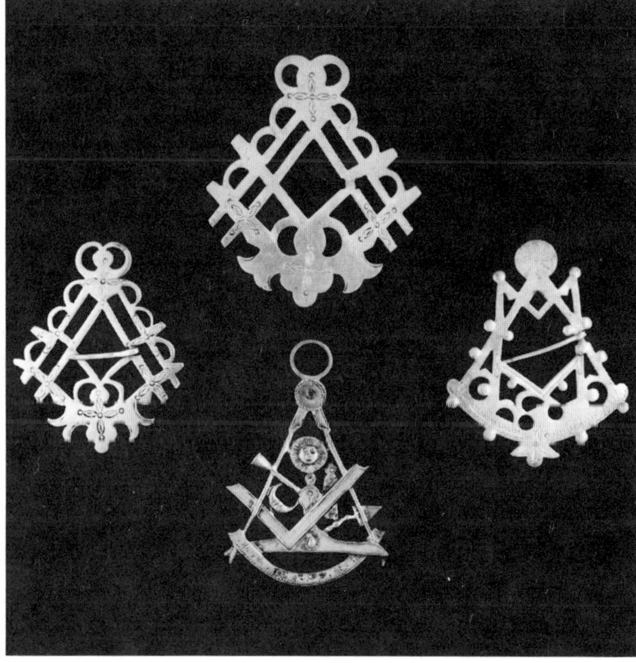

24

The heart-shaped brooch has been called the national badge of the Iroquois because of its popularity among them. It is found in both single and double forms, often surmounted by a crown. The design is thought to have come to North America from Scotland, where it was a popular love token and betrothal symbol. The "Luckenbooth" brooch, as it was known in Scotland, may have been introduced by British-trained silversmiths such as Robert Cruickshank or James Hanna. Another possibility is that the Indians requested the brooch after seeing it worn by Scottish traders and settlers.

25

Masonic emblems were favoured by the Iroquois in the eighteenth century. The Order of Freemasons flourished in England and Scotland early in that century, and many of the British officers and traders in North America were members. In fact, in 1775, Joseph Brant, a Mohawk-Iroquois war chief, was made a member of the Order while on a visit to London. In New England, Freemasonry was active as early as 1730, and by the time of the American Revolution it was well established. The Iroquois adopted the Masonic emblem of the compass and square to represent the "Council Fire", a meeting of chiefs.

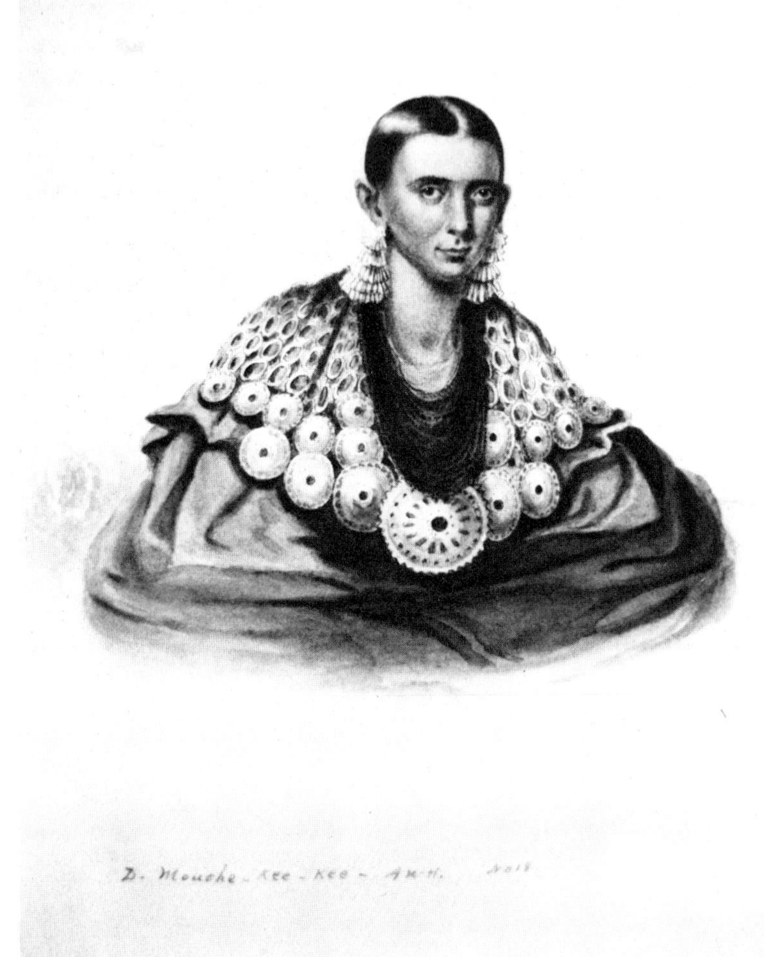

26

D-Mouche-Kee-Kee-Awh

This Potawatomi woman displays an elaborate array of circular brooches. George Winter, the artist, described her thus: "No Pottawattamie squaw equalled her in regard to dress; she was . . . plated with silver brooches, the very ne plus ultra *of an Indian woman's toilette."*

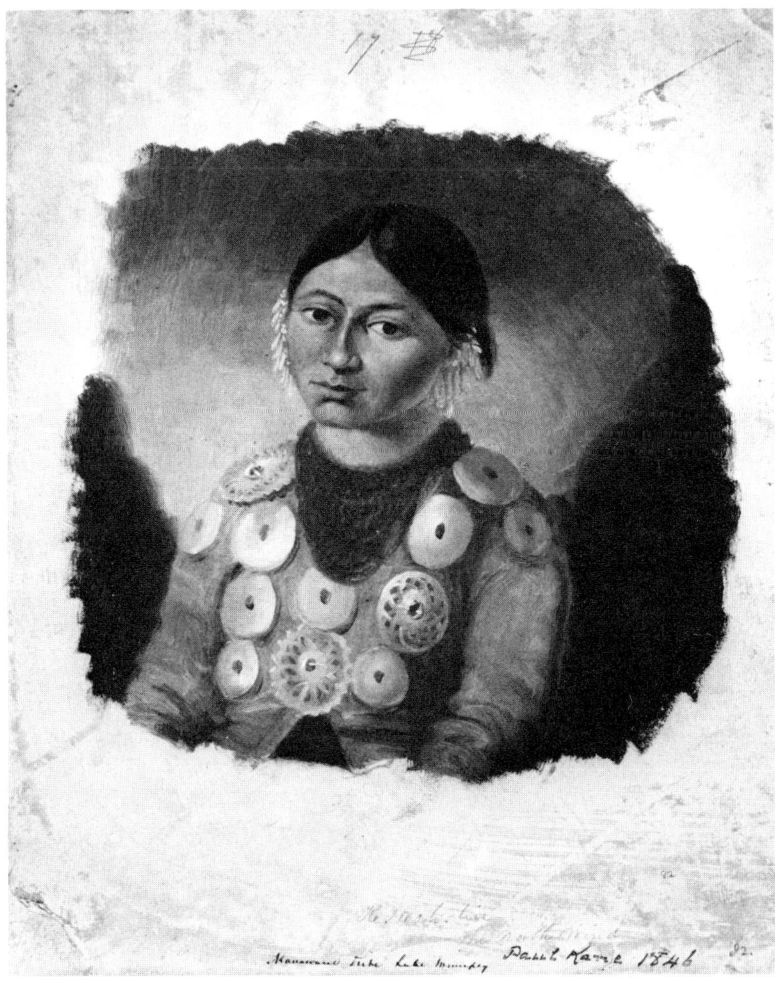

27

Ke-Wah-Ten, or the North Wind

Brooches were the most popular and versatile of silver ornaments. Among Indian women, in particular, the wearing of large numbers of brooches on the bodice was fashionable, quantity being a measure of status and wealth. The suggestion that this fashion was derived from a similar style prevalent among German women in eighteenth-century Pennsylvania has not been substantiated.

Indians of the southern Great Lakes and upper Mississippi regions – the Iroquois, Winnebago, Menomini, Fox and Sauk – and even among the Sioux of the Dakotas. More common among the northern Indians are the ear-wheels. These are circular ornaments decorated with a variety of pierced designs; the discs often had smaller silver pieces fastened to them. In the deep south, among the Choctaw and Creek, triangular ear-ornaments were preferred; these have also been found among some groups of the Shawnee tribe. Isaac Weld, Jr., in his *Travels through the States of North America,* described the wearing of earrings as follows:

> Instead of boring their ears, the men slit them along the outward edge from top to bottom, and . . . hang heavy weights to them in order to stretch the rim thus separated as low down as possible.*

It was apparently fashionable to wear several ornaments in each ear.

According to Weld, nose-rings were not as common as earrings, and were worn primarily by men. Finger-rings, by contrast, were the adornment mainly of women, although evidence from the Red Deer River burial (see p. 47) suggests that Ojibwa men may have worn several rings on each hand.**

Various kinds of bands were worn by almost all Eastern Woodland Indians. Armbands, legbands, bracelets and headbands were all common ornaments. They were made of thin sheets of silver of varying widths, with holes drilled at the ends for ties, thus making the pieces adjustable in size. Armbands were worn either singly or in pairs at the middle of the upper arm, wristbands or bracelets on the lower arm, and legbands on the ankle, at mid calf or just below the knee. Headbands, rarer than the other forms, were usually more ornate. They were often worn two or three at a time, incorporated into an Indian headdress or as trimming on a European top hat. The only distinctly regional design to be found in these bands is an interesting combination of pierced openings in the shapes of hearts and triangles, with a row of heart bangles dangling around the lower edge of the headband. Arm, leg and head

*Quoted in Marius Barbeau, "Indian Trade Silver", *Proceedings and Transactions of the Royal Society of Canada,* ser. 3, vol. 34, sec. 2 (1940), p. 39.

**The Red Deer rings are not of silver, but their presence indicates that Ojibwa men did wear that form of adornment.

bands fashioned in this style by unknown craftsmen are believed to have been worn by Algonquin Indians.

Some popular silver jewellery had aboriginal prototypes. The silver bands described above are obvious copies of the bark, leather and beadwork bands worn by many Indian peoples. Another example of traditional usage is found in the circular gorget, or moon. In pre-contact times, medallion-like objects made of shell or stone were suspended from the neck on a leather thong. Most prevalent among the southeastern tribes, such as the Cherokee and Creeks, they were also found as far north as Ontario among the Ojibwa. The circular gorget was worn in the same manner as the aboriginal decoration, and it is frequently difficult to differentiate between silver and other kinds of circular ornaments that appear in Indian portraits of the trade silver period. The previous existence of such adornments might help to explain the popularity of European and colonial medals among North American Indians.

One of the rarest and most problematical pieces of trade silver is the animal effigy. Although a variety of animal forms have been found, many silver experts doubt their authenticity because no documented instance has been found of their having been used in trade. Of the silver effigies now in existence, the silver beaver is the most numerous, and many have been attributed to Robert Cruickshank of Montreal. These beavers could well have been made at the request of Ojibwa Indians of the northwestern Great Lakes area, where beaver effigy pendants made of stone have been found in the prehistoric levels of a Lake Superior site and similar pendants of catlinite have been found in later levels of a Lake Michigan site. Like their aboriginal prototypes, the silver effigies could have been worn suspended from the neck.

A variety of silver hair-ornaments produced for the Indian trade also appear to be copied directly from aboriginal prototypes. The tubular silver hair-pipes, about 4 centimetres long, that were widely popular among not only the Plains Indians but also some eastern peoples were modelled on the shell beads found in New York and Ontario. The shell hair-pipes were probably first copied in glass, then in metals, and later in various other materials. Also called hair-bobs, these pipes were worn in large numbers, each encircling several strands of hair. By 1763, Philadelphia silversmiths were making hair-pipes for the Indians of the Ohio Valley, and by 1800 pipes were also made in Montreal. It

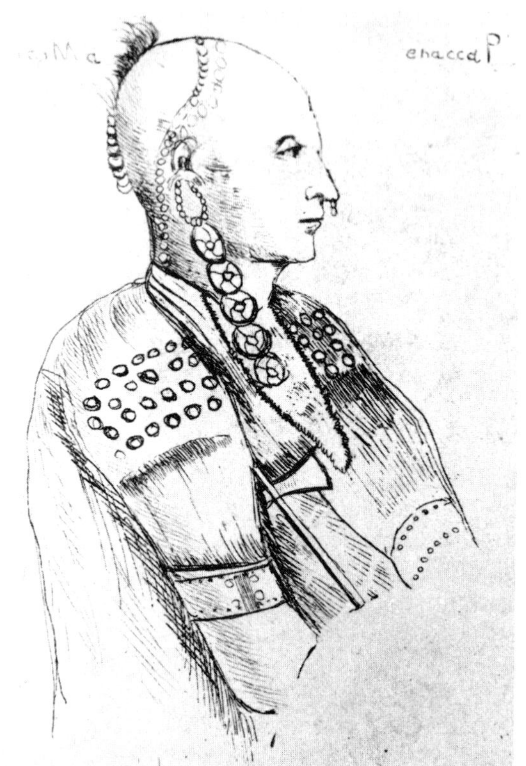

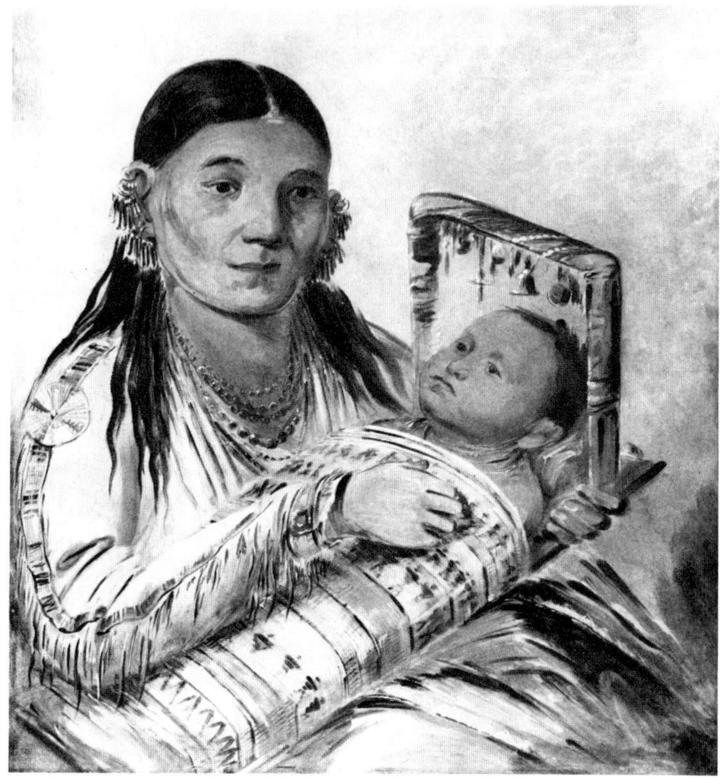

28

Paccane, a Miamis

Ear ornaments were a popular trade good. Both men and women wore ear-wheels similar to those illustrated in this sketch. Nose ornaments of silver were less common, although some were manufactured for the Indian trade. This man is also wearing armbands, brooches and hair ornaments, probably of silver.

29

Chee-Ah-Ka-Tchee, Wife of Not-To-Way

Silver ornaments were sometimes used for purposes other than personal adornment. Here an Iroquois woman has hung some silver trinkets on a cradleboard as a plaything, or perhaps as an amulet, for her child.

BREWETT,

A Celebrated Miami Chief.

30

Brewett, a Celebrated Miami Chief

This portrait, from a sketch made at the Treaty of Massinnewa in 1827, illustrates the popular style of wearing several crescent gorgets one above the other. Brewett also wears silver earrings, nose-ring, headband, and arm and wrist bands.

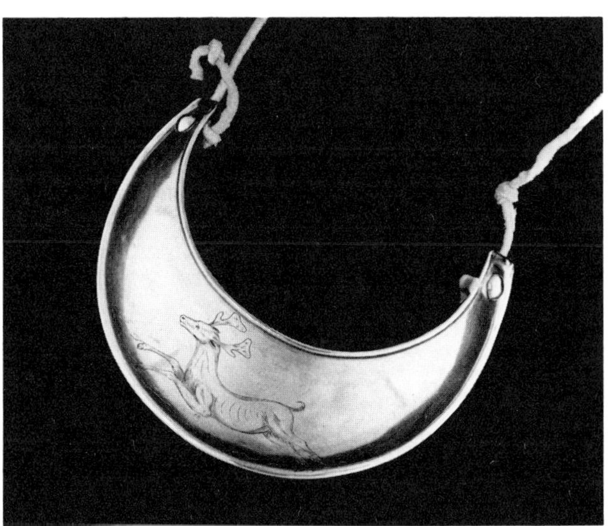

31

Animal imagery is a significant part of Woodland Indian tradition. There are legends woven about all the animals found in the region, and special powers are attributed to them. The Iroquois legend of the turtle, for instance, explains that the earth was formed from a lump of mud on the turtle's back. Iroquois clans usually bear the name of an animal—Turtle, Bear, Eel, Wolf, for example. It is believed that the engraved animal designs on some pieces of trade silver are clan symbols or personal signatures of the owner.

Some of the engraving has been done with the flourish of a professional engraver. The deer on this gorget is an example of the highly stylized animals the Indians sometimes wanted engraved on trade silver. On other pieces the engraving looks more amateurish, and may have been done by the owner.

appears from archaeological evidence that hair-pipes of shell, bone and silver were worn all together at the turn of the nineteenth century.

Where extremely long hair was fashionable, the more elaborate silver hair-plates were also traded. Although popular on the plains, hair-plates were traded to the eastern Indians between 1750 and 1821. When twenty or more of these silver discs were worn along a single plait of hair, the effect resembled that achieved in the following passage:

> They divide [the hair] and plat from 10 to 25 tresses about one inch broad; on those quaittes they stick pieces of gum three or four inches square and an inch apart, which every morning, after washing and freshening, they carefully daub with red or white clay, always painting the patches of gum one color and the intervening spaces another. This decoration at a distance has nearly the same effect as a Saulteur (Ojibwa) head covered with silver brooches.*

Perhaps the oldest form of trade silver, and one of the few without an Indian prototype, is the cross. Introduced by the earliest French missionaries to North America, the cross and the crucifix were first distributed among aboriginal converts, but during the fur trade era they became a popular trade item, usually without religious significance. The cross circulated well into the nineteenth century.

Several forms, of varying degrees of ornateness, have been found of the single-barred, or Latin, cross; the double-barred Lorraine, or Patriarchal, cross; and the triple-barred, or Papal, cross. The Papal cross, rarest of the three, was usually the most ornate. Crosses of the fur trade era vary in length from 2.5 to 25 centimetres, with an occasional exception measuring as much as 45 centimetres. Of the marked crosses that have been discovered, the majority appear to have been produced in Montreal, many of them by Robert Cruickshank. Indians wore the larger crosses on the breast, suspended on a chain or string, and the smaller ones as ear ornaments.

There are no clear indications of tribal or regional preferences for these various forms of silver, with the exception of the various Iroquoian brooch

---

*Norman Feder, "Plains Indian Metalworking", Pt. 1, *American Indian Tradition,* vol. 8, no. 2, pp. 57–8.

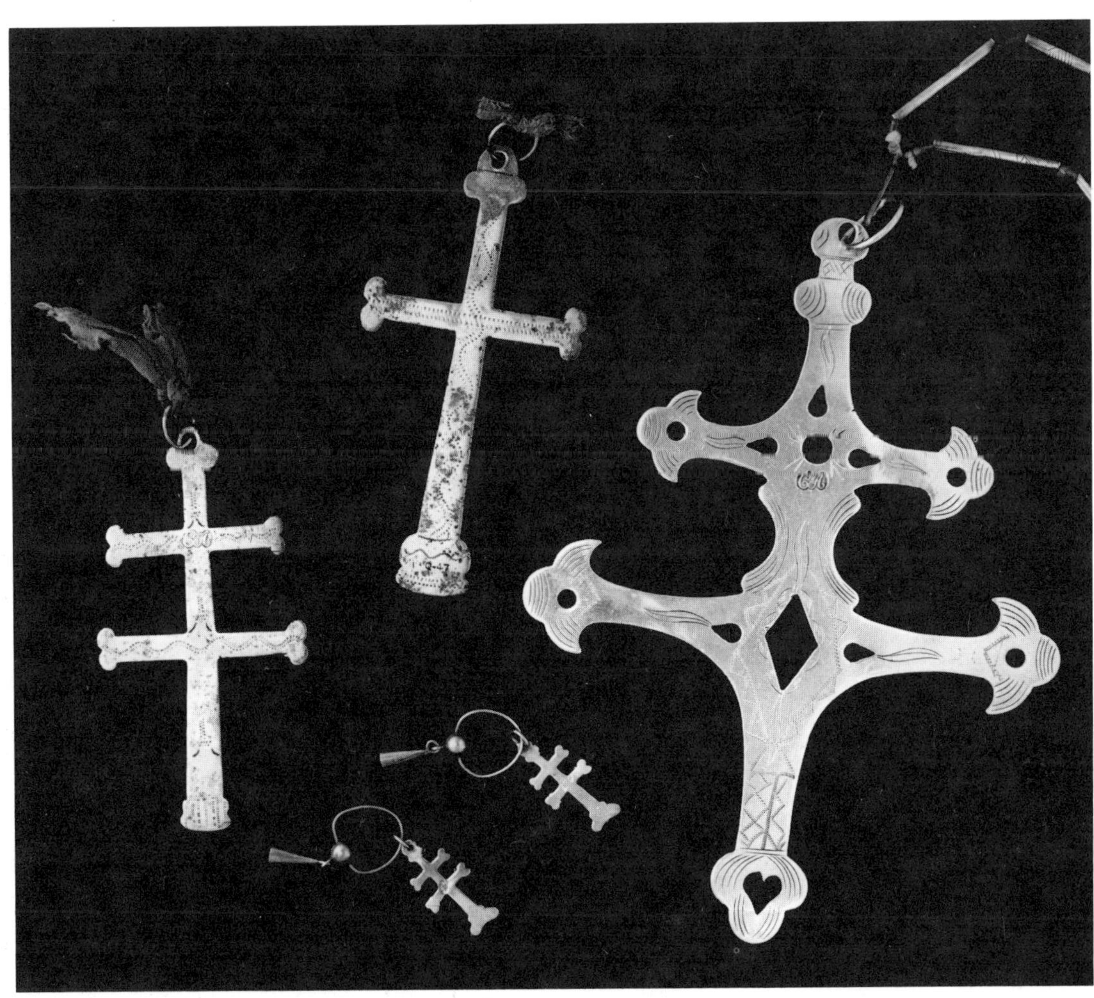

32

The cross was introduced in North America by Christian missionaries, who gave crosses of copper or brass (rarely of silver) to their Indian converts. It quickly achieved secular popularity, and was manufactured in large quantities for the fur trade. The most common styles were the single-barred Latin cross and the double-barred Lorraine cross.

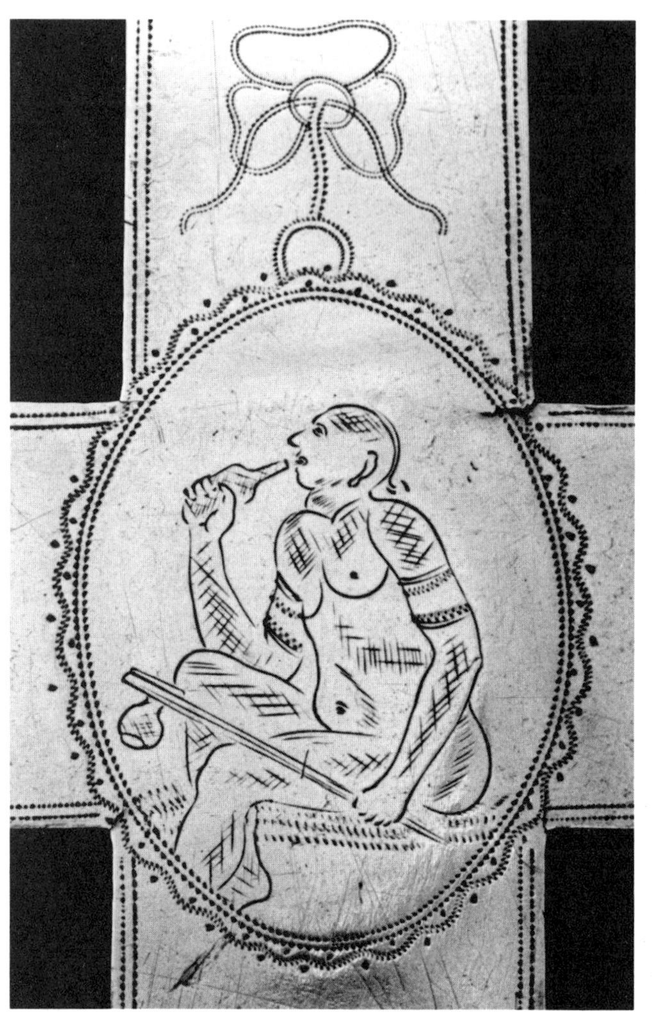

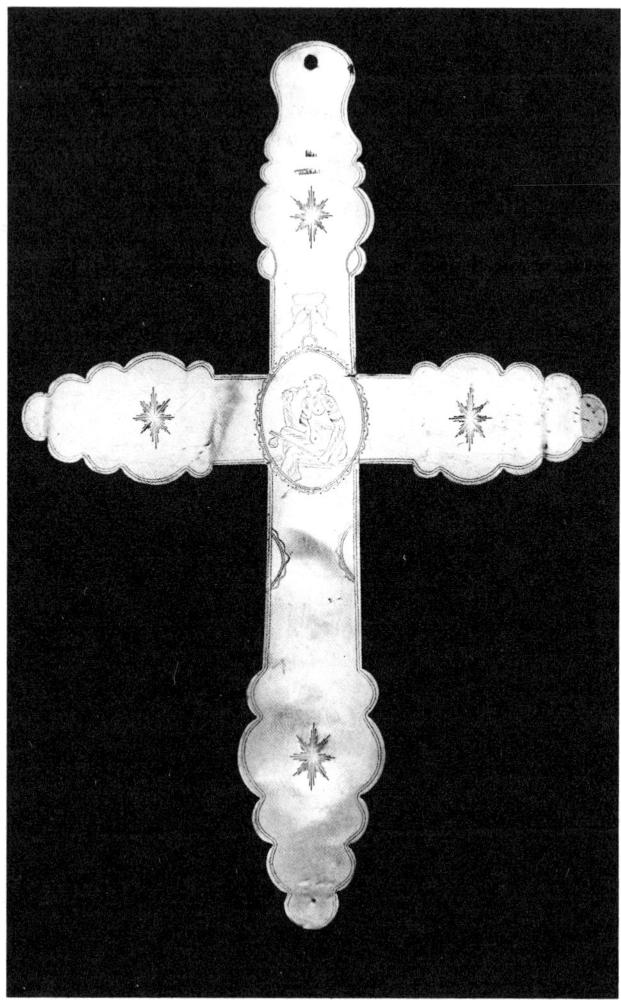

33

Evidence of the secular use of a sacred symbol is provided by this silver cross made for the fur trade by Pierre Huguet dit *Latour. The large single-barred chest ornament bears the engraving of an Indian apparently drinking whisky out of a bottle.*

designs. For purposes of identification, however, the designs engraved on all forms of trade silver might give possible clues. Most decorative designs appealed to some element of Indian culture or some regional characteristic that might increase interest in the piece.

One of the most popular engraved designs was the scene, or tableau. An order for trading goods sent from Fort Albany to England in 1796 included the following:

> Gorgets, with the following engravings. Vizt. to represent Albany, two or three Houses, some Indian Tents and Indian Men & Women, No 12.*

Other popular scenes included a white man and an Indian in an alliance ceremony. Because of their large size, engravings of this nature were usually found on gorgets.

Much more personal were the animal engravings found on many silver pieces. These fall into two categories, imaginative and representational. It is thought that the representations of animals were clan or personal symbols, designating ownership of the article. Totemic symbols of this kind were often used by Indian chiefs when signing agreements with Europeans. The imaginative figures, on the other hand, would be more likely to have some religious or mythological significance.

Among Algonquian tribes, the use of floral patterns was well established before the coming of the European. Floral designs are variations on the double-curve motif well known in Algonquian art – two opposing curves stemming from a single base. This design is thought to represent the "celestial tree", a symbol of peace and of the origin of the world. Leaves and branches of the coniferous trees indigenous to the eastern woodlands were also a popular design.

How the silver ornaments produced by Canadian, American and European craftsmen came to be decorated with distinctively Indian designs is uncertain. Quimby speculates that "the Indians made drawings of the animals for the trader, who in turn submitted them to the silversmith for engraving, or in some cases it may have been the trader who actually engraved

*Quoted in Barbeau, p. 37.

64

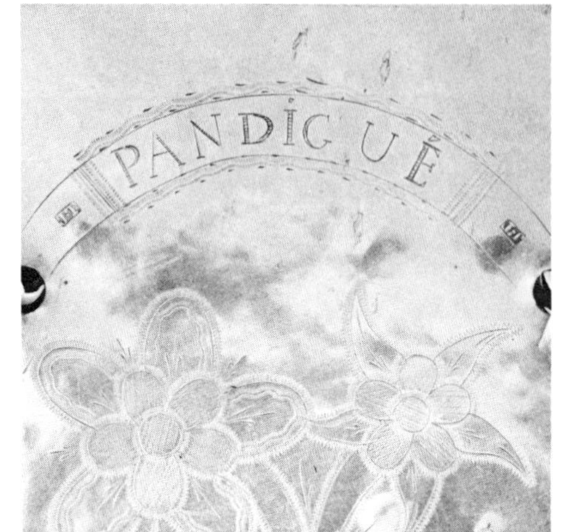

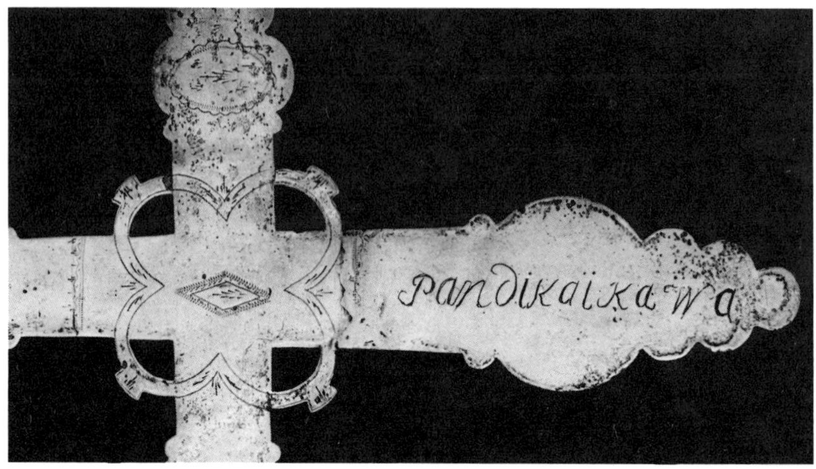

The Delaware Deputies sent from Ohio to [illegible] Ratify and Confirm the [illegible] Treaty [illegible] by [illegible] for themselves and the rest of the whole Nation Confirm the whole of the said Treaty [illegible] the same having been fully Explained and Clearly understood by them. [illegible] the Great King of England and to be Stiled such for the Future, [illegible] British Crown [illegible] Subjection so far as the same can be Consistent with the Indians Native Rights. In Testimony whereof they have hereunto Affixed their proper Marks and Seals [illegible]

The Shawanese Deputys sent from Ohio to Subscribe to a Treaty of Peace before Sir William Johnson [illegible] they are duly Authorized Agree to every Article of the Treaty Subscribed to by the Delawares, so far as the same can be Extended to the Shawanese, and do engage faithfully to abide thereby, the same having been fully Explained to and Clearly understood by them. [illegible] of the Great King of England and to be Stiled such for the Future [illegible] to the British Crown [illegible] Submission and Subjection so far as the same be Consistent with their Native Rights. In Testimony whereof they have hereunto Affixed their proper Marks and Seals at Johnson Hall the 13th day of July 1765.

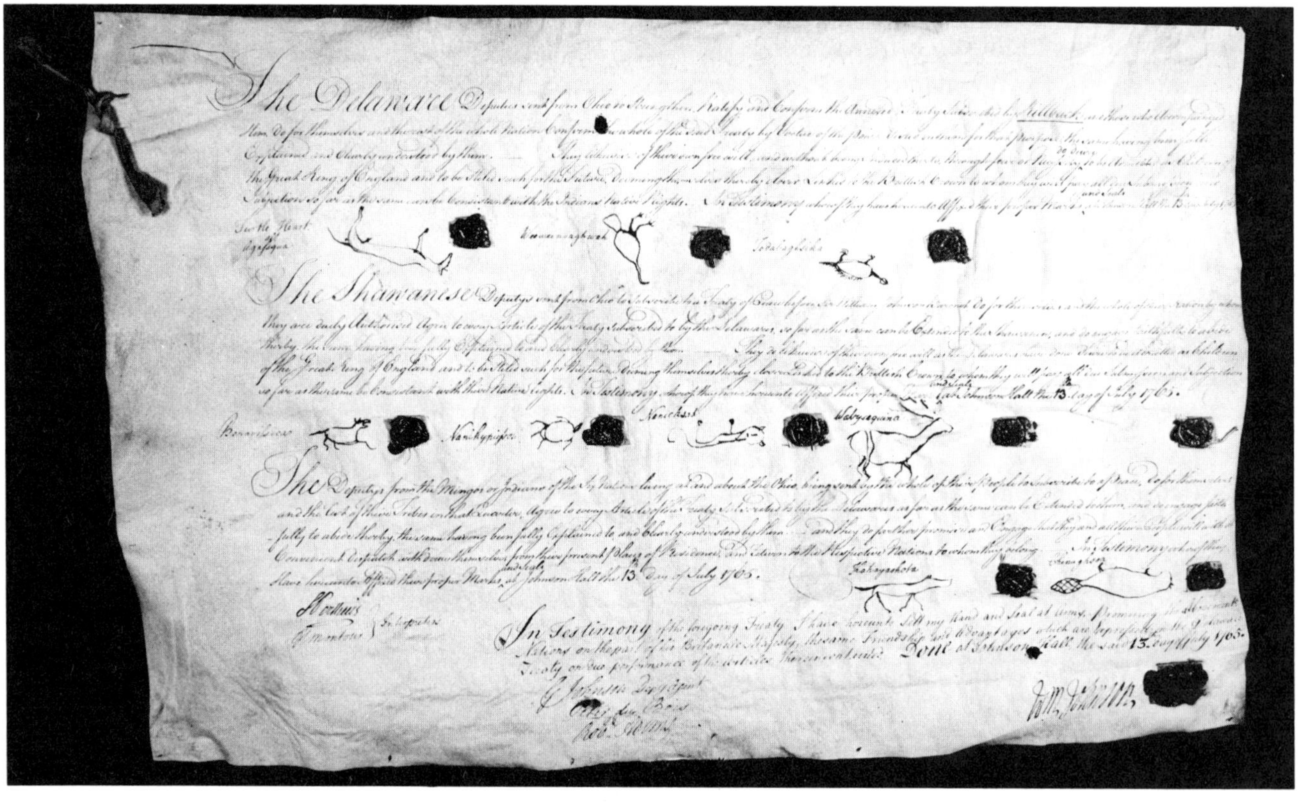

The Deputies from the Mingoes or Indians of the Six Nations living at and about the Ohio, being sent by the whole of their People to Subscribe to a Peace, do for themselves and the rest of their Tribes in that Quarter, Agree to every Article of the Treaty Subscribed to by the Delawares as far as the same can be Extended to them, and do engage faithfully to abide thereby, the same having been fully Explained to and Clearly understood by them [illegible] and they do further promise and Engage that they and all their People will with all Convenient dispatch withdraw themselves from their present Place of Residence, and return to the Respective Nations to whom they belong. In Testimony whereof they have hereunto Affixed their proper Marks and Seals at Johnson Hall the 13th Day of July 1765.

In Testimony of the foregoing Treaty I have hereunto Sett my Hand and Seal at Arms, Promising the [illegible] Advantages which are Expressed on the [illegible] Nations on the part of his Britannic Majesty, the same Friendship [illegible] Treaty on due performance of the Articles therein contained. Done at Johnson Hall the said 13th day of July 1765.

G. Johnson Dep. Agent
[illegible]
Robt. Adems

Wm. Johnson

the ornaments" *, although the latter is highly unlikely. In any case, there is a wide range of refinement in the engravings, from the highly stylized to the very crude. Another possible explanation for the engravings might be found among the Indians themselves. Perhaps the Indian recipients inscribed their own designs on the silver. There is some evidence to indicate that by the early 1800s the Iroquois had begun working silver, and could conceivably have altered the pieces already in circulation.

---

*George Irving Quimby, *Indian Culture and European Trade Goods* (Madison: University of Wisconsin Press, 1966), p. 97.

34

Many items of personal adornment identify their owners by the name or symbol they carry. The large gorget bears the name "Pandigué" as well as the maker's mark of Jonathan Tyler, a Montreal silversmith. The cross bears the name of Pandikaikawa, an Indian chief who was the son of Chief Panamas, the Ojibwa who signed the surrender of Mackinac Island to Britain during the War of 1812.

35

This document, dated 13 July 1765, is a treaty between the British and the Delaware, Shawnee and Mingo tribes. The Indians' signatures are pictures of various animals, used to represent either their clan association or personal totem. Sir William Johnson signed for the British.

VI / IROQUOIS SILVERSMITHS

As THE RESULT OF THE DECLINING DEMAND FOR FURS in Europe, the inroads into the beaver population of eastern Canada, and the opening up of western and northern sources of supply, fur trading in the eastern regions fell sharply towards the end of the eighteenth century. With the amalgamation of the Hudson's Bay Company and the North West Company in 1821, competition became less vigorous, and traders were no longer concerned with winning the Indians with more attractive trade goods than their opponents had to offer. These factors combined to bring a virtual end to the trade in silver articles with the Great Lakes and East Coast Indians.

By this time silver had become a customary part of Indian costume and ceremony, and a few Indians had acquired from the white man the techniques of the silversmith. Having begun working with other metals early in the period of contact with whites, Indian craftsmen would find it relatively easy to adapt the techniques of cruder metalcraft to the working of silver. It is believed that, among the Iroquois at least, silversmithing was first practised shortly after 1800. In 1851, Lewis H. Morgan wrote that "most of the silver ornaments in later years have been made by Indian silversmiths, one of whom may be found in nearly every Indian village."* It is not known whether this was the case with other Indian tribes with whom silver was traded. In any case, among the Iroquois the craft appears to have gradually died out, and by the early years of the twentieth century only a few aged smiths were still working.

In 1907, anthropologist M. R. Harrington described an interview with one of the remaining silversmiths, Chief Levi Joe of the Onondaga tribe on the Six Nations Reserve in Ontario.** Using patterns and methods he had learned

---

**League of the Ho-de'-no-sau-nee, or Iroqouis*, enl. ed., 2 vols. in 1 (New York: Dodd, Mead, 1904), vol. 2, p. 50.

**"Iroquois Silverwork", *Anthropological Papers of the American Museum of Natural History*, vol. 1, pt. 6 (1908), pp. 351–69.

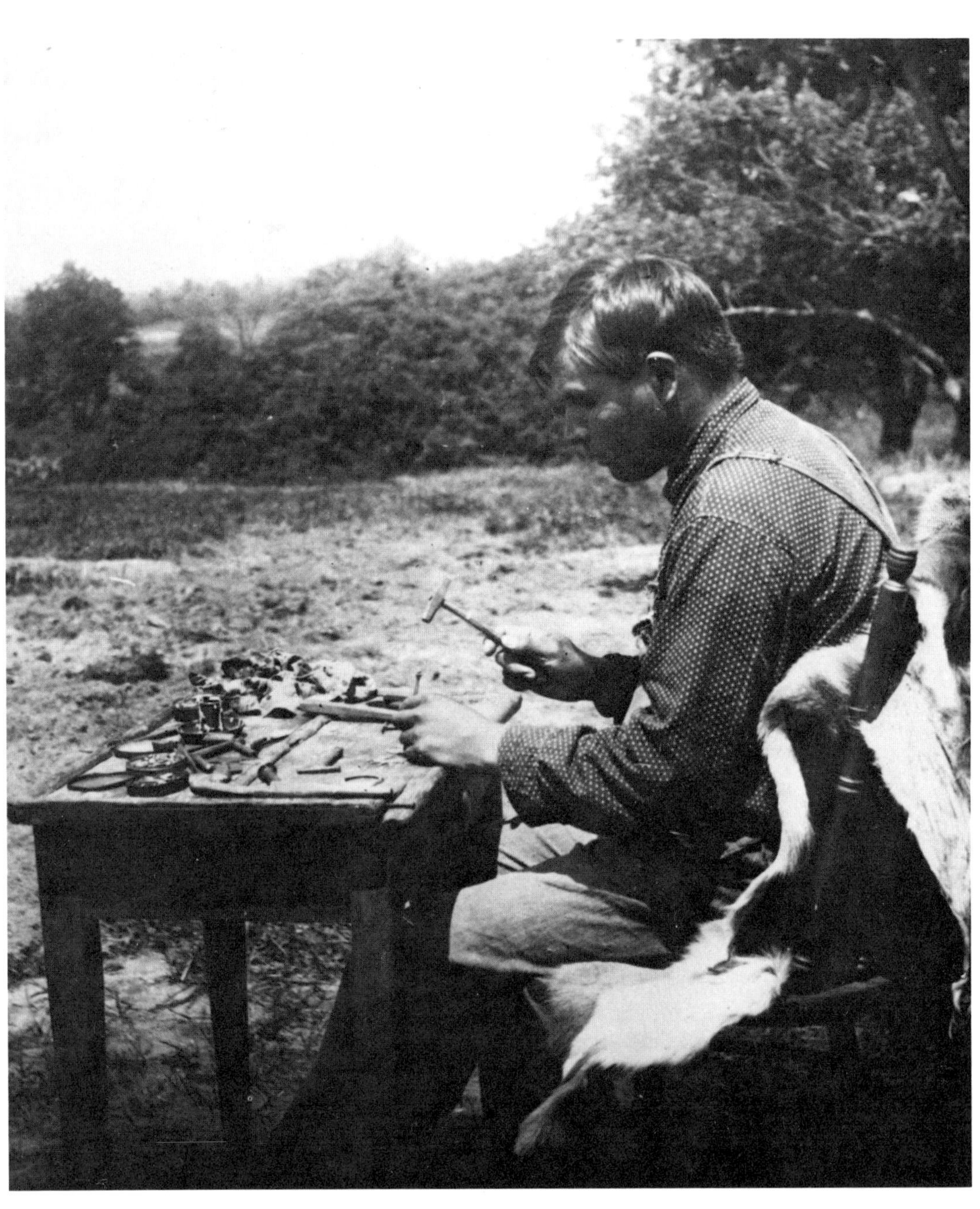

from his grandfather, the Chief made several ornaments in Harrington's presence.

In converting a Canadian dime to a brooch, the Chief laid the silver coin on the anvil and beat it with a large hammer until its diameter increased by over 2 centimetres and its thickness was greatly reduced. He then smoothed the now blank face of the silver with a file. For the star brooch he intended to make he had cut a pattern out of tin.

> Laying this pattern where he could see it, he perforated the centre of the blank with one of the awls. Then using the pincers as dividers, holding their jaws apart with one of the chisels, he laid off a circle to mark out the central opening of the brooch, the tip of the pincers making distinct scratches. . . . The points about the periphery, where the rays of the star were to terminate in bosses, were then marked out and the arms themselves indicated.*

When an accurate pattern was available, it was placed upon the blank, and its outline was traced directly into the silver with an awl. The bosses at the tips of the star were made by laying the edge of the blank over the smallest hole on the die-plate, and forcing the silver into it with a stamp driven by a hammer. Then, the outline of the star was cut with curved and straight chisels, and the surplus metal trimmed off. Edges were smoothed with a file and the surface decorated with engraving. Once completed, the brooch was perforated near the edge of the central opening, and the pin hinged there. Arm

*Ibid., p. 363.

36

Indian silversmiths began to make ornaments for their people after silver ceased to be available through the fur trade. The craft seems to have been practised in Iroquois villages through the last half of the nineteenth century, but died out soon after 1900. This Iroquois silversmith was photographed at work in the early twentieth century.

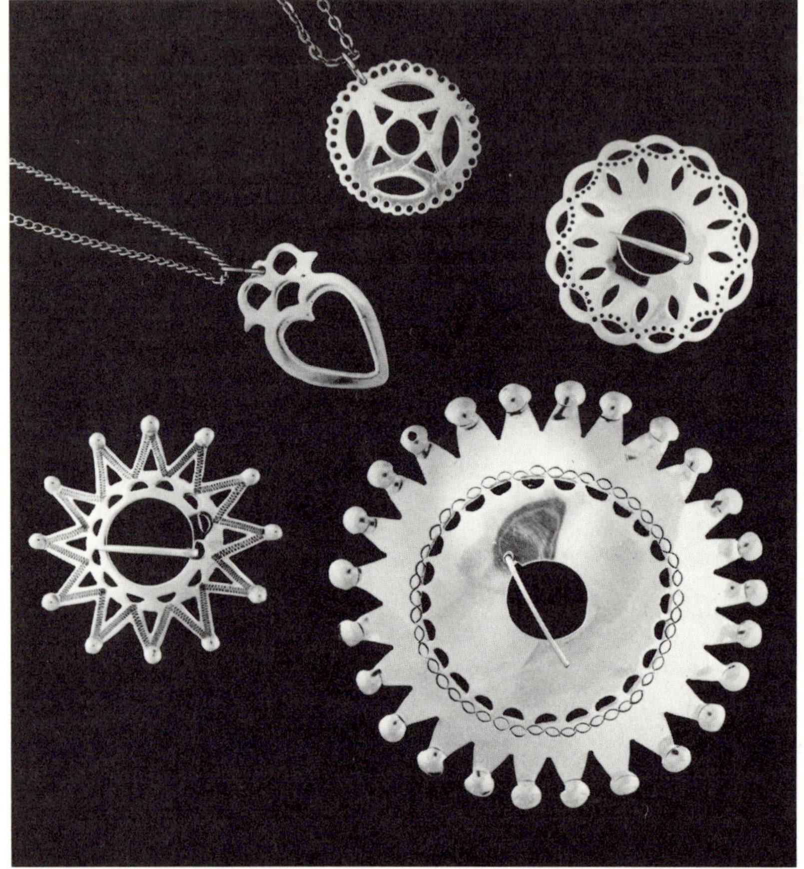

37

Several Iroquois silversmiths have recently revived the craft practised briefly by their ancestors in the nineteenth century. These pieces fashioned by silversmiths on the Six Nations Reserve in southern Ontario are copies of some of the eighteenth-century designs of European and colonial silversmiths.

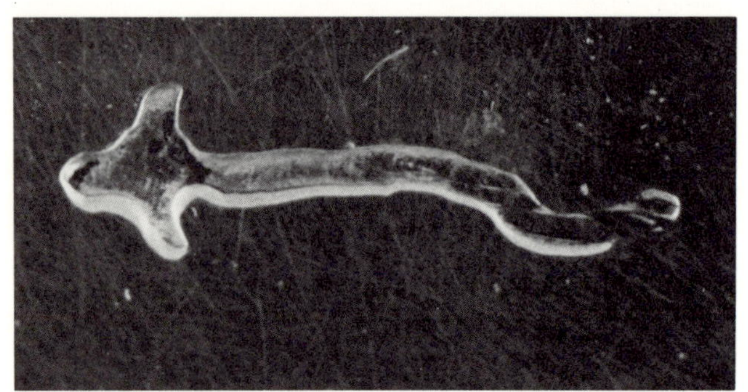

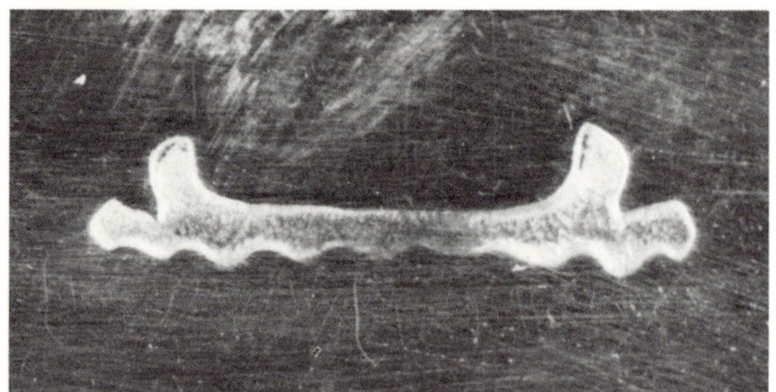

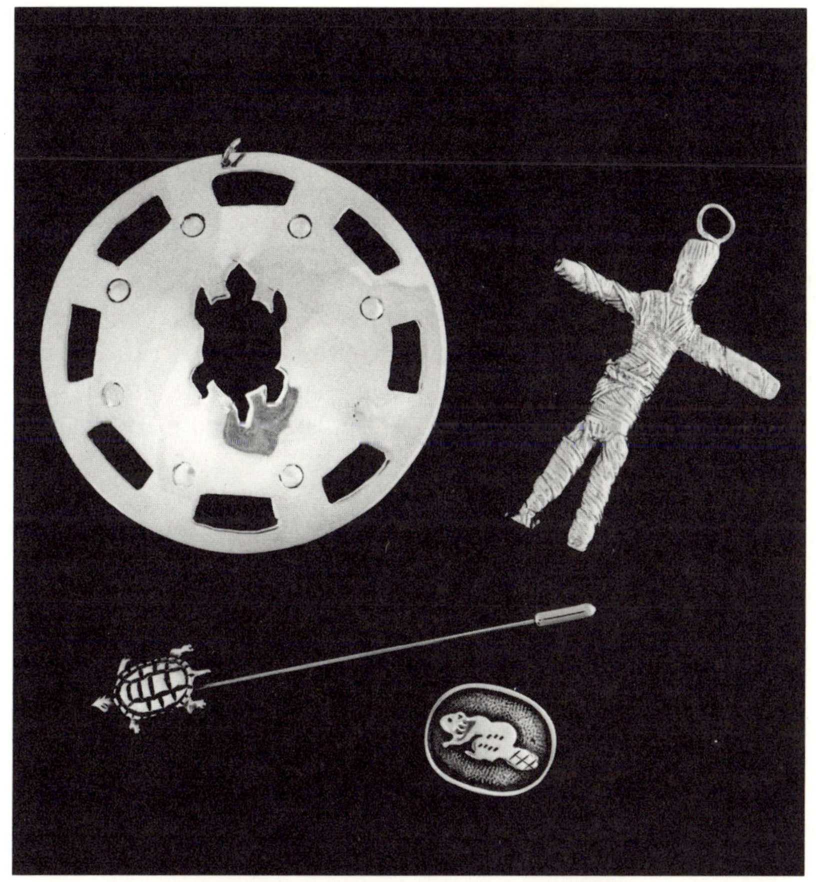

38

Modern Iroquois silversmiths are creating new designs that, while adapted from traditional trade-silver patterns, are nevertheless distinctively their own. Many of the pieces are based on the animal symbols of Iroquois clans or on other characteristic symbols of Iroquois life.

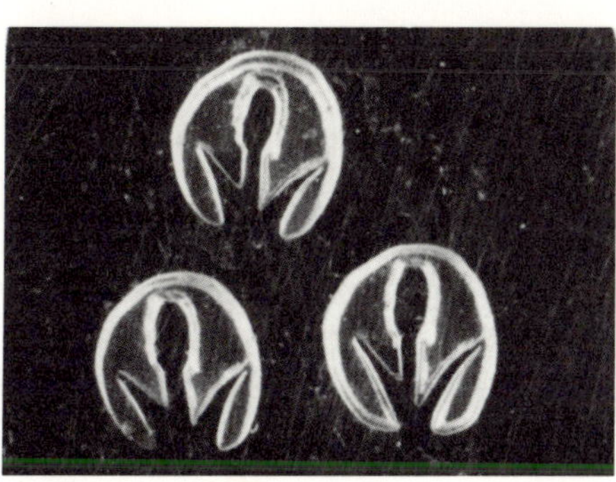

39

Following the practice of eighteenth-century colonial silversmiths, modern Iroquois craftsmen sign their work with their own distinctive makers' marks. Arthur Powless, a member of the Eel clan of the Onondaga Nation, has adopted the eel as his mark. Elwood Green uses a depiction of his Indian name, Floating Canoe, and his son Anthony marks his jewellery with three cattails.

and head bands were hammered from silver first cast in shallow rectangular moulds, and then decorated in the same fashion as the brooches.

With the passing of the old silversmiths early in the twentieth century, the craft appeared to have died out among the Iroquois. Old silver ornaments were worn on ceremonial occasions, but new ones were not being made. Silver jewellery became very rare.

Today, on the Six Nations Reserve, a few Iroquois silversmiths have revived the craft. Having studied the old trade patterns found in museum collections and publications, they now make brooches and pendants in both traditional forms and modern adaptations. Of course, their methods have been modified by modern technology. They use an electric drill to pierce the blank silver in the initial cut, but, other than that, their main tools are a variety of files and chisels, a small soldering torch, and a few preserving chemicals. Their jewellery can be distinguished from eighteenth-century silver by its uniform thickness, consistent sterling content, and distinctive makers' marks. Jewellery marked with the sign of the eel is crafted by Arthur Powless of Ohsweken, Ontario, on the Six Nations Reserve. The canoe-shaped mark is the sign of Elwood Green, of Caledonia, whose Iroquois name is Floating Canoe. His son Anthony marks his jewellery with three cattails.

The work of the modern Iroquois silversmiths is an important manifestation of the creative force of cultural contact. While the metal and the techniques were contributed by Europeans, most of the forms and designs are Indian in origin. The uses and significance of trade silver are distinctly Indian. Each band and brooch is a testimony to the Indian influence on the North American fur trade.

CATALOGUE

The dates given for the silversmiths represent the earliest and latest known references to each of them, except for the British silversmiths, whose dates indicate when the pieces were made.

LENDERS TO THE EXHIBITION

The National Museum of Man wishes to thank the institutions that generously responded to our requests to borrow from their collections for this exhibition. They are listed below, along with the abbreviations that identify them in the catalogue. (Objects from this museum's collection carry the abbreviation NMM.)

Alabama	Alabama Department of Archives and History, Montgomery
ANS	American Numismatic Society, New York
Bk. Canada	Bank of Canada, National Currency Collection, Ottawa
Glenbow	Glenbow Museum, Calgary
McCord	McCord Museum, Montreal
MHS	Missouri Historical Society, St. Louis
MMFA	Montreal Museum of Fine Arts, Montreal
Heye	Museum of the American Indian, Heye Foundation, New York
NGC	National Gallery of Canada, Ottawa
NGC, Birks	National Gallery of Canada, Henry Birks Collection of Canadian Silver, Ottawa
NMAS	National Museum of Antiquities of Scotland, Edinburgh
NBM	New Brunswick Museum, Saint John
OMC	Ottawa Masonic Corporation, Ottawa
Parks	Parks Canada, Western Region, Calgary
PMA	Provincial Museum of Alberta, Edmonton
PAC	Public Archives of Canada, National Medal Collection, Ottawa
Putnam	Putnam Museum, Davenport, Iowa
ROM	Royal Ontario Museum, Toronto
U. Sask.	University of Saskatchewan, Saskatoon

I / GIFTS OF SILVER

In the exchange of gifts that took place at Indian–European ceremonial councils, the Indians received a variety of goods, including clothing, weapons and silver ornaments. These Huron leaders have posed in their finery for the painter Henry D. Thielcke. They are wearing an Indian adaptation of European military dress, heavily decorated with silver armbands, gorgets, medals and earrings.

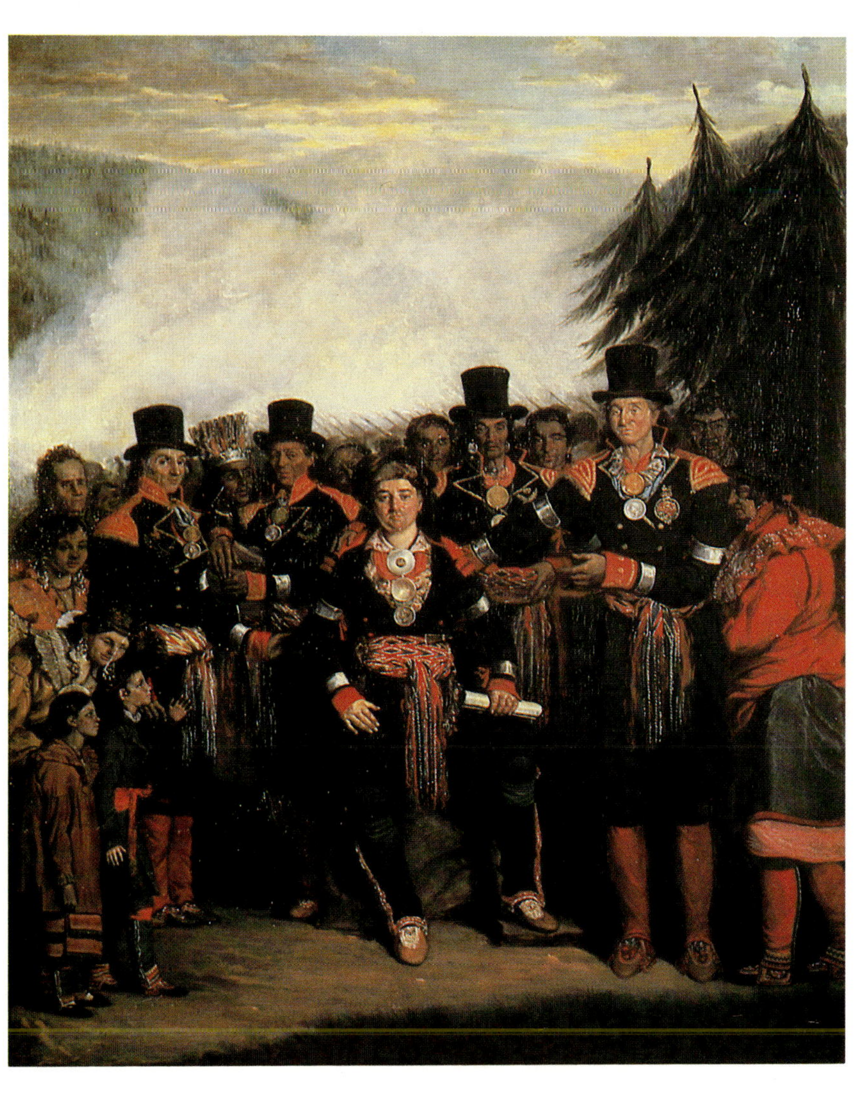

1/British Medal
OBV.: GEORGIUS III DEI GRATIA
REV.: Royal arms of Britain
SIZE: 7.7 cm diam.
COLL.: McCord (M5932)

2/Wampum Belt
MATERIALS: Shell beads, rawhide
DATE: 1750–1820
SIZE: 68 cm l. × 10 cm w.
COLL.: NMM (III-I-35)

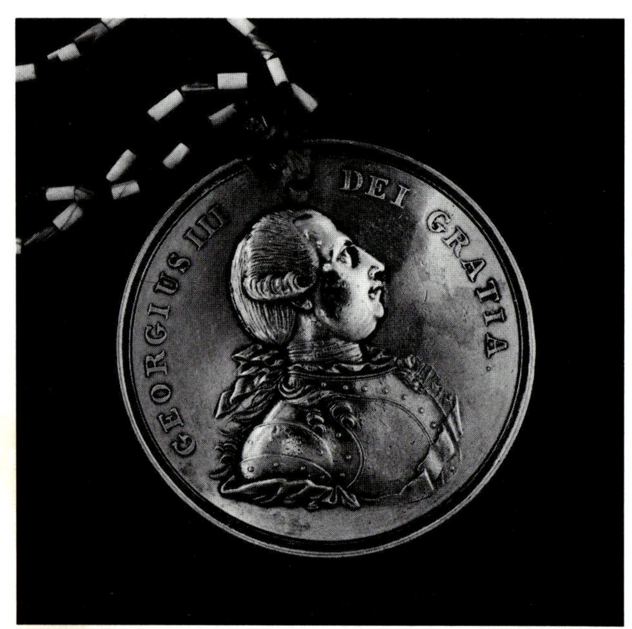

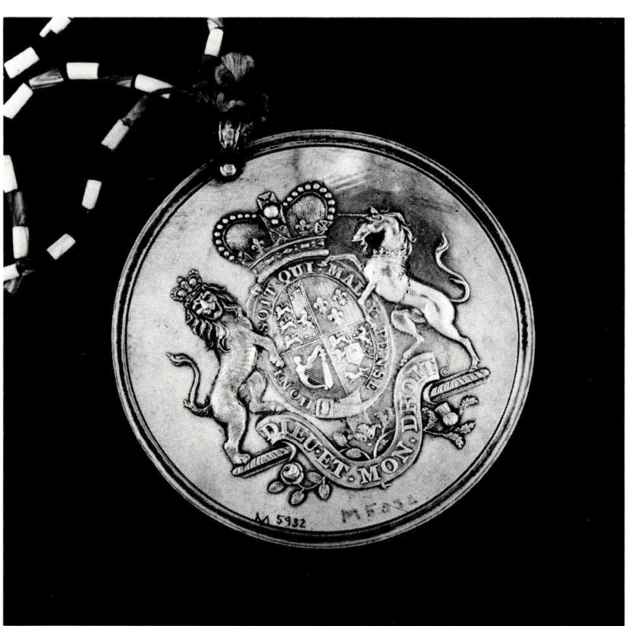

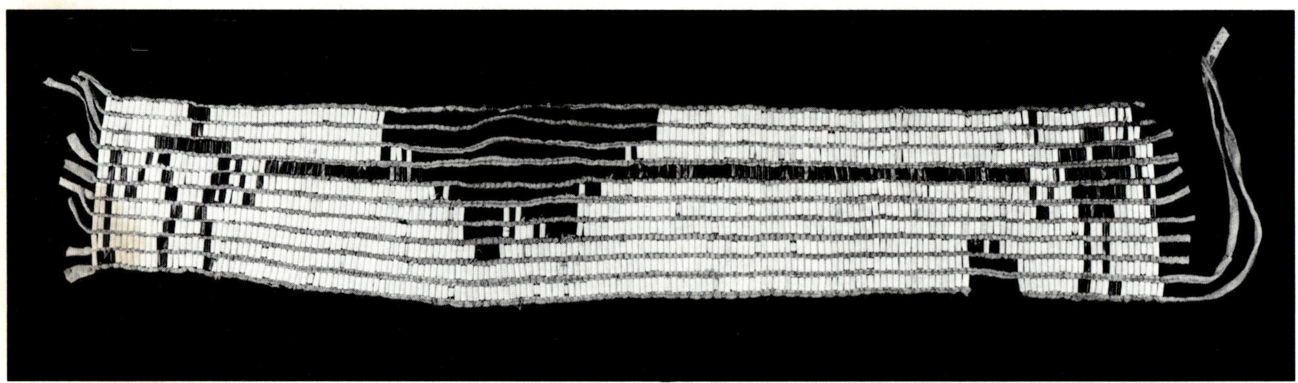

3/British Medal
OBV.: GEORGIVS II DEI GRATIA
REV.: LET US LOOK TO THE MOST HIGH WHO BLESSED OUR FATHERS WITH PEACE/1757
SIZE: 4.9 cm diam.
COLL.: PAC (H1608)

4/French Medal and Chain
OBV.: LUD. XV REX CHRISTIANISSIMUS
REV.: REX COELESTI OLEO UNCTUS REMIS 25 OCT. 1722
SIZE: 3.2 cm diam.
COLL.: NMM (III-H-470)

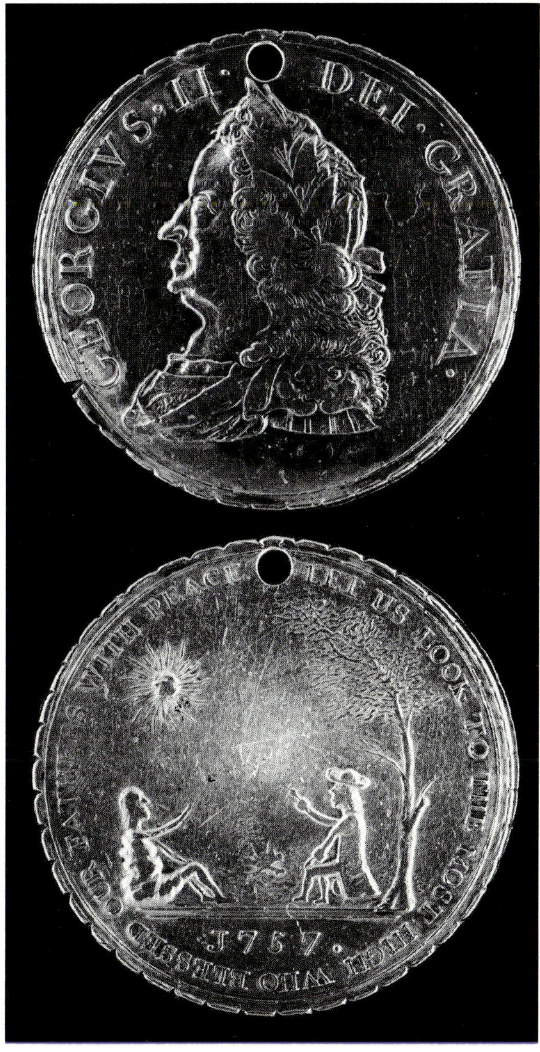

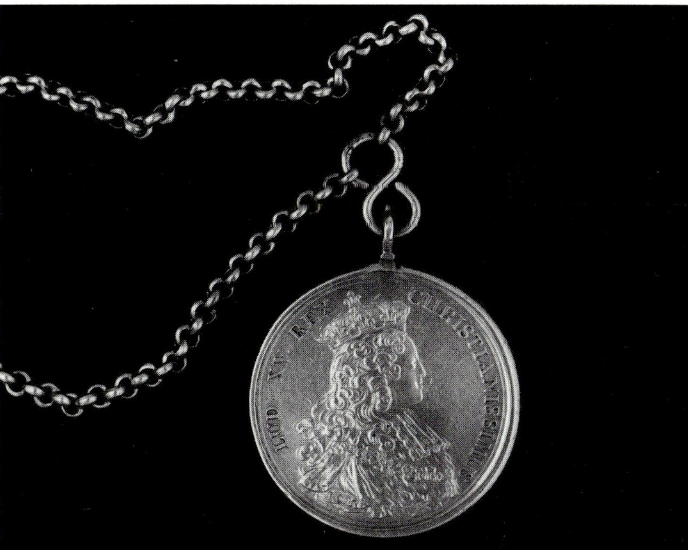

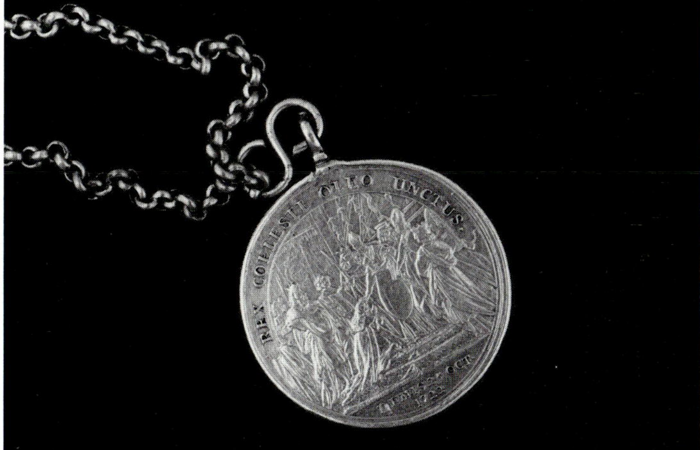

5/Calumet
MATERIALS: Wood, lead
DATE: 1750–1850
SIZE: 81.0 cm l. × 11.5 cm h.
COLL.: NMM (III-G-884a, b)

6/Luckenbooth Brooch
MATERIALS: Silver
DATE: 1700–50
SIZE: 4.9 cm h. × 2.8 cm w.
COLL.: NMAS (NGA-202)

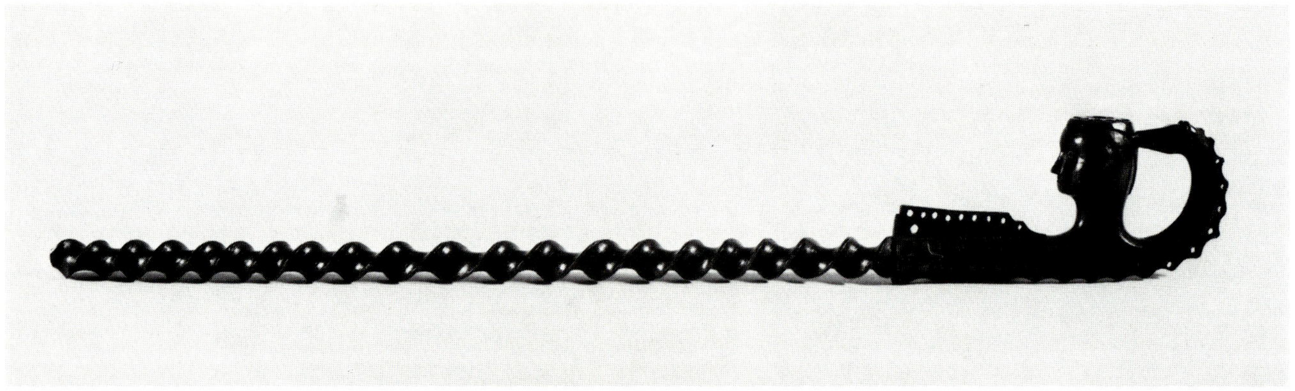

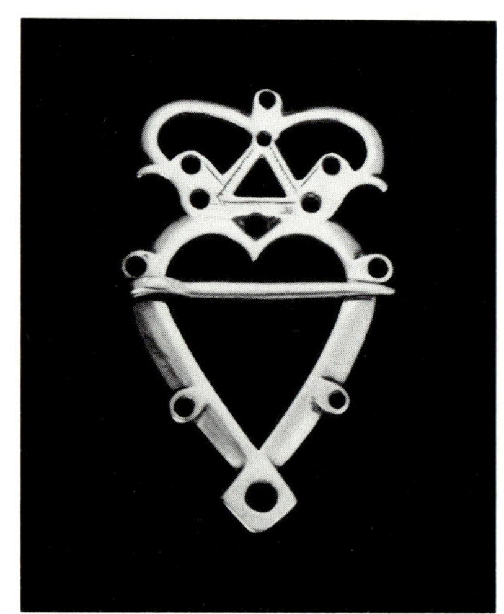

II / THE MEDAL TRADITION

Medals were the earliest form of silver presented to the Indians. At first they were used to secure friendly relations with Indian tribes, and later to confirm military alliances. In this portrait by George Catlin, the famous Seneca chief and orator Red Jacket wears the George Washington medal presented to him by the president in 1792. The first of the presidential medals, it was originally struck in 1789, but was modified in 1792 because of Indian dislike of the rendering of the female figure on the original medal. This later version, illustrated on page 86, shows Washington offering the peace pipe to an Indian.

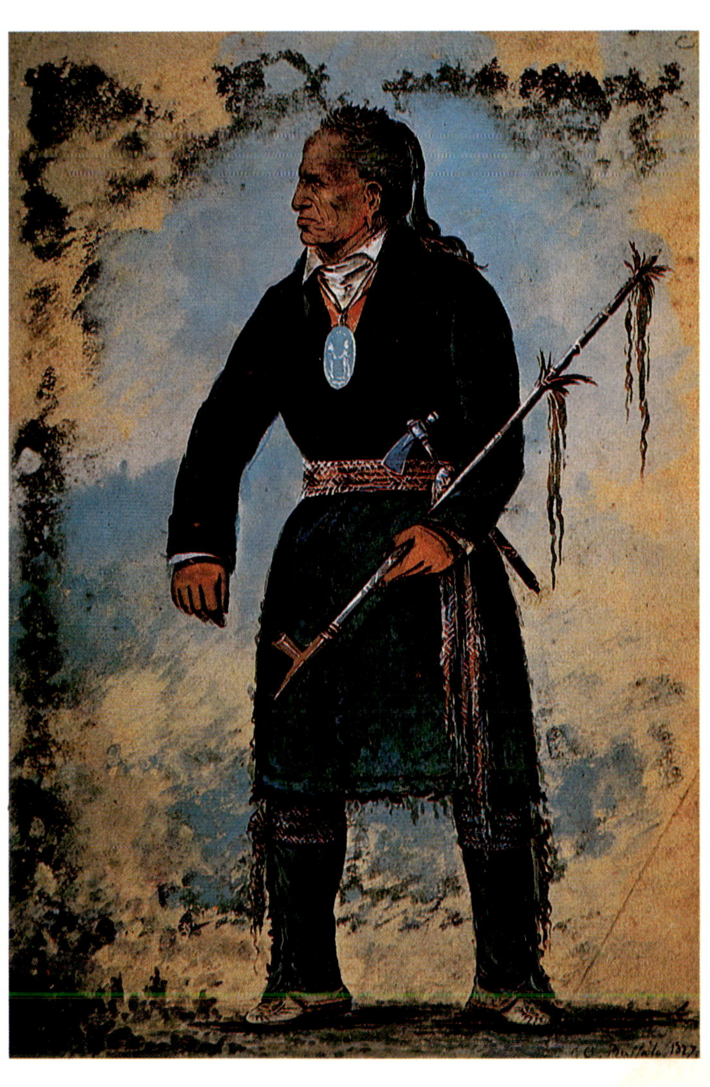

7/British Medal
OBV.: GEORGIUS III DEI GRATIA
REV.: Royal arms of Britain
SIZE: 7.7 cm diam.
COLL.: MMFA (953.Ds.23)

8/Spanish Medal
OBV.: CARLOS IIII REX DE
HISPANA Y DE LAS INDIAS
REV.: AL MERITO Y FIDELIDAD.
SIZE: 6.4 cm h. × 6.0 cm w.
COLL.: ANS

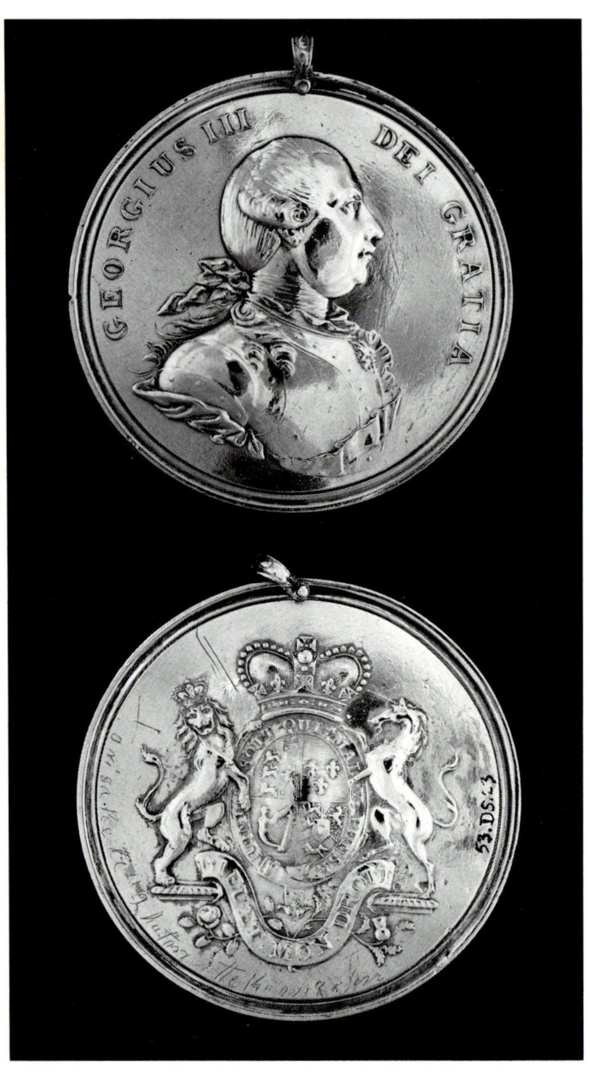

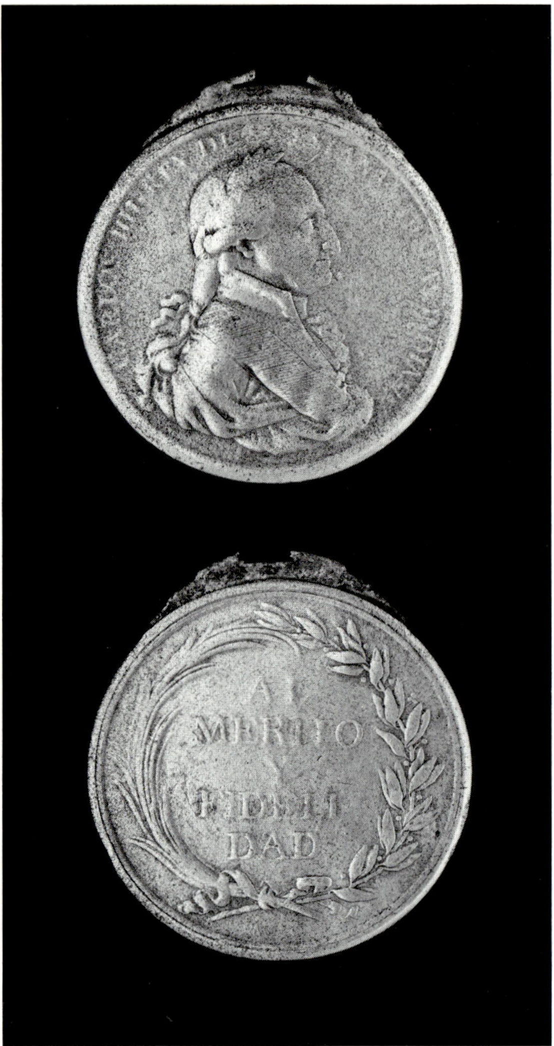

9/French Medal
OBV.: LUDOVICUS XV REX CHRISTIANISSIMUS
REV.: HONOS ET VIRTUS
SIZE: 5.1 cm diam.
COLL.: PAC (H1253)

10/British Medal (pewter)
OBV.: MONTREAL
REV.: Tankalkel MOHICKANS
SIZE: 4.5 cm diam.
COLL.: PAC (H1609)

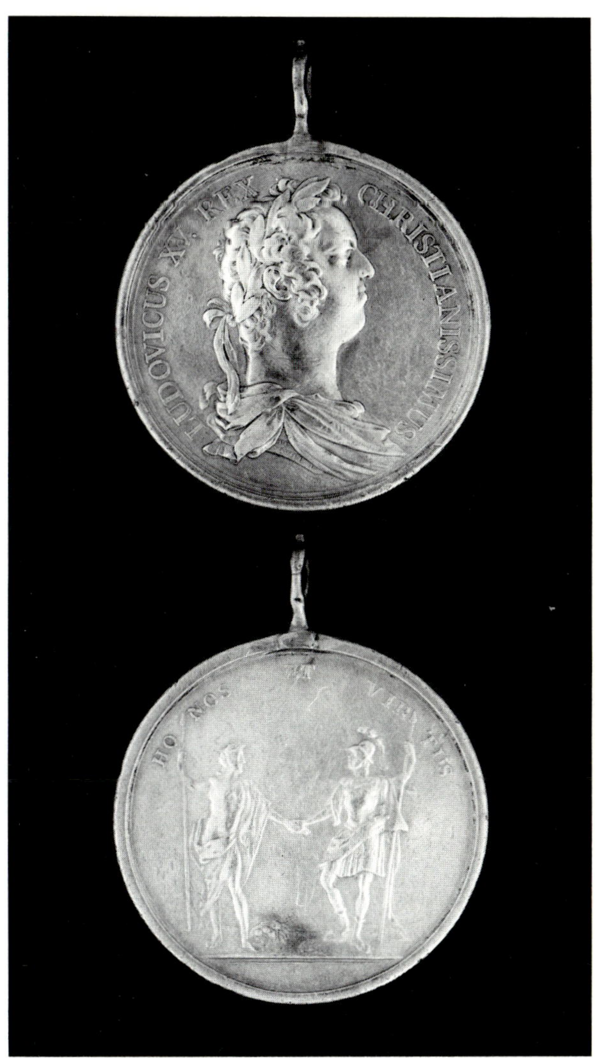

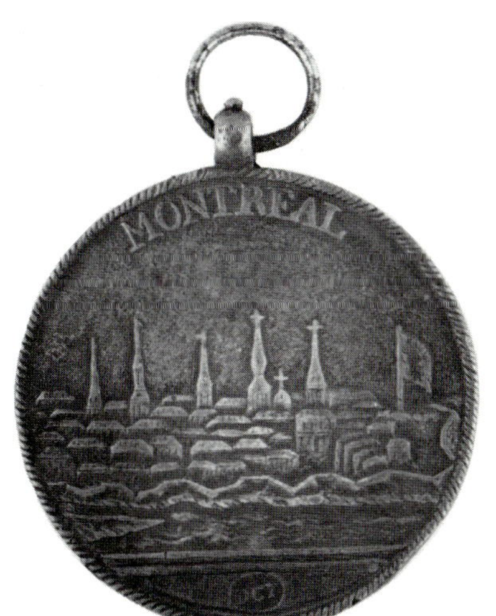

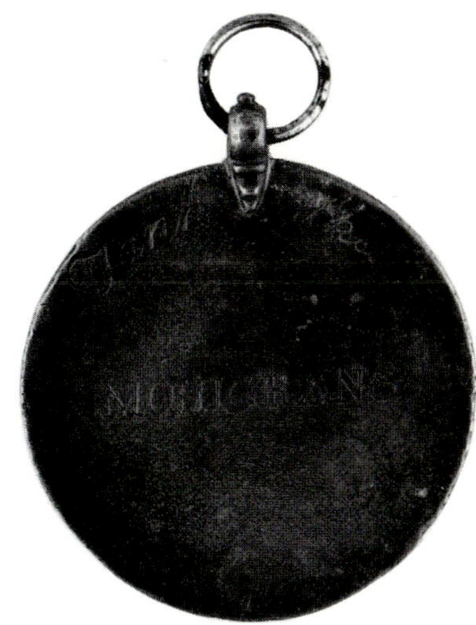

11/British Medal (1763)
OBV.: GEORGIUS III DEI GRATIA
REV.: Lion, wolf, faint background
SIZE: 6.1 cm diam.
COLL.: PAC (H1611)

12/British Medal
OBV.: GEORGIUS III D.G.M. BRI. FRA. ET HIB. REX F. D.
REV.: HAPPY WHILE UNITED 1764
SIZE: 5.6 cm diam.
COLL.: PAC (H1612)

13/Altered French Medal
OBV.: (Bust of Louis XV) Georgius III Rex Dei Gratia
REV.: HONOS ET VIRTUS/1775
SIZE: 5.6 cm diam.
COLL.: ANS

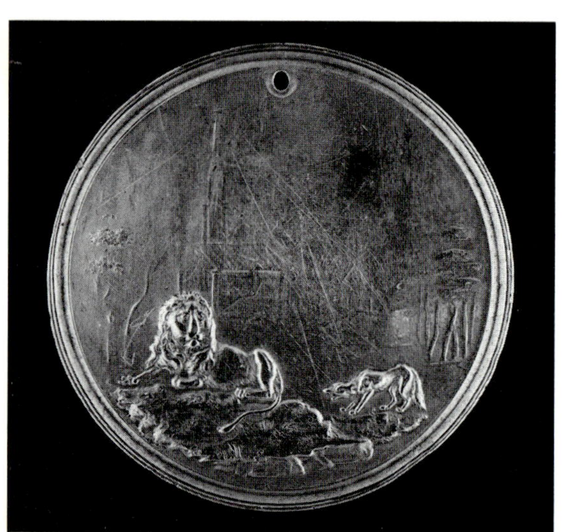

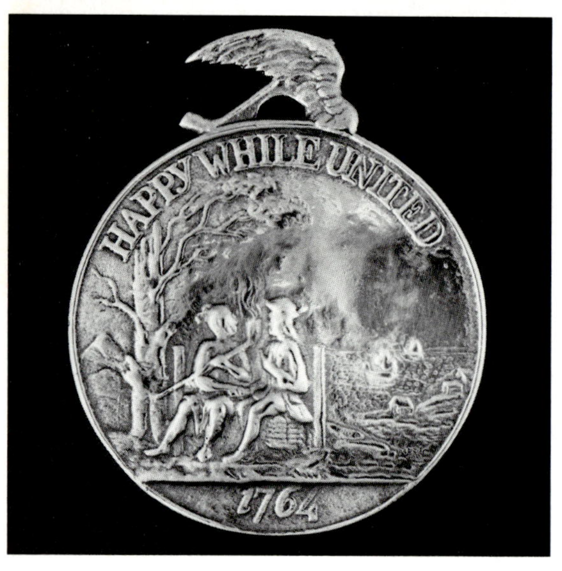

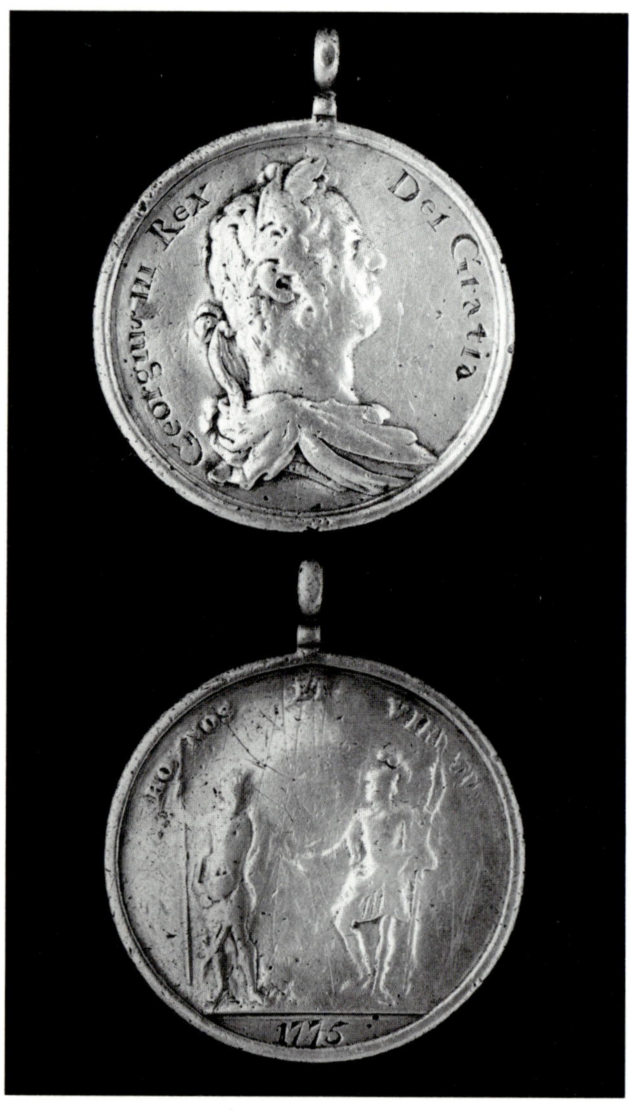

14/Wampum Belt
MATERIALS: Shell beads, rawhide
DATE: Unknown
SIZE: 79.0 cm l. × 6.5 cm w.
COLL.: McCord (M1909)

15/British Medal (c. 1812)
OBV.: GEORGIUS III DEI GRATIA
REV.: Royal arms of Britain
SIZE: 7.9 cm diam.
COLL.: MMFA (953.Ds.12)

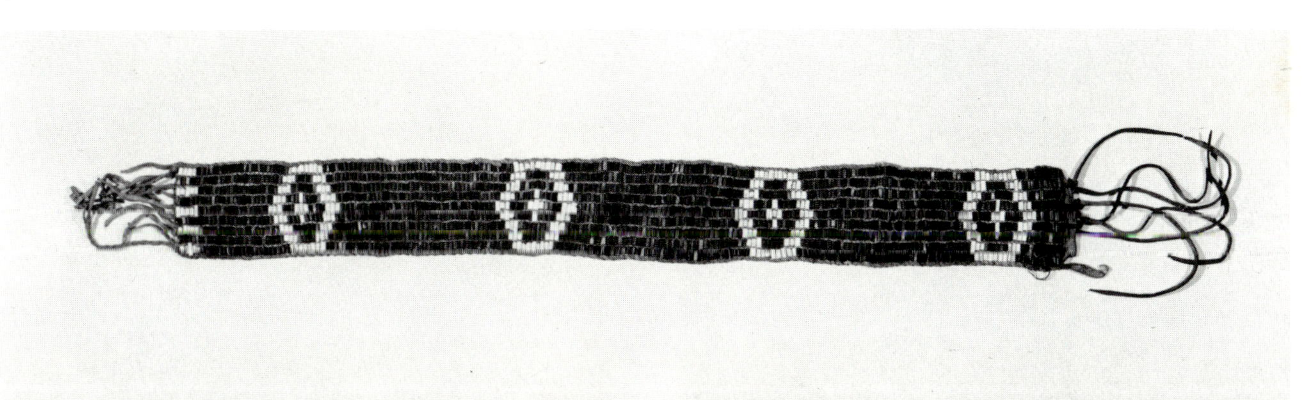

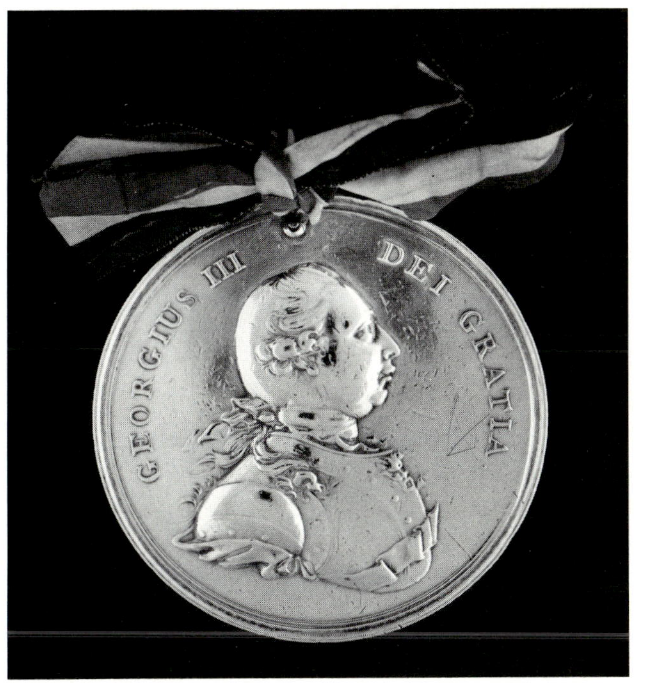

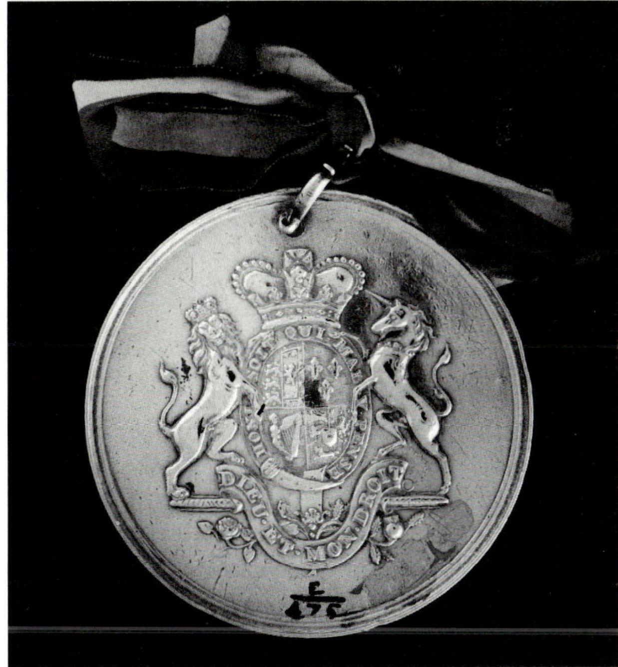

16/American Medal
OBV.: JAMES MONROE PRESIDENT OF THE U.S., A.D. 1817
REV.: PEACE AND FRIENDSHIP
SIZE: 7.6 cm diam.
COLL.: ANS

17/British Medal (copper)
OBV.: GEORGIUS III D: G. BRITANNIARUM REX. FID. DEF. &c
REV.: Coat of arms of the Hudson's Bay Co.
SIZE: 4.9 cm diam.
COLL.: PAC (H1620)

18/British Medal
OBV.: PRESENTED TO JOSEPH M. ITKOBEITCH, CHIEF OF THE MICMAC INDIANS AT RESTIGOUCHE, BY THE MINISTER OF WAR AND COLONIES, BY COMMAND OF THE QUEEN. 25, JAN: 1842.
REV.: VICTORIA DEI GRATIA BRITANNIARUM REGINA FID: DEF:
SIZE: 6.8 cm diam.
COLL.: PAC (H1632)

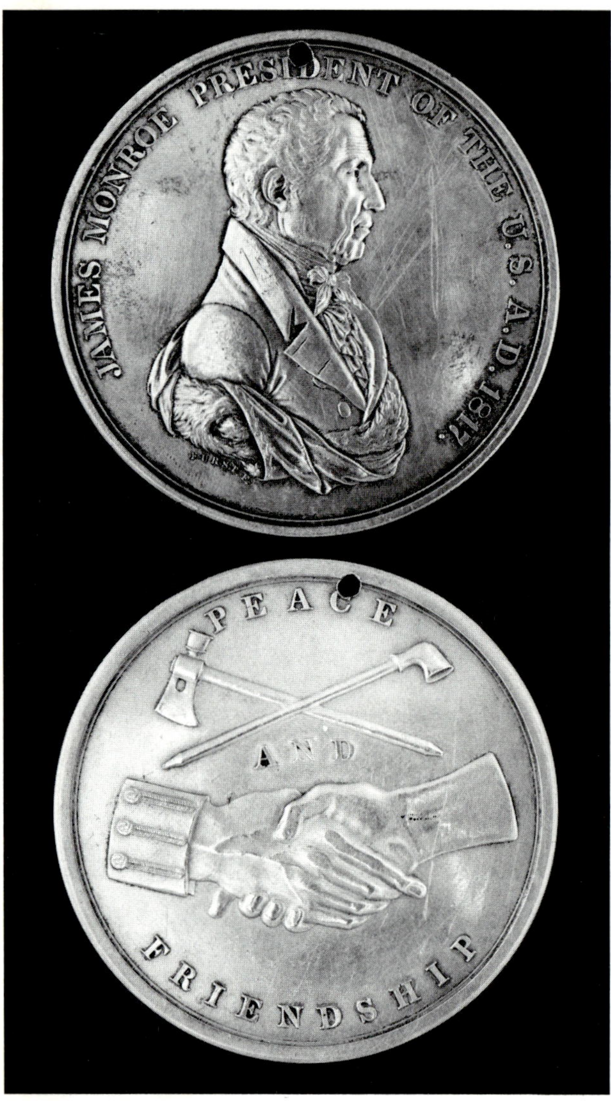

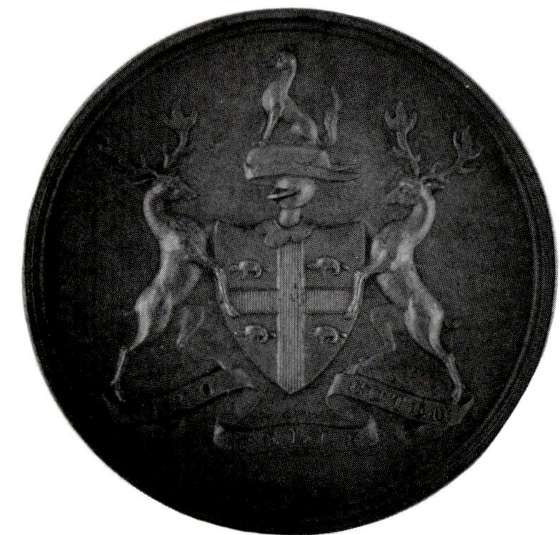

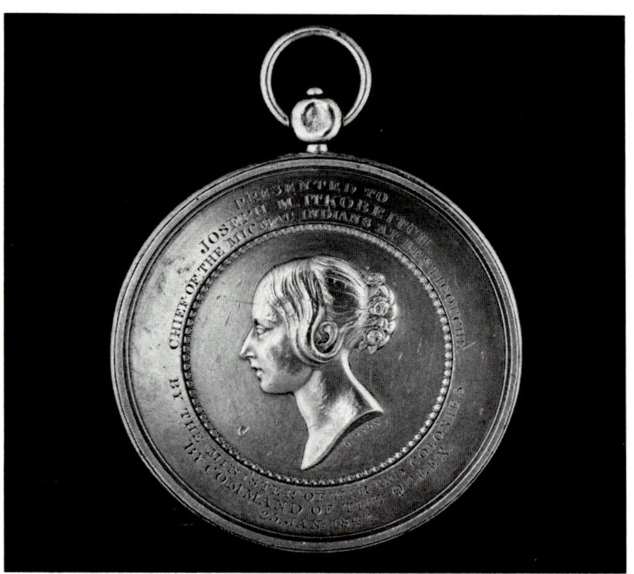

19/British Medal
OBV.: VICTORIA DEI GRATIA BRITANNIARUM REGINA F: D:/1860 (Re-struck for the Prince of Wales visit to Canada in 1860)
REV.: Royal arms of Britain/1840
SIZE: 7.6 cm diam.
COLL.: MMFA (953.Ds.14)

20/British Medal
OBV.: GEORGIVS V DEI GRA: REX ET IND: IMP:
REV.: INDIAN TREATY N° 11/1921
SIZE: 7.7 cm diam.
COLL.: PAC (H1643)

21/Canadian Medal
OBV.: ELIZABETH II D. G. REGINA
REV.: PRESENTED TO THE CHIEFS OF THE MANITOBA INDIAN BROTHERHOOD FOR THEIR BANDS BY HER MAJESTY THE QUEEN TO COMMEMORATE MANITOBA'S CENTENNIAL THE PAS JULY 11, 1970.
SIZE: 8.9 cm diam.
COLL.: PAC (1970-78)

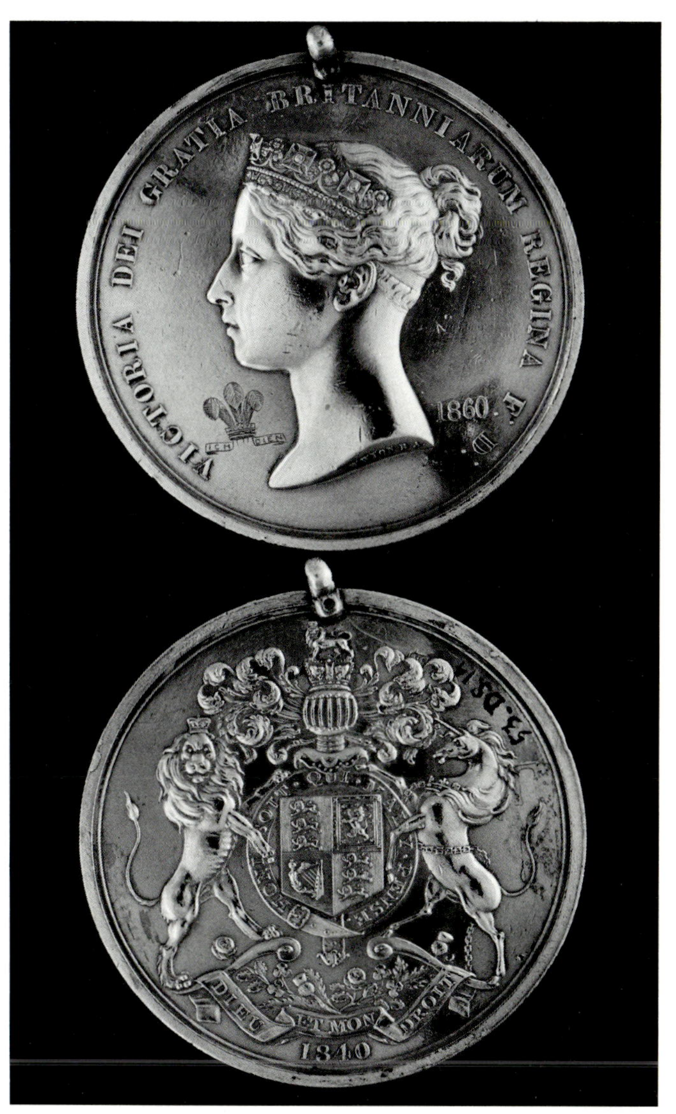

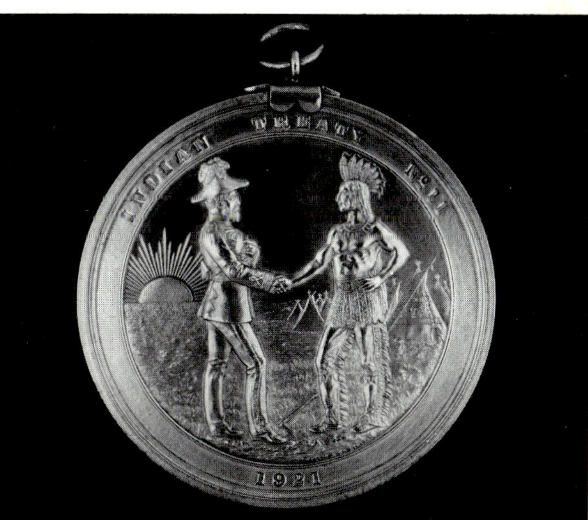

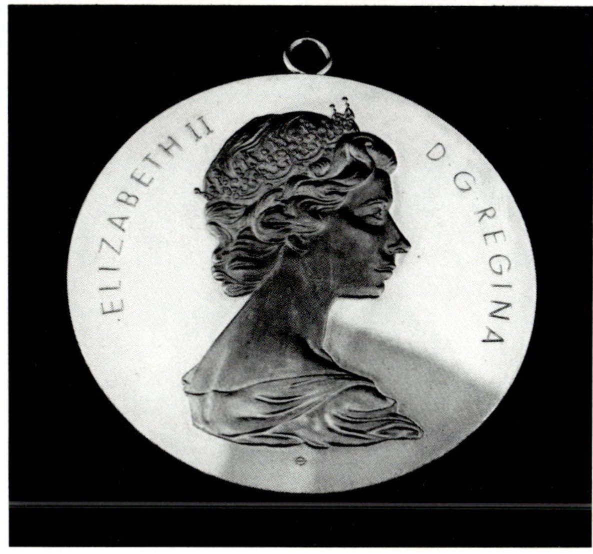

22/American Medal
OBV.: GEORGE WASHINGTON
PRESIDENT. 1792.
REV.: Great Seal of the United States
SIZE: 18.3 cm h. × 12.3 cm w.
COLL.: PAC (H1653)

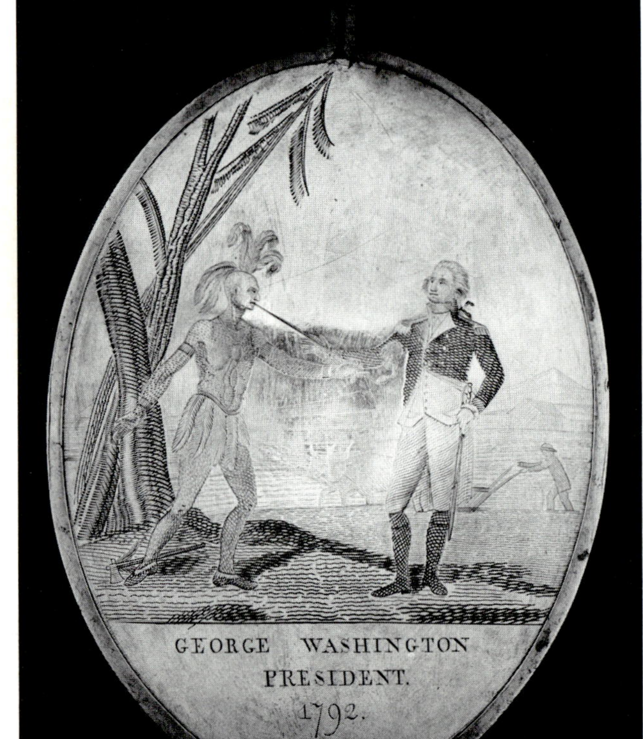

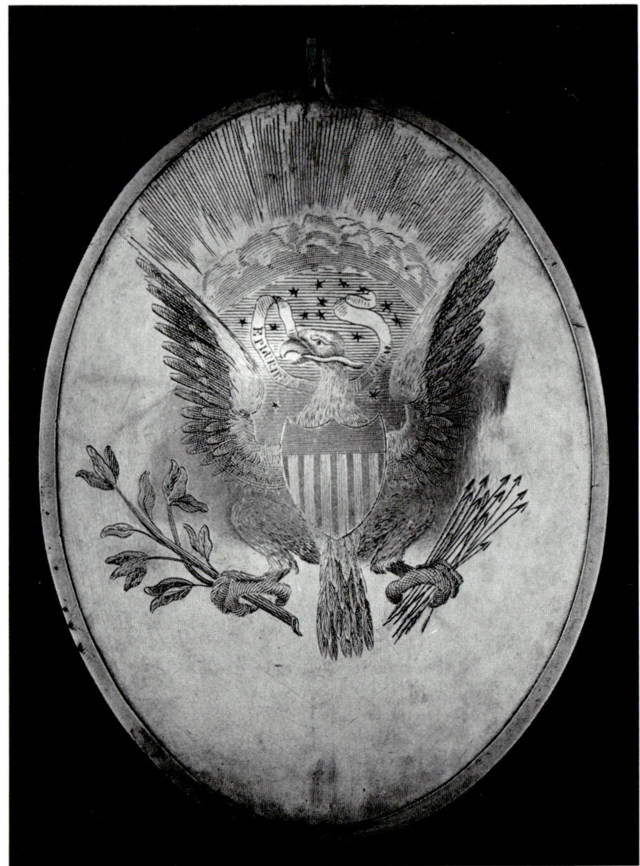

III / TRADING CEREMONIES

Meetings of Indians and whites retained a ceremonial character even after the fur trade replaced the earlier diplomatic negotiations. Rounds of trade were often preceded by gift-giving ceremonies and celebrations, which sometimes lasted several days. Although the trader viewed the barter of goods for furs as a straightforward commercial transaction, the Indian continued to perceive it as a mutual pledge of loyalty and friendship. Painter Peter Rindisbacher shows a group of Indians firing their guns in a formal leave-taking at a Wisconsin fort in 1815.

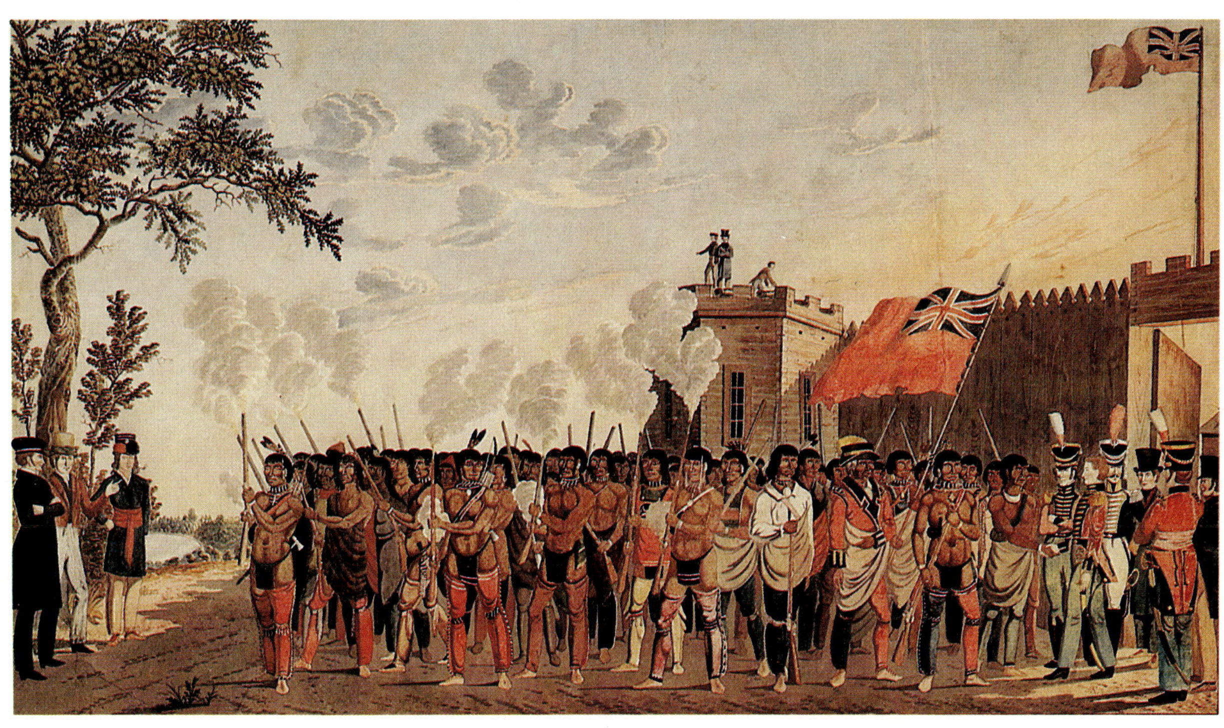

23/Hudson's Bay Company Brass Trade Tokens
VALUE: 1, 1/2, 1/4 and 1/8 "made" beaver
DATE: Late nineteenth century
SIZE: Largest, 2.9 cm diam.
COLL.: Heye (24/1222 and 18/18684)

24/British Medal
OBV.: GEORGIUS III DEI GRATIA
REV.: Royal arms of Britain
SIZE: 7.9 cm diam.
COLL.: NMM (III-H-472)

25/British Medal
OBV.: Busts of George III and Queen Charlotte
REV.: Royal arms of Britain
SIZE: 3.9 cm diam.
COLL.: PAC (H1282)

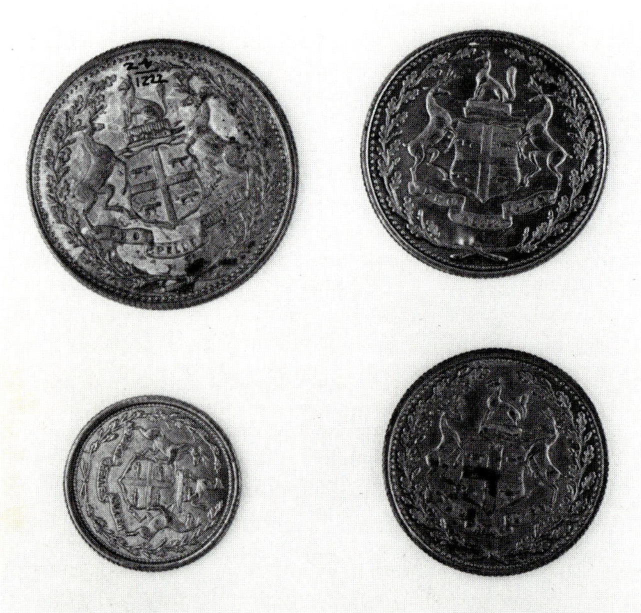

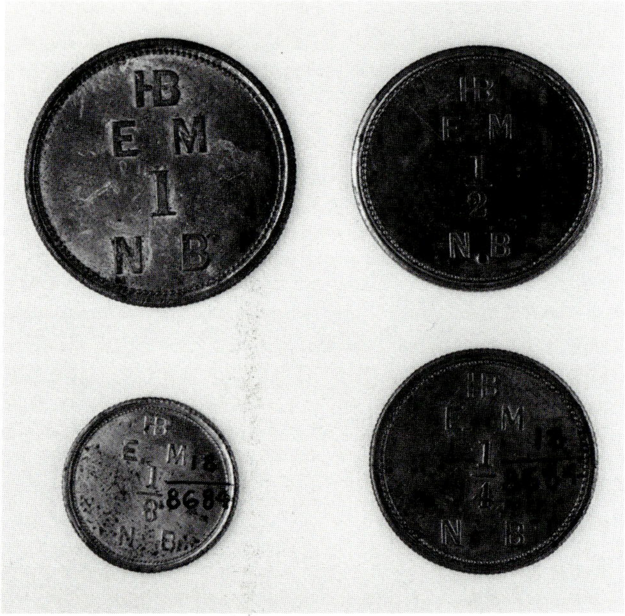

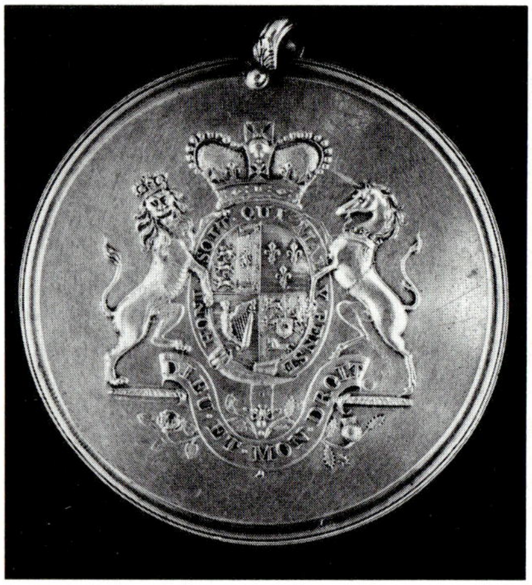

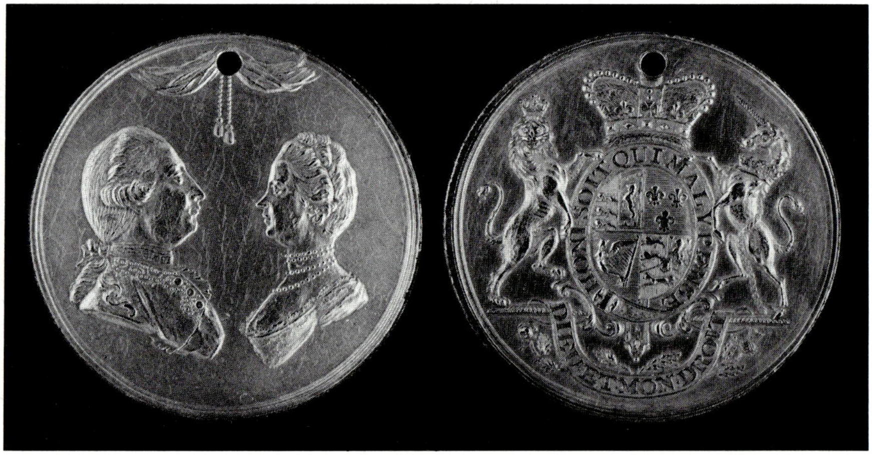

26/Headband
MARK: SM
MAKER: Salomon Marion
(Montreal, 1782–1832)
SIZE: 58 cm l. × 7 cm w.
COLL.: NMM (III-L-17)

27/Round Brooch
MARK: C (bust) (lion)
MAKER: Unknown
SIZE: 17 cm diam.
COLL.: Heye (1/2133)

28/Round Brooch
MARK: None
MAKER: Unknown
SIZE: 10.2 cm diam.
COLL.: NMM (III-H-475)

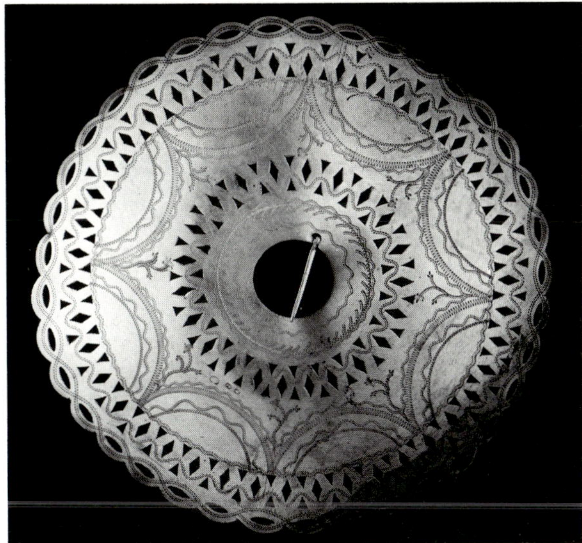

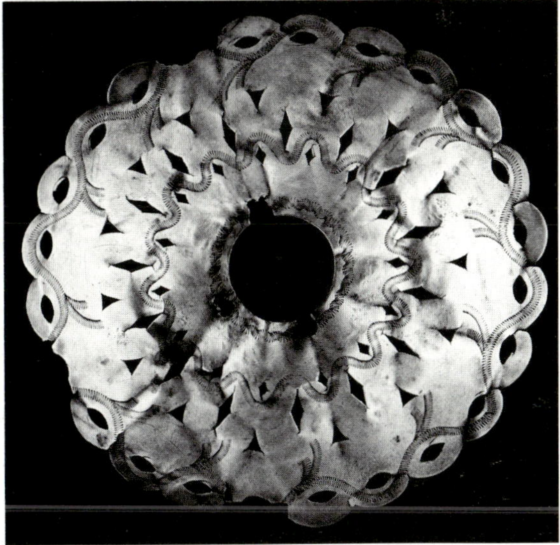

29/Pair of Legbands
MARK: JT
MAKER: Jonathan Tyler
(Montreal, 1817–28)
SIZE: 38.7 cm l. × 7.8 cm w.
COLL.: McCord (M172.1, 2)

30/Round Brooch
MARK: MONTREAL
MAKER: Unknown
SIZE: 11.4 cm diam.
COLL.: NGC, Birks (C465)

31/Round Brooch
MARK: None
MAKER: Unknown
SIZE: 9.2 cm diam.
COLL.: Heye (2/9711)

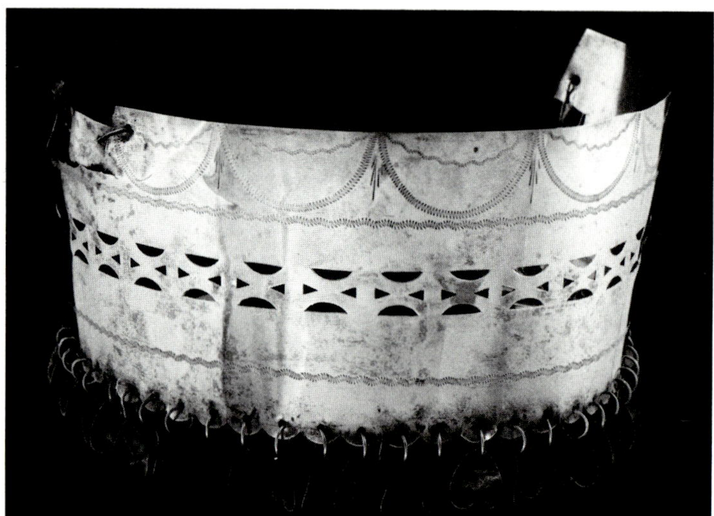

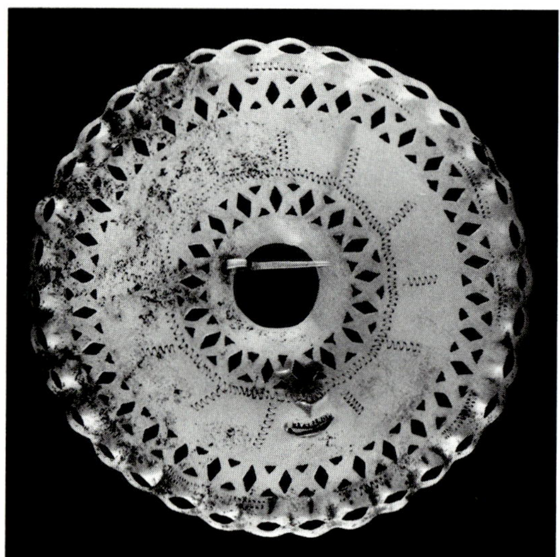

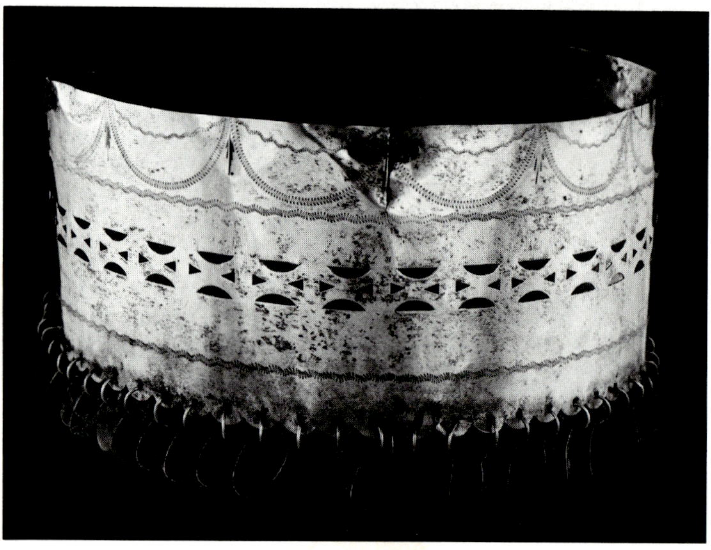

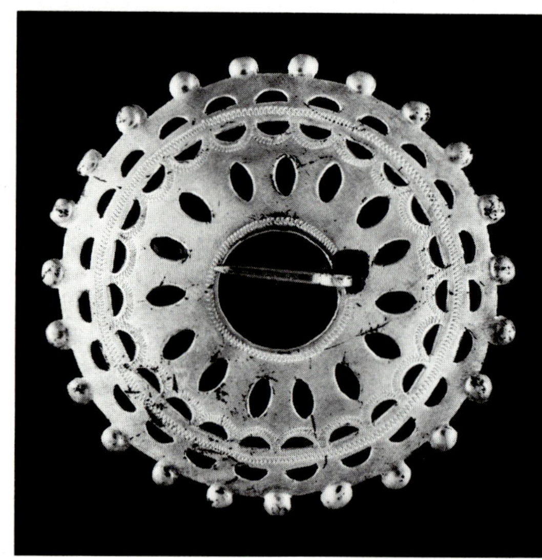

32/Pair of Armbands
MARK: PB AB WB
MAKER: Peter, Ann and William Bateman
(London, late 18th century)
SIZE: 23.2 cm l. × 5.4 cm w.
COLL.: NMM (III-H-478a, b)

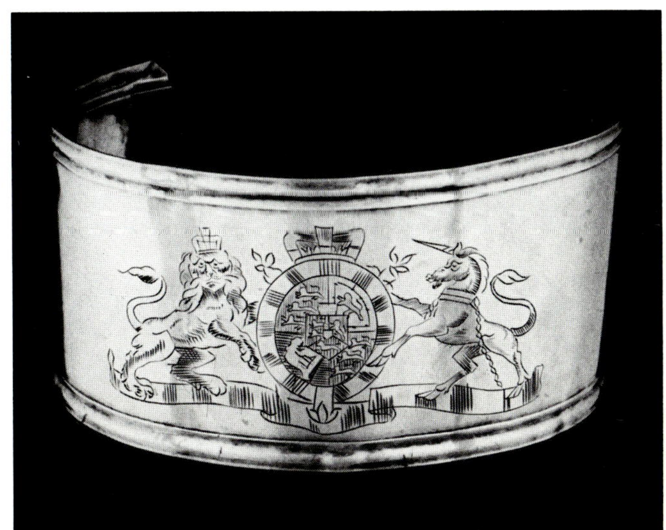

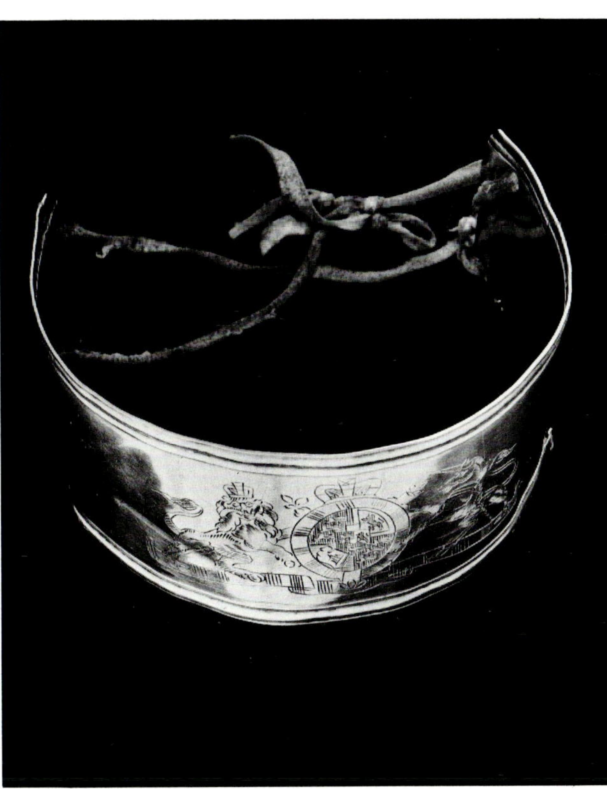

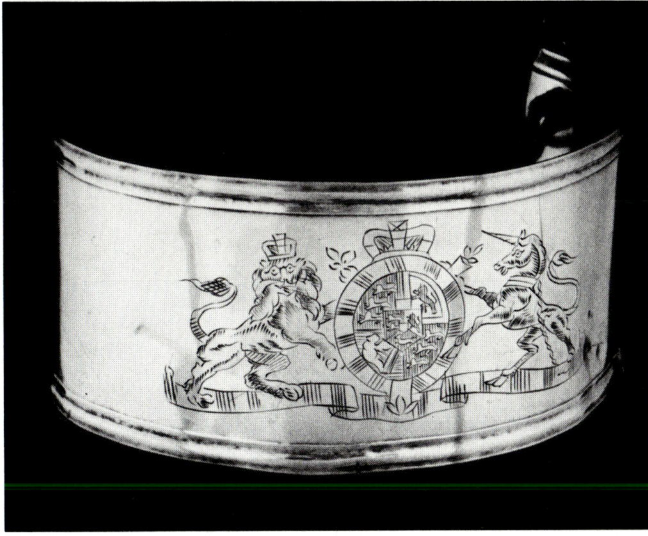

33/Pair of Armbands
MARK: MONTREAL
MAKER: Unknown
SIZE: 34.1 cm l. × 6.8 cm w.
COLL.: McCord (M173.1, 2)

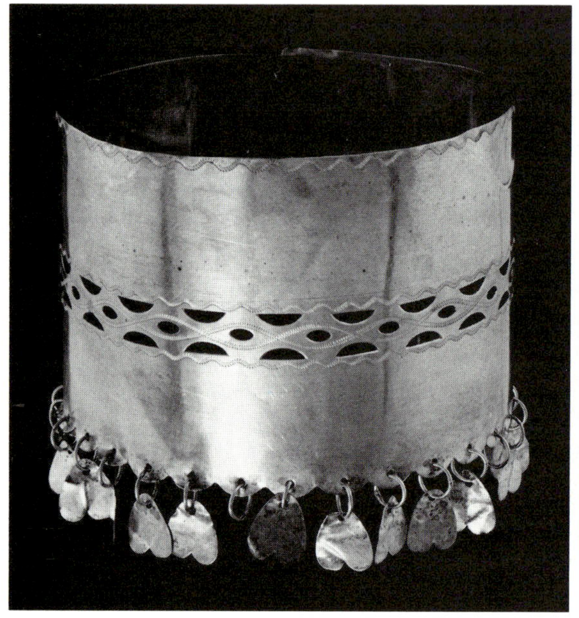

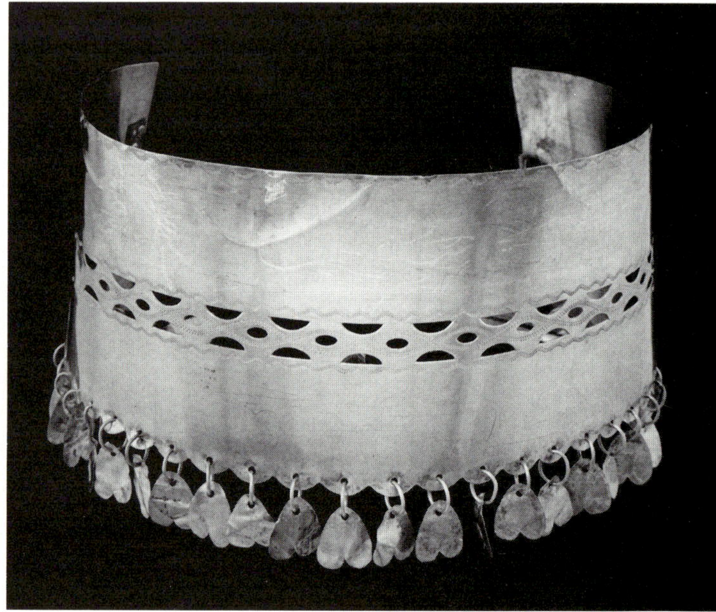

IV / SILVER AS A TRADE GOOD

Silver ornaments were popular with the Indians throughout the fur-trade period. Along with copper pots, whisky, tobacco, beads, bells, pipes, cloth, knife blades and axe heads, silver "trinkets" were traded all along the fur-trade routes deep into the interior. According to a "Standard of Trade" list for 1795, one beaver pelt could be traded for any of the following: 2 silver crosses, 6 small silver brooches, 24 hawkbells, 2 ostrich feathers, 1 small brass kettle, 8 knives, or 2 hatchet heads.

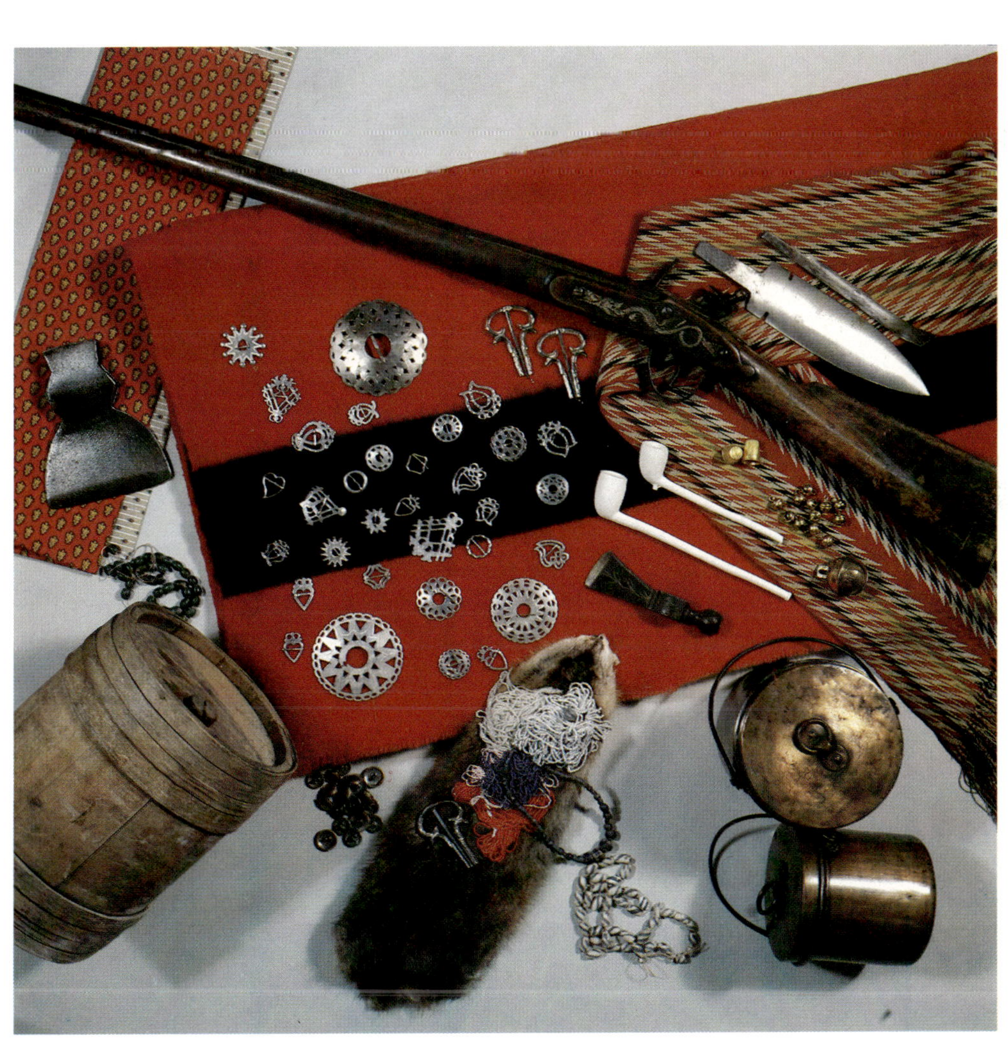

34/Luckenbooth Heart Brooches
MARK: None
MAKER: Unknown
SIZE: Average, 3.0 cm h. × 2.3 cm w.
COLL.: ROM (951x75.16)

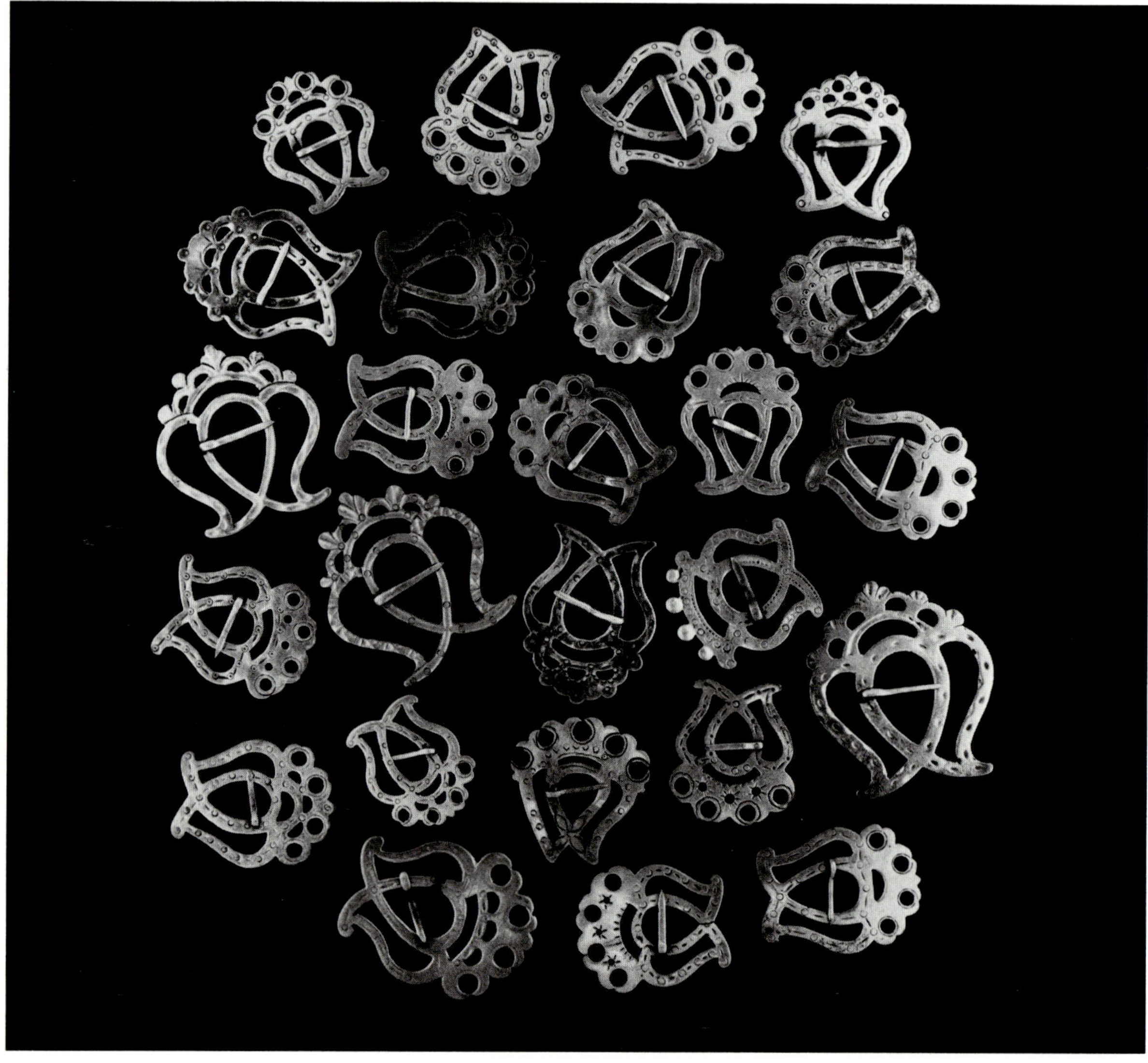

35/Council Square Brooches
MARK: None
MAKER: Unknown
SIZE: 2.4 cm square
COLL.: ROM (951x75.17)

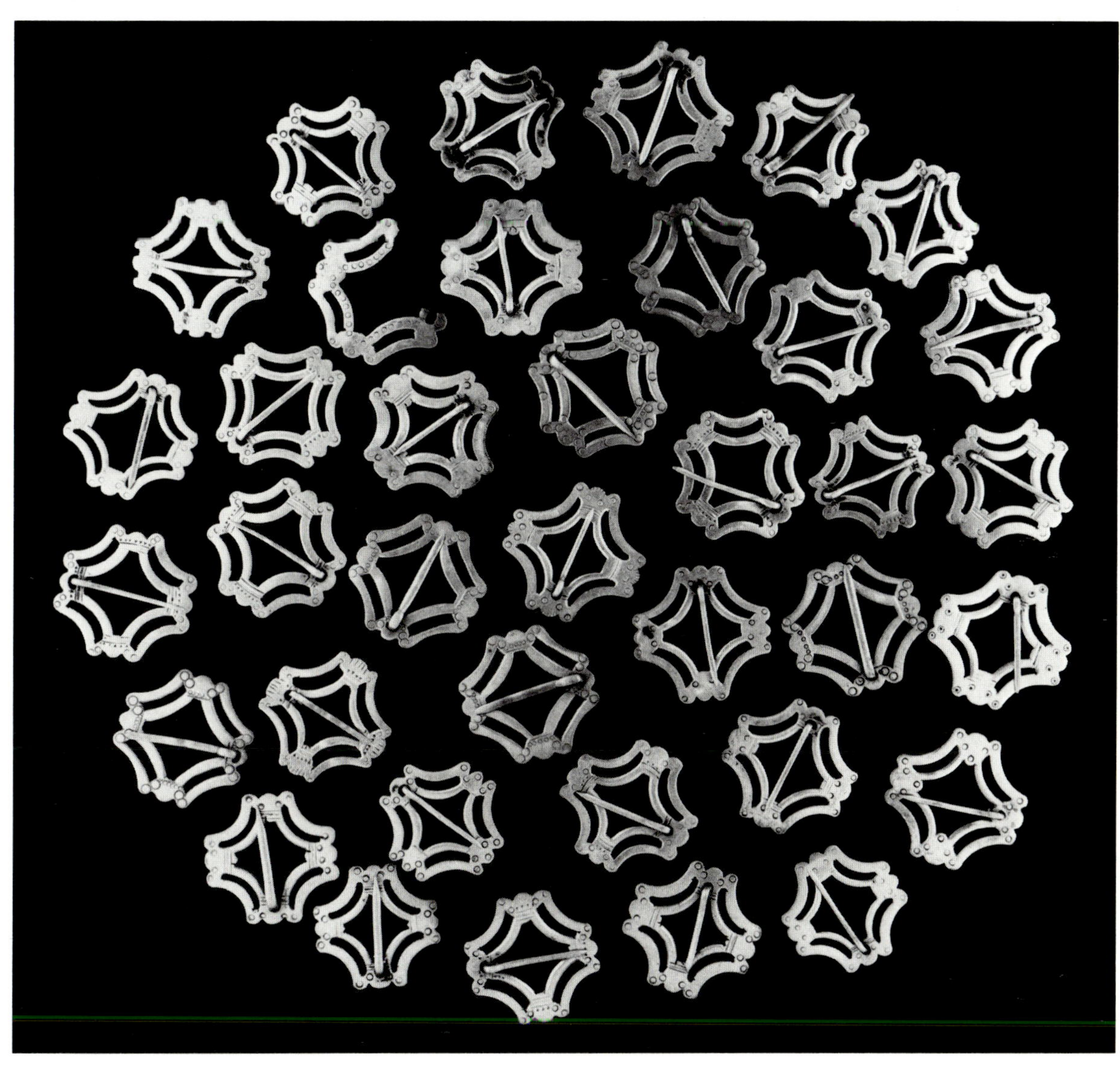

36/Ring Brooches
MARK: None
MAKER: Unknown
SIZE: 1.5 cm diam.
COLL.: ROM (951x75.18)

37/Round Brooch
(German silver)
MARK: FS
MAKER: François Sasseville
(Quebec, 1797–1864)
SIZE: 8.9 cm diam.
COLL.: NGC, Birks (Q514)

38/Brooch with Leaf Motif
MARK: TP
MAKER: Thomas Powis
(Quebec, 1781)
SIZE: 8.3 cm diam.
COLL.: NGC, Birks (U182)

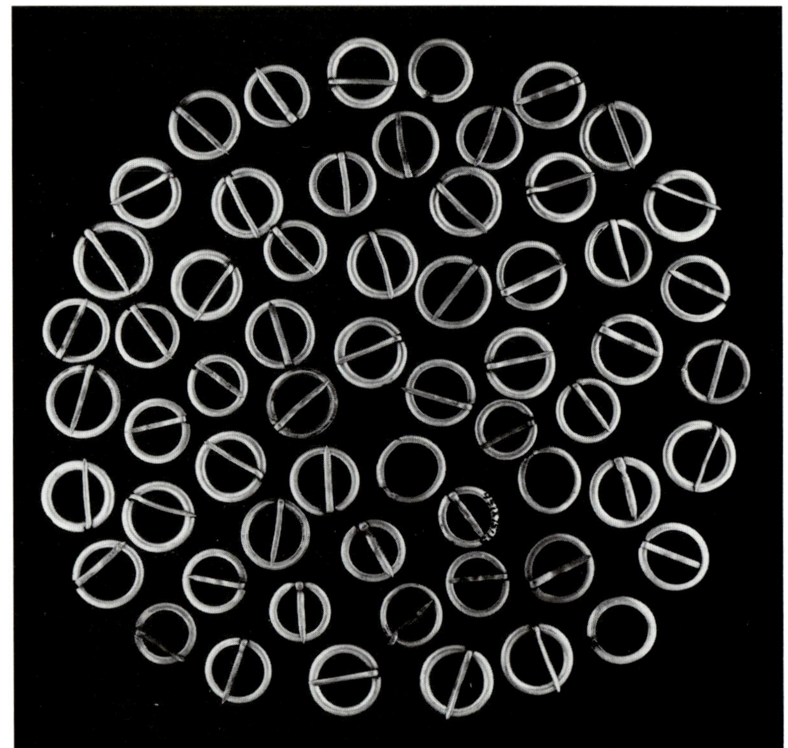

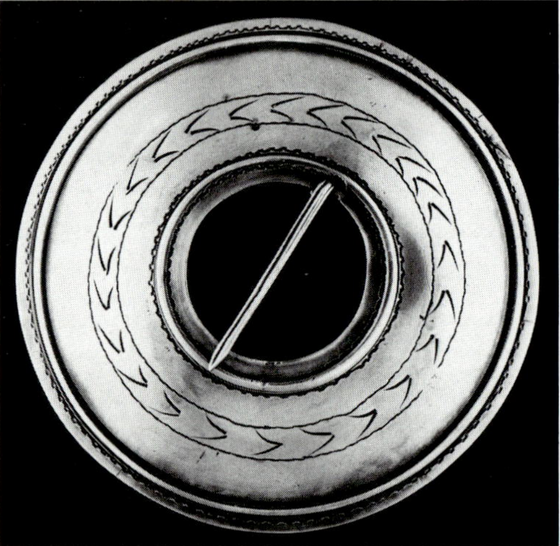

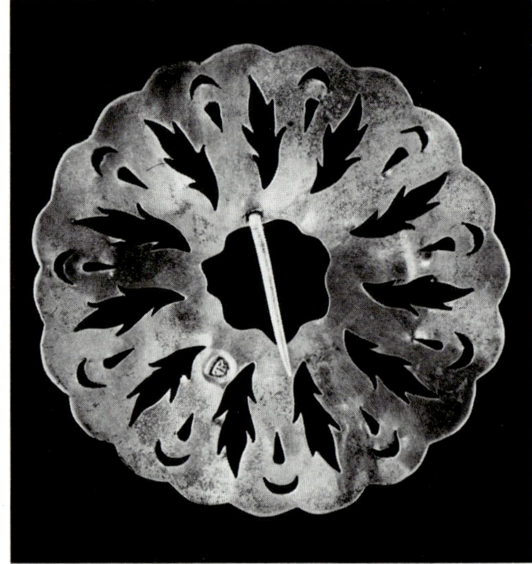

39/Two Crosses
MARK: RC
MAKER: Robert Cruickshank (Boston, Montreal, 1767–1809)
SIZE: 2.3 cm h. × 1.6 cm w.
COLL.: PMA (H69.3.1137 and H69.3.1079)

40/Round Brooch
MARK: RC
MAKER: Robert Cruickshank (Boston, Montreal, 1767–1809)
SIZE: 3.4 cm diam.
COLL.: Parks (16R-7B4-1)

41/Ear-Wheel
MARK: RC
MAKER: Robert Cruickshank (Boston, Montreal, 1767–1809)
SIZE: 7.2 cm diam.
COLL.: U. Sask. (FfMj-1001-3)

42/Lorraine Cross
MARK: CA
MAKER: Charles Arnoldi (Montreal, 1779–1817)
SIZE: 9.4 cm h. × 4.0 cm w.
COLL.: Heye (4/425)

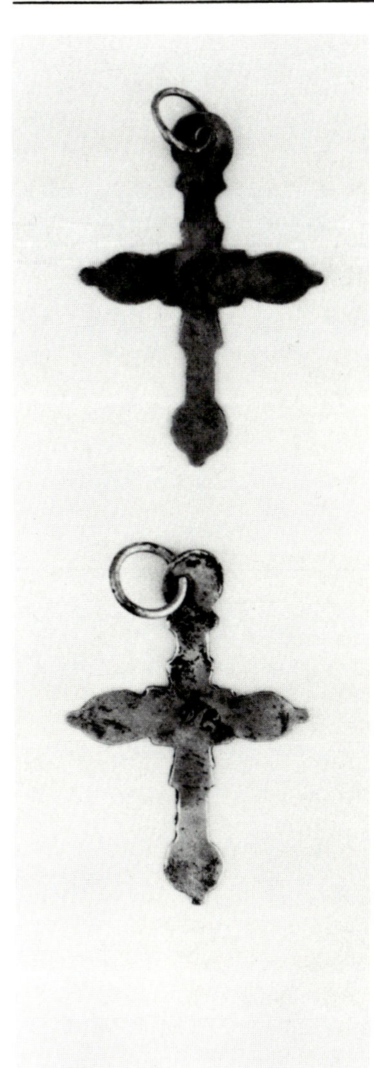

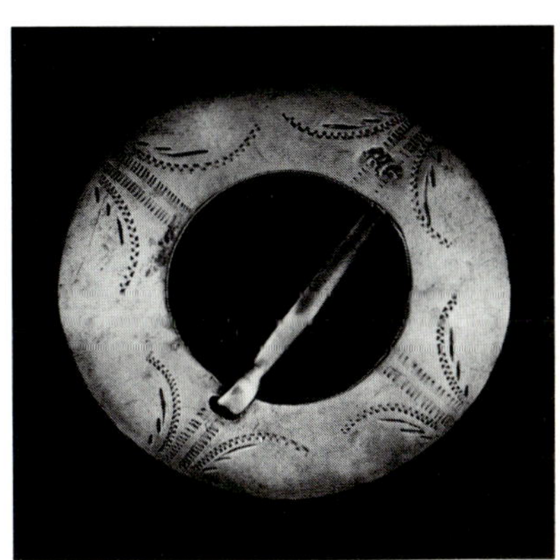

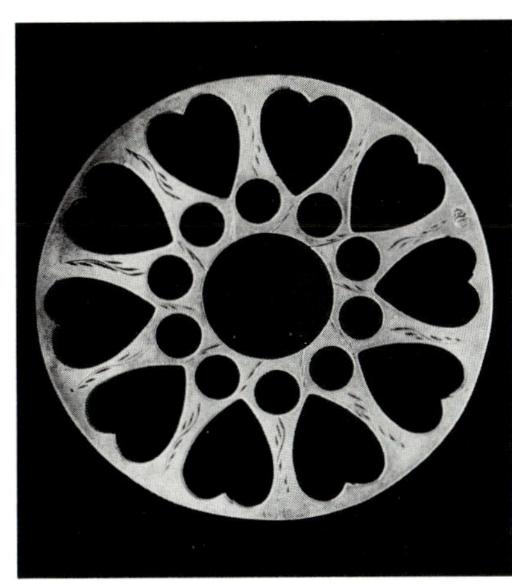

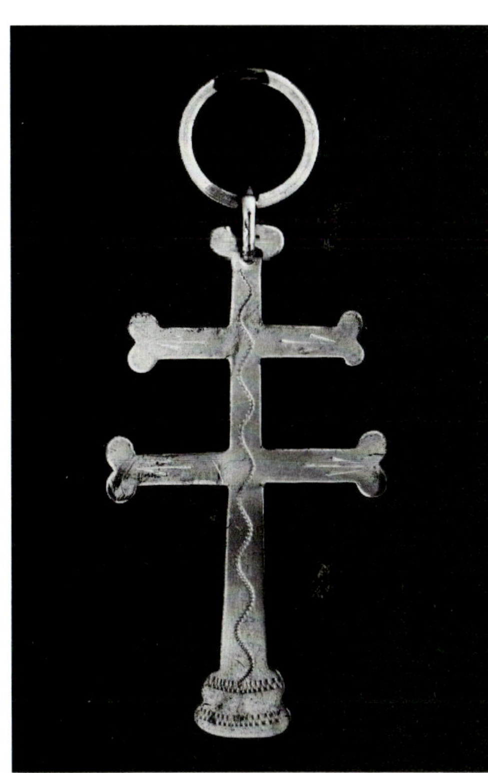

43/Pair of Armbands
MARK: RC
MAKER: Robert Cruickshank
(Boston, Montreal, 1767–1809)
SIZE: 24.7 cm l. × 8.0 cm w.
COLL.: Alabama
(12.14.52 and 12.15.52)

44/Crescent Gorget
MARK: HB (British hallmarks)
MAKER: Hester Bateman (London, 1781)
SIZE: 14.4 cm w. × 10.8 cm h.
COLL.: Alabama (2.17.54)

45/Round Brooch
MARK: IS
MAKER: Jonas or "Widow" Schindler
(Quebec, Montreal, 1760–1823)
SIZE: 6.4 cm diam.
COLL.: Putnam (AR14742)

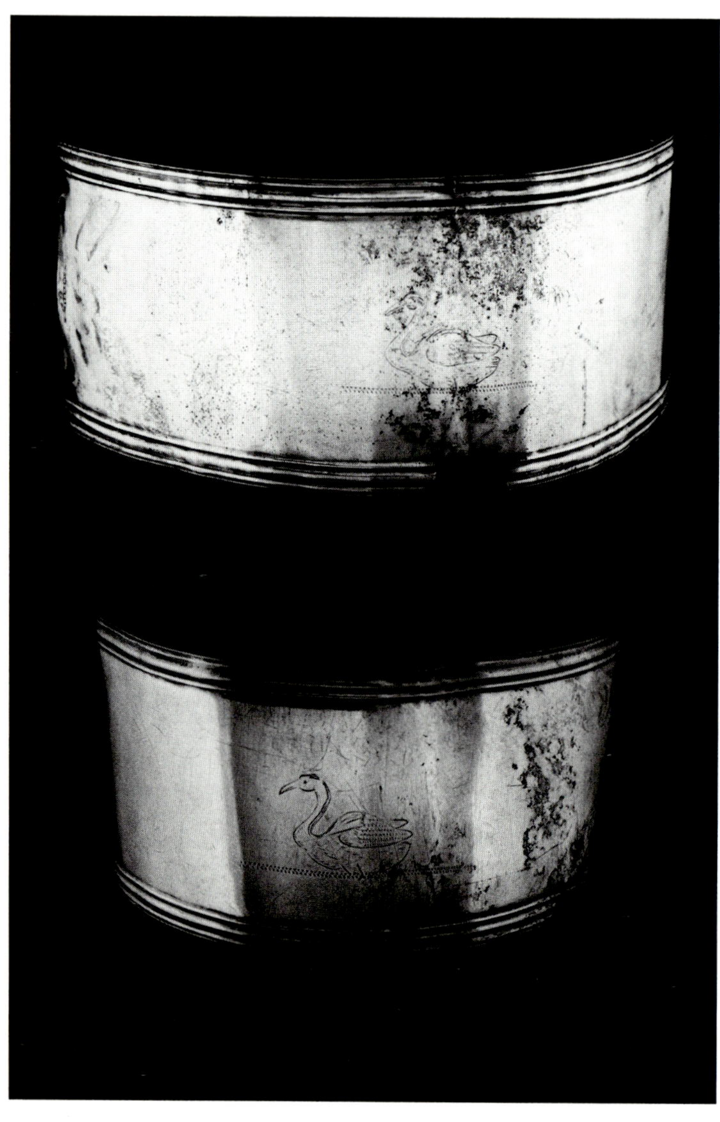

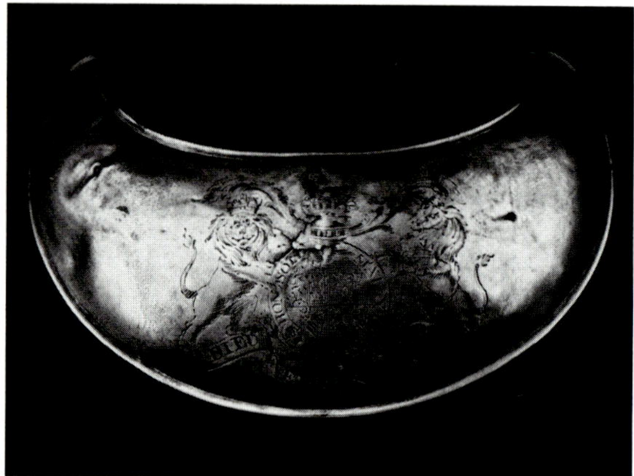

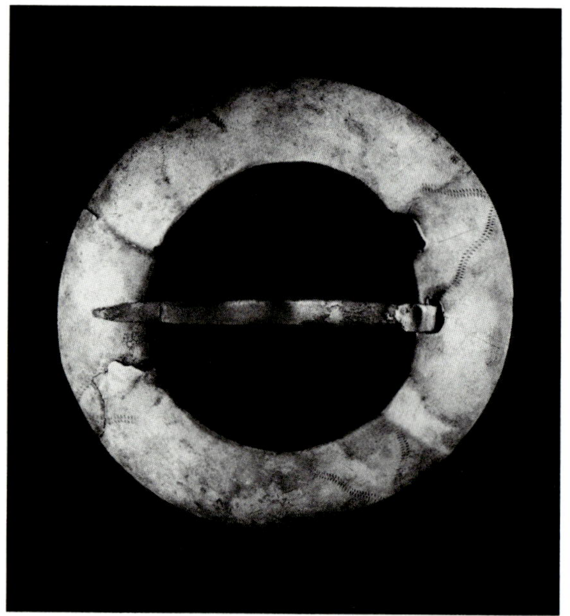

46/Locket
MARK: RC
MAKER: Robert Cruickshank
(Boston, Montreal, 1767–1809)
SIZE: 5.5 cm h. × 4.0 cm w.
COLL.: Heye (1/2143)

47/Lorraine Cross
MARK: CA
MAKER: Charles Arnoldi
(Montreal, 1779–1817)
SIZE: 8.1 cm h. × 4.2 cm w.
COLL.: NMM (III-Q-42)

48/Crescent Gorget
MARK: RC
MAKER: Robert Cruickshank
(Boston, Montreal, 1767–1809)
SIZE: 12.5 cm w. × 4.6 cm h.
COLL.: NMM (VIII-F-26745)

49/Round Brooch
MARK: PH
MAKER: Pierre Huguet
dit Latour, Sr. or Jr.
(Montreal, 1771–1829)
SIZE: 6.3 cm diam.
COLL.: NMM (III-I-1026)

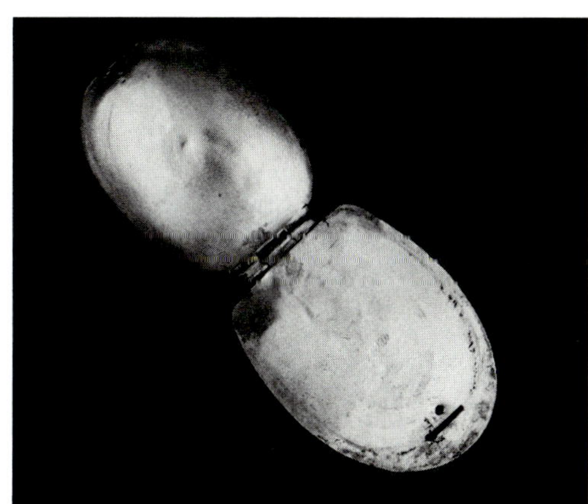

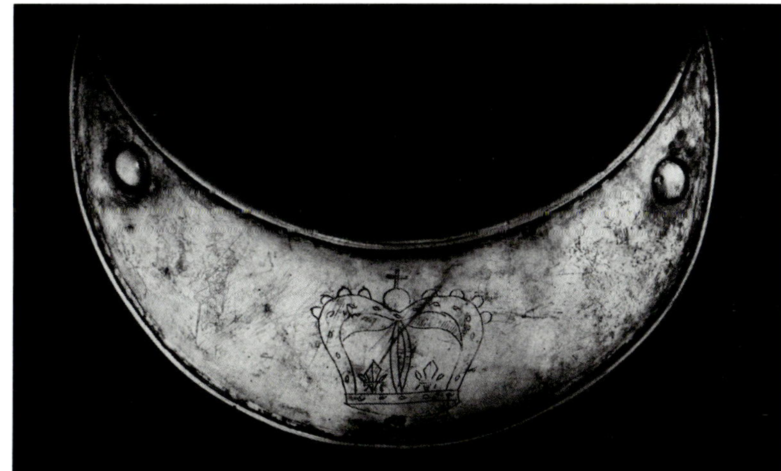

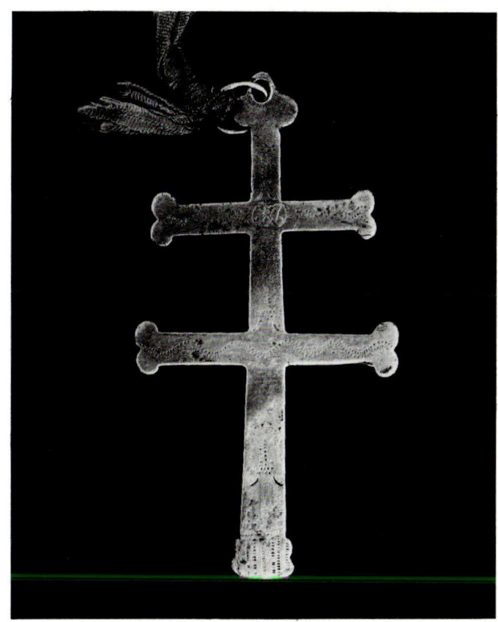

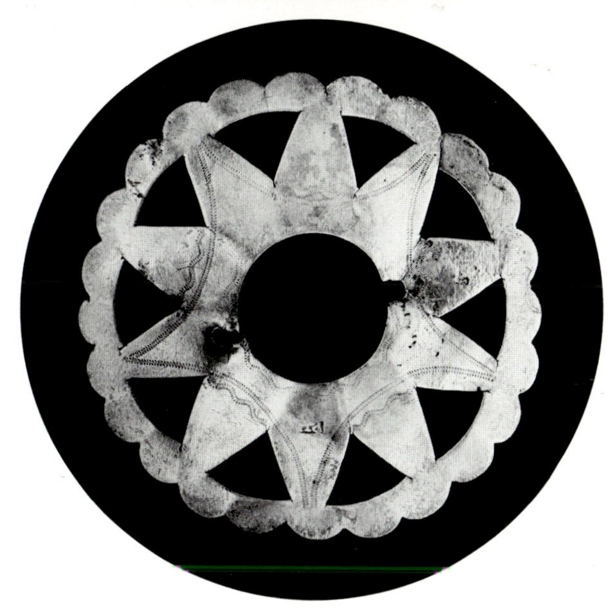

50/Round Brooch
MARK: JT
MAKER: Jonathan Tyler
(Montreal, 1817–28)
SIZE: 20.8 cm diam.
COLL.: NMM (III-L-195)

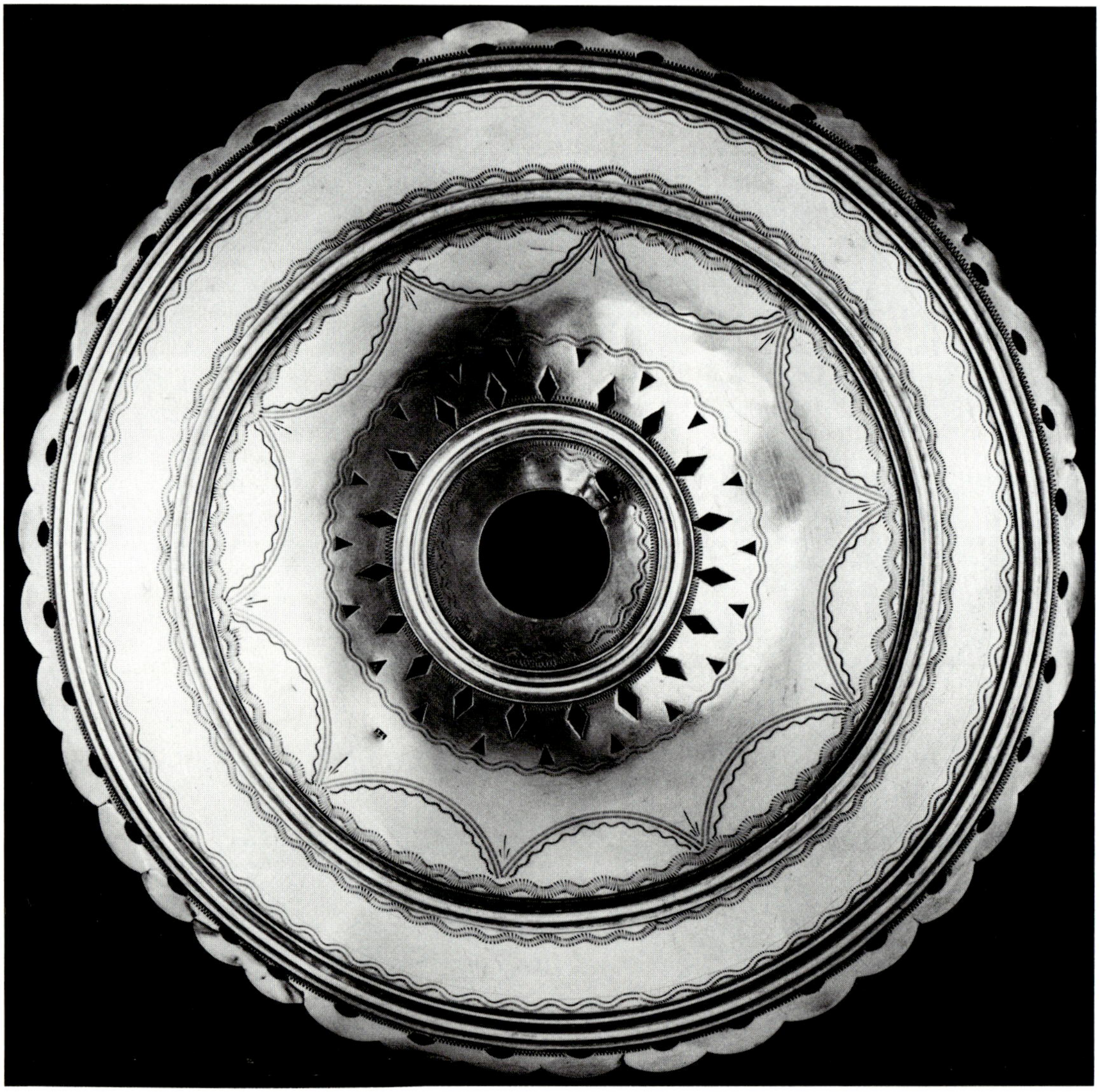

V / THE SILVERSMITHS

Making silver ornaments for the fur trade was the main source of income for colonial silversmiths, although the Hudson's Bay Company imported their requirements from Britain. This unusual piece, made by Pierre Huguet *dit* Latour of Montreal, is a silver cover designed to secure a well-wrapped child to its cradleboard. Most of the thousands of brooches, armbands, wristbands, earrings and hair-pipes made for the fur trade were small – crafted with an eye to using as little silver as possible. Only occasionally were the silversmiths called upon to create elaborate pieces such as this cradleboard cover.

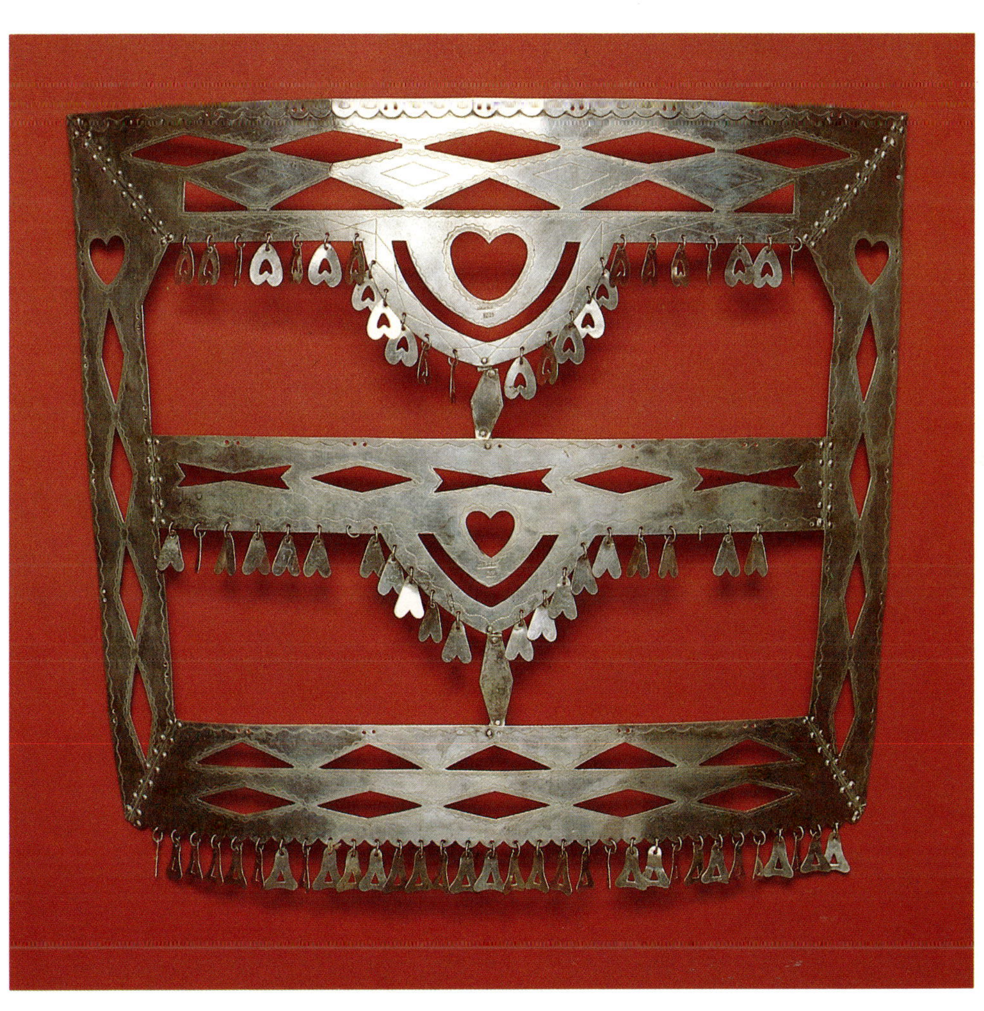

51/Ewer (handle missing)
MARK: CA
MAKER: Charles Arnoldi
(Montreal, 1779–1817)
SIZE: 14.9 cm h.
COLL.: NGC, Birks

52/Lorraine Cross
MARK: CA
MAKER: Charles Arnoldi
(Montreal, 1779–1817)
SIZE: 14 cm h. × 7 cm w.
COLL.: Heye (1/2674)

53/Spoon
MARK: IS
MAKER: Jonas or "Widow" Schindler
(Quebec, Montreal, 1760–1823)
SIZE: 21.5 cm l. × 4.3 cm w.
COLL.: NMM (A-1965)

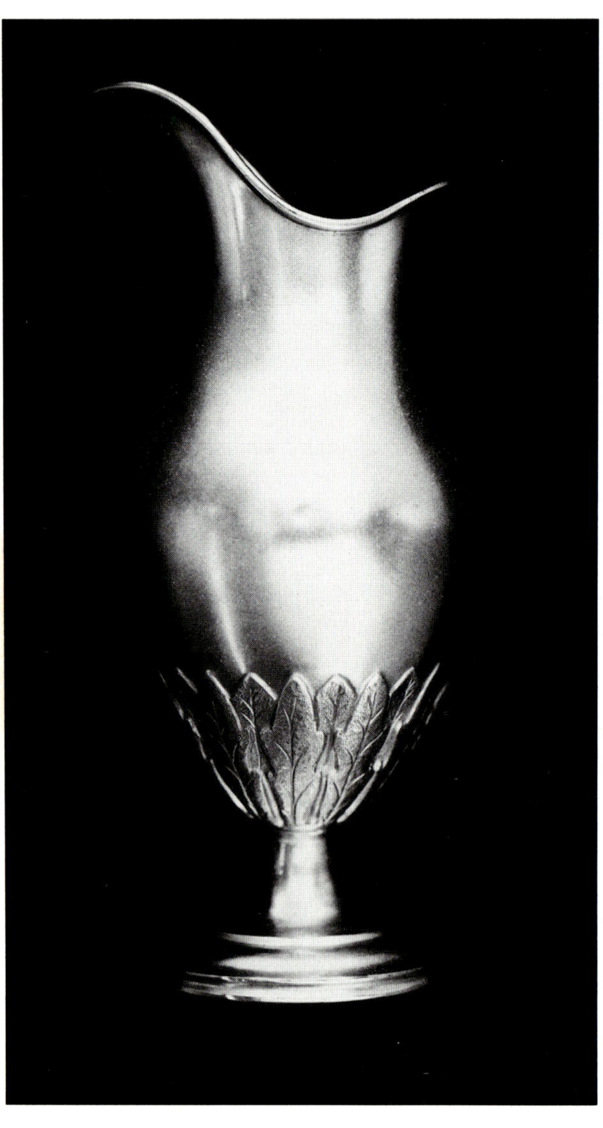

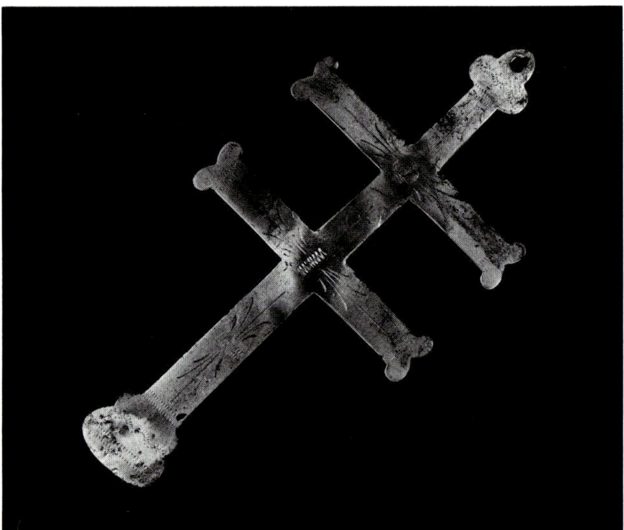

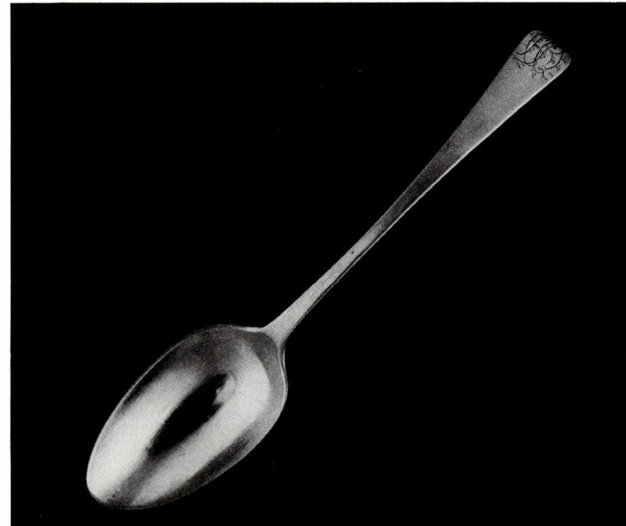

54/Pair of Armbands
MARK: IS
MAKER: Jonas or "Widow" Schindler
(Quebec, Montreal, 1760–1823)
SIZE: 25.4 cm l. × 6.0 cm w.
COLL.: NGC, Birks (C487 and C488)

55/Serving Ladle
MARK: NR
MAKER: Narcisse Roy
(Montreal, 1765–1819)
SIZE: 36.0 cm l. × 9.3 cm w.
COLL.: NMM (A-1699)

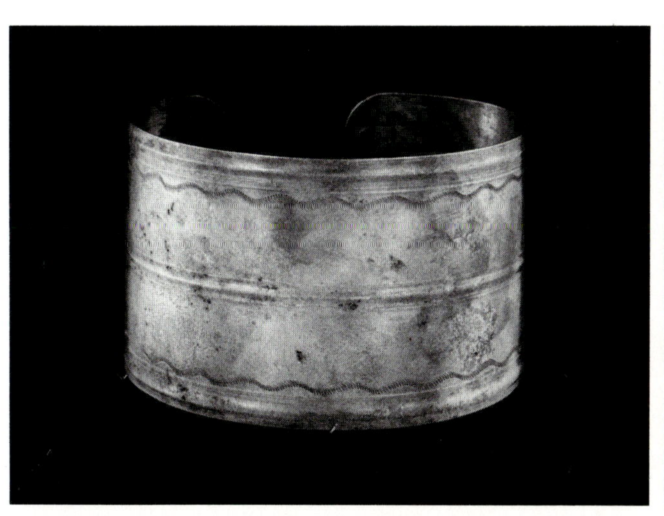

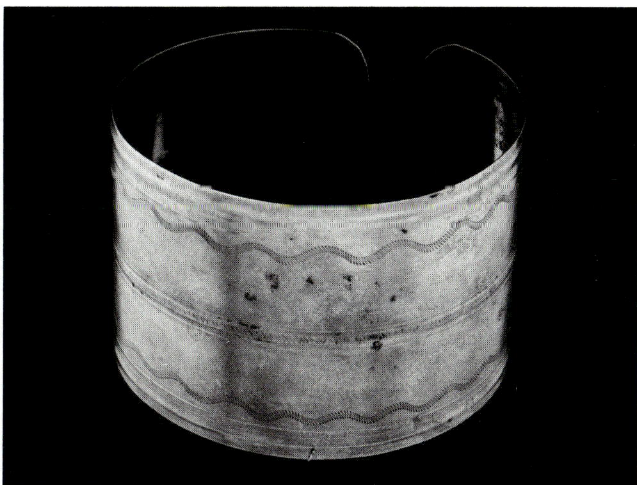

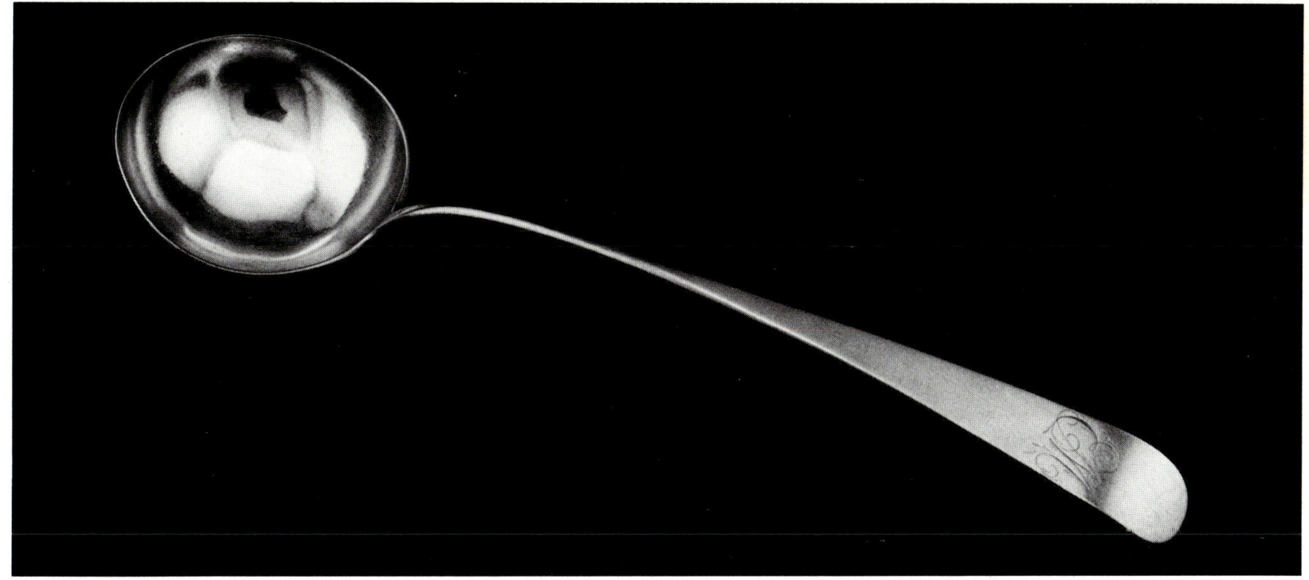

56/Crescent Gorget
MARK: NR
MAKER: Narcisse Roy
(Montreal, 1765–1819)
SIZE: 12 cm w. × 10 cm h.
COLL.: U. Sask. (FfMj-1001-5)

57/Round Brooch
MARK: RC
MAKER: Robert Cruickshank
(Boston, Montreal, 1767–1809)
SIZE: 7.3 cm diam.
COLL.: Heye (1/2134)

58/Ciborium with Lid
MARK: RC
MAKER: Robert Cruickshank
(Boston, Montreal, 1767–1809)
SIZE: 26.3 cm h.; 12.3 cm diam.
COLL.: NMM (A-1690)

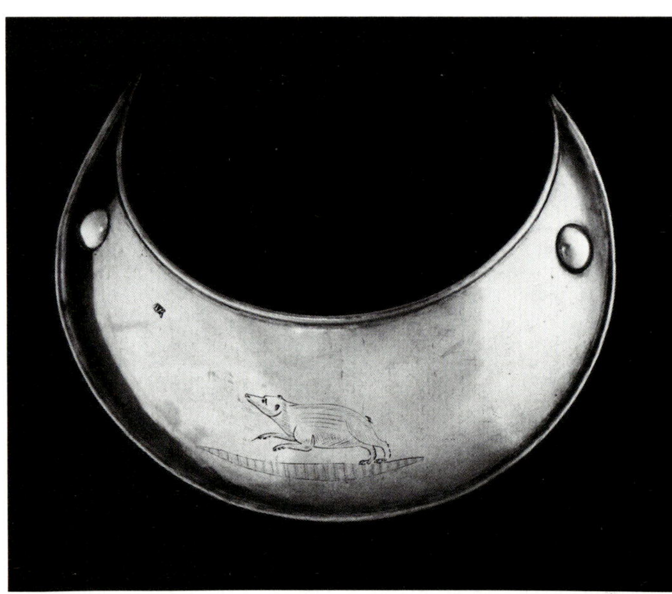

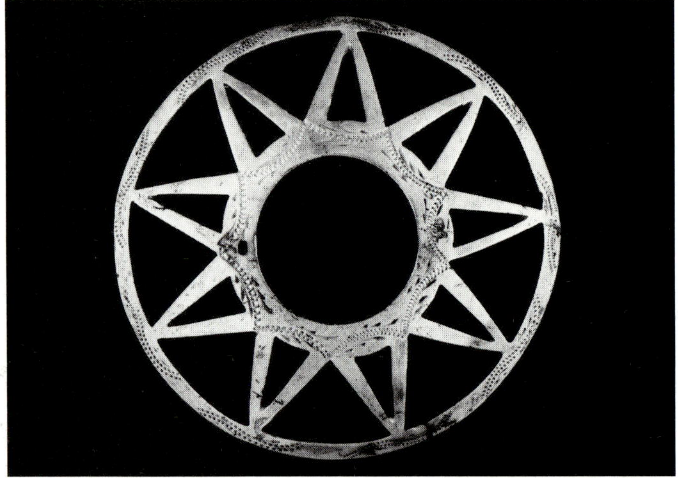

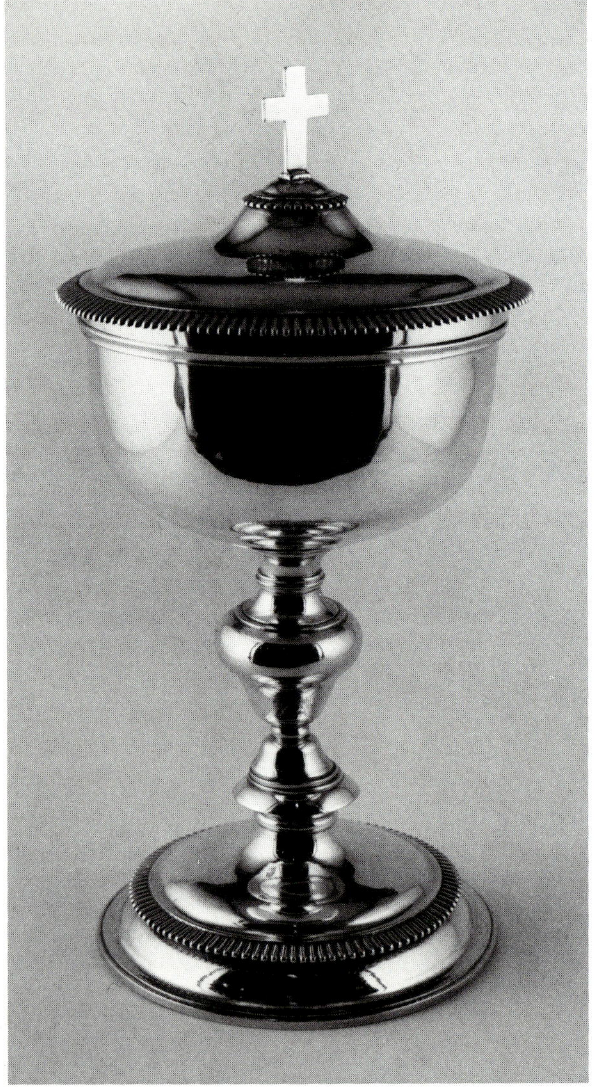

59/Round Brooch
MARK: JT
MAKER: Jonathan Tyler
(Montreal, 1817–28)
SIZE: 14 cm diam.
COLL.: McCord (M411)

60/Baptismal Pot
MARK: PH
MAKER: Pierre Huguet *dit* Latour, Sr. or Jr.
(Montreal, 1771–1829)
SIZE: 6.8 cm h.
COLL.: NMM (A-1694)

61/Crown
MARK: PH MONTREAL
MAKER: Pierre Huguet *dit* Latour, Sr. or Jr.
(Montreal, 1771–1829)
SIZE: 51.6 cm l. × 9.0 cm h.
COLL.: NGC, Birks (C392)

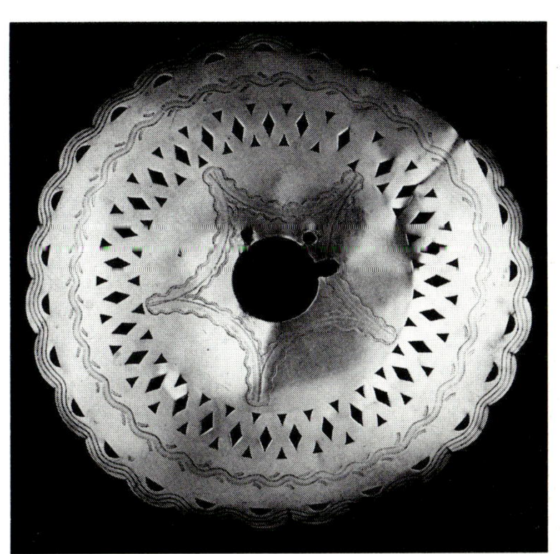

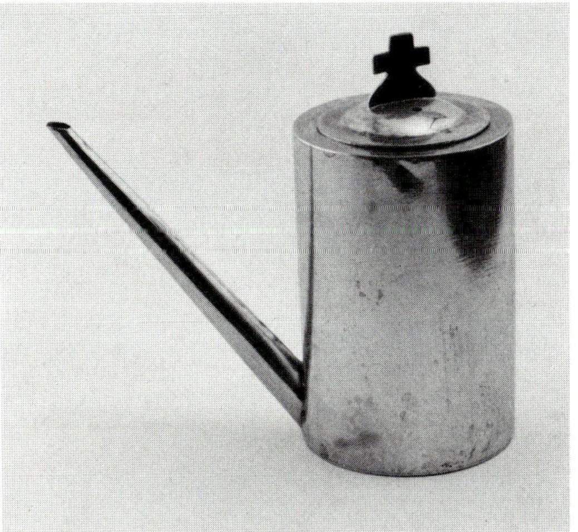

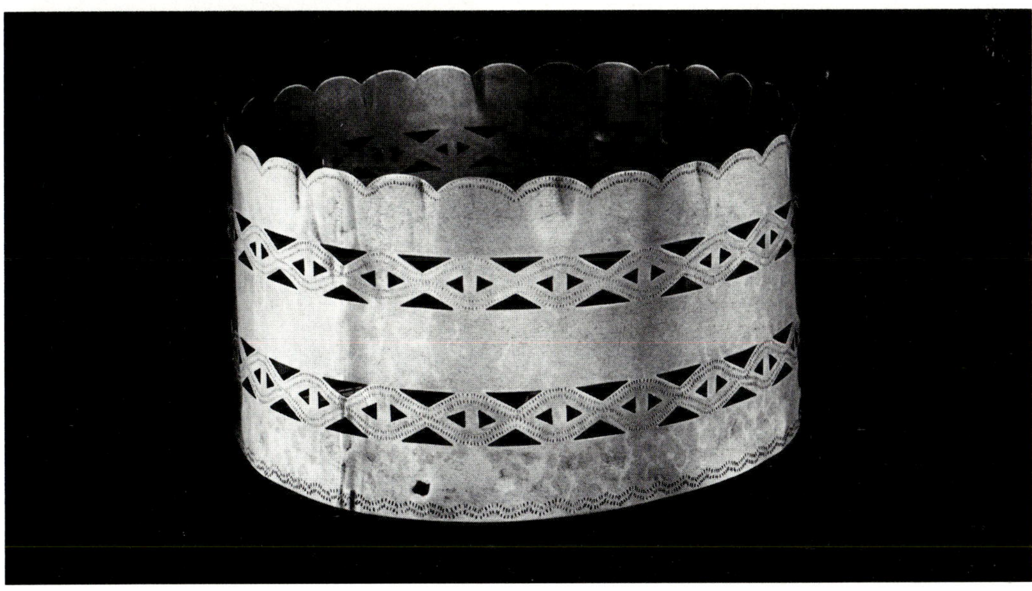

62/Round Gorget
MARK: IK
MAKER: Possibly John Kinzie (Chicago, 1780–1812)
SIZE: 16.8 cm diam.
COLL.: Heye (1/2139)

63/Crescent Gorget
MARK: HB (British hallmarks)
MAKER: Hester Bateman (London, 1770–71)
SIZE: 14.2 cm w. × 12.8 cm h.
COLL.: Alabama (12.7.52)

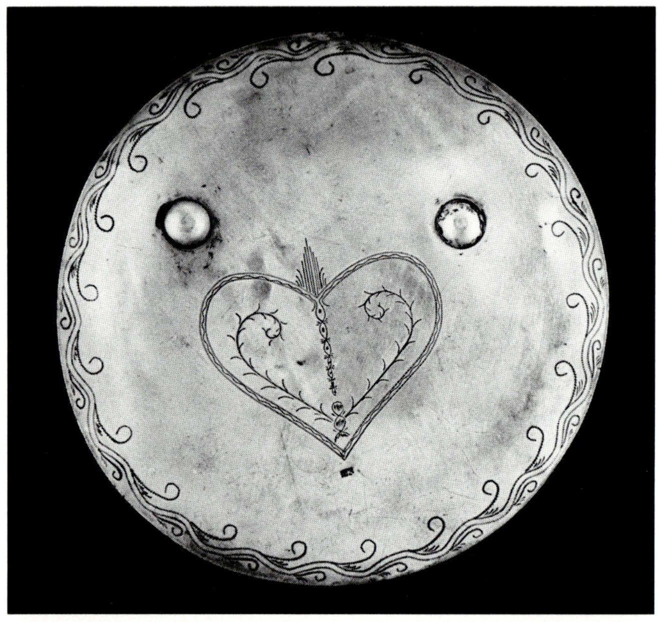

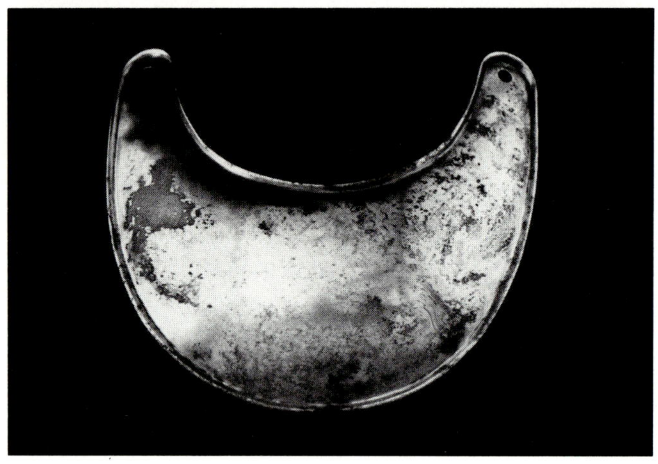

VI / THE MANUFACTURE OF SILVER ORNAMENTS

Zacharie Vincent, also known as Telari-o-lin, was a Huron from Lorette, Quebec. He painted this self-portrait in the mid-nineteenth century. Like most Indian trade silver, the large round brooch, headband and armbands he is wearing were made from coin silver. This was done by melting down coins, rolling the silver into thin sheets, and cutting out the desired shapes. The pieces would then be decorated with engraved or cut-out designs.

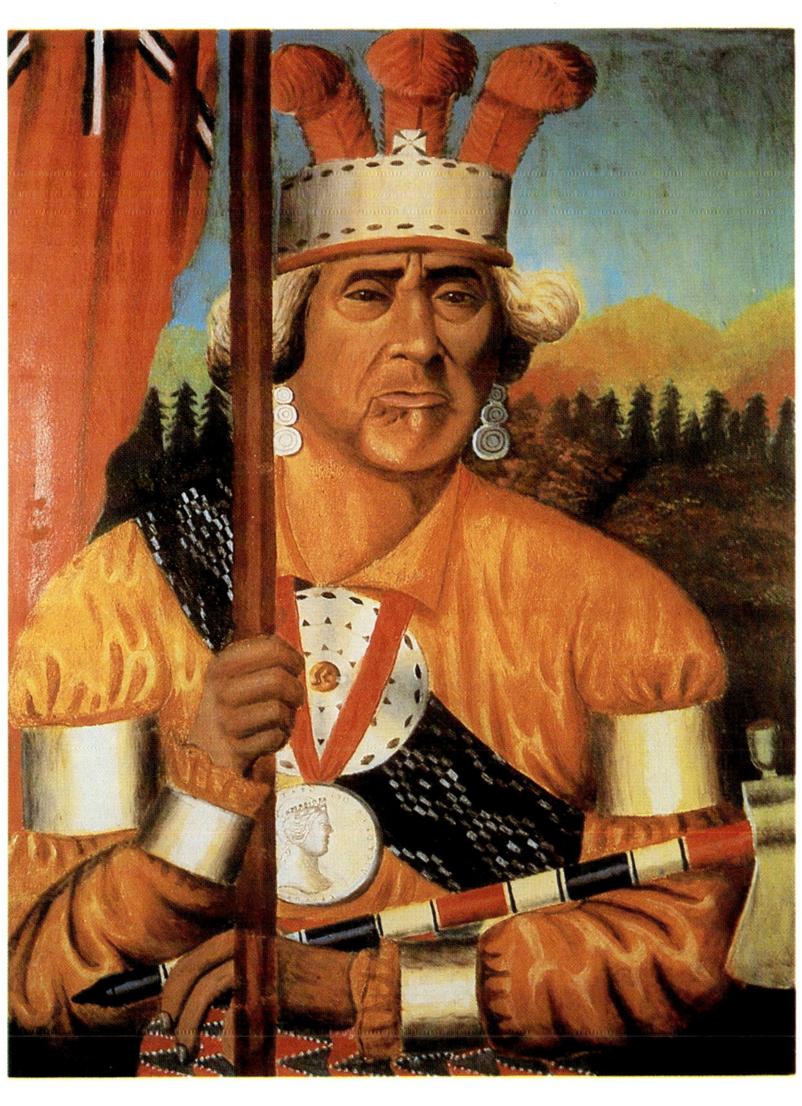

64/Crown
MARK: FS QUEBEC
MAKER: François Sasseville
(Quebec, 1797–1864)
SIZE: 41.9 cm l. × 8.9 cm h.
COLL.: NGC, Birks (Q360)

65/Heart-shaped Brooch
MARK: None
MAKER: Unknown
SIZE: 4.6 cm h. × 4.6 cm w.
COLL.: MHS

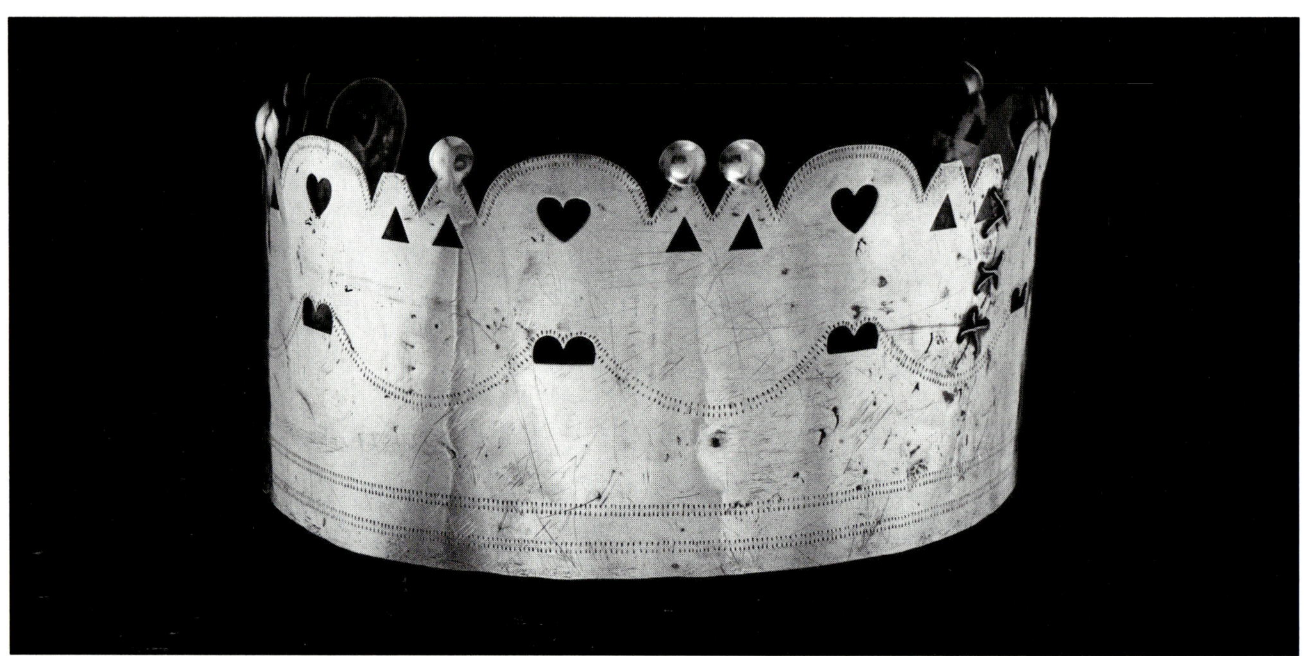

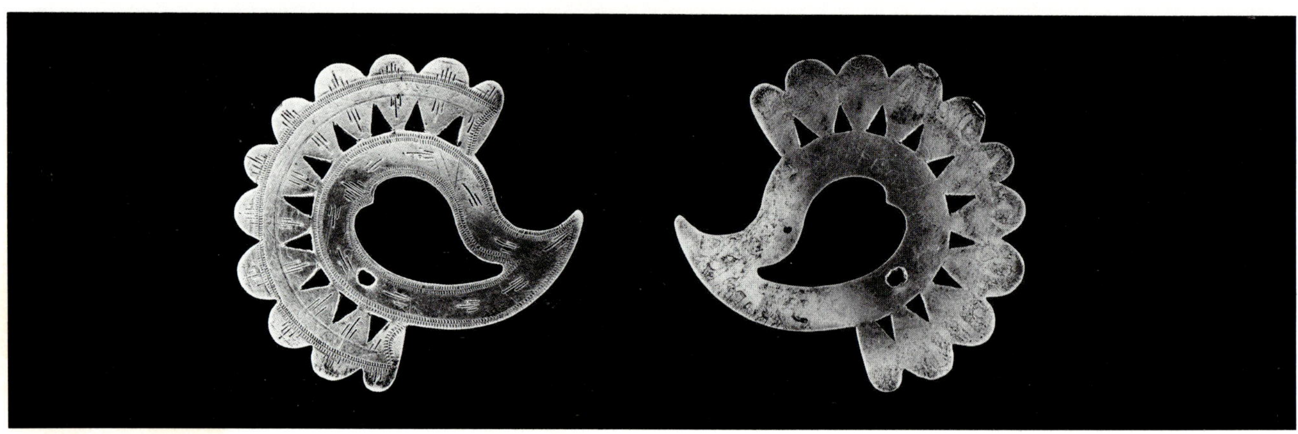

66/Spanish Silver Coin
VALUE: 8 reales
DATE: 1768
SIZE: 3.9 cm diam.
COLL.: Bk. Canada (M35302)

67/Round Brooch
MARK: None
MAKER: Unknown
SIZE: 4.8 cm diam.
COLL.: Heye (2/5144)

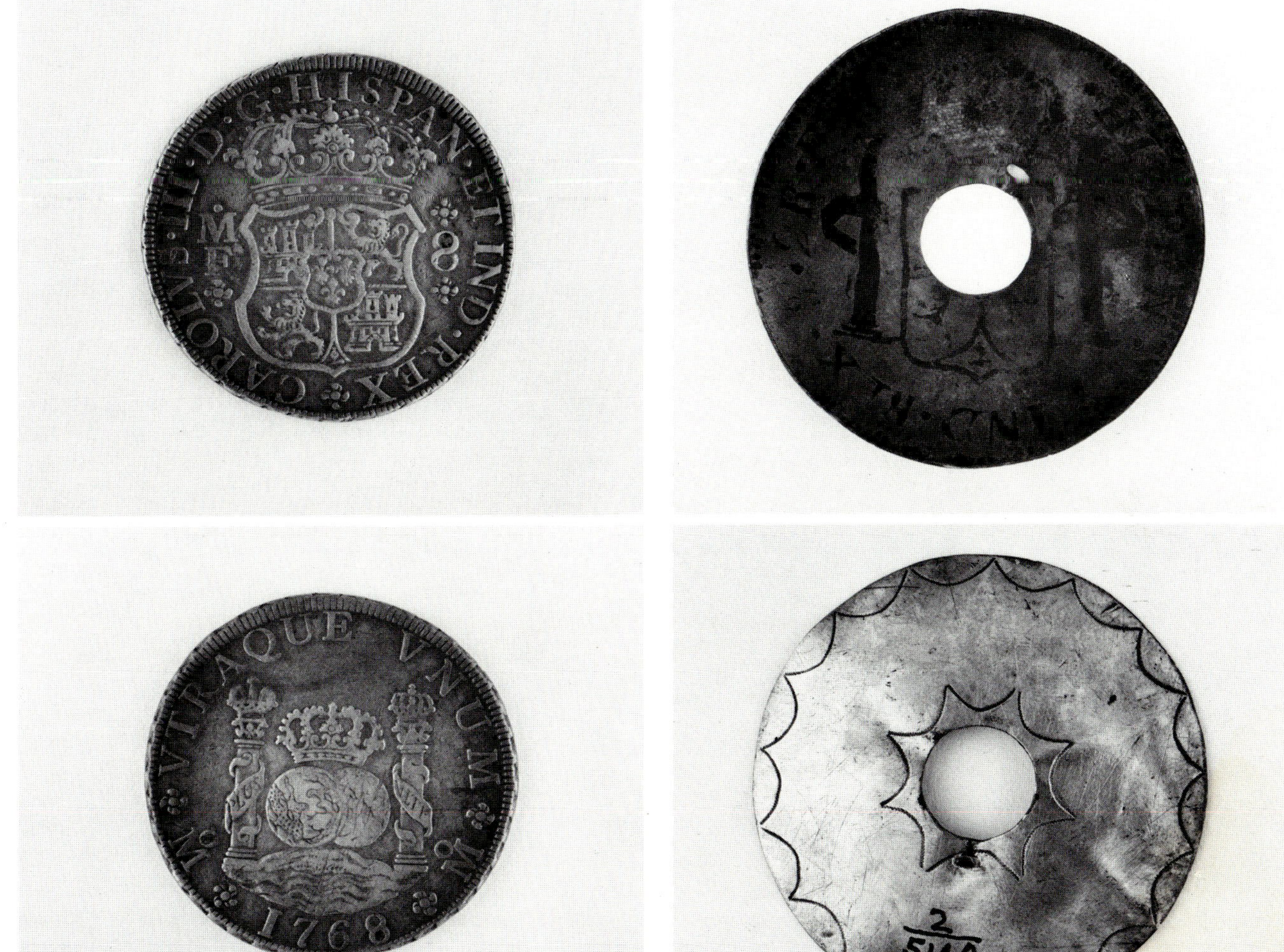

68/Round Brooch
MARK: JT
MAKER: Jonathan Tyler
(Montreal, 1817–28)
SIZE: 18.1 cm diam.
COLL.: NMM (III-L-15)

69/Pipe
MARK: None
MAKER: Unknown
SIZE: 32 cm l. × 4 cm h.
COLL.: Heye (11/6008)

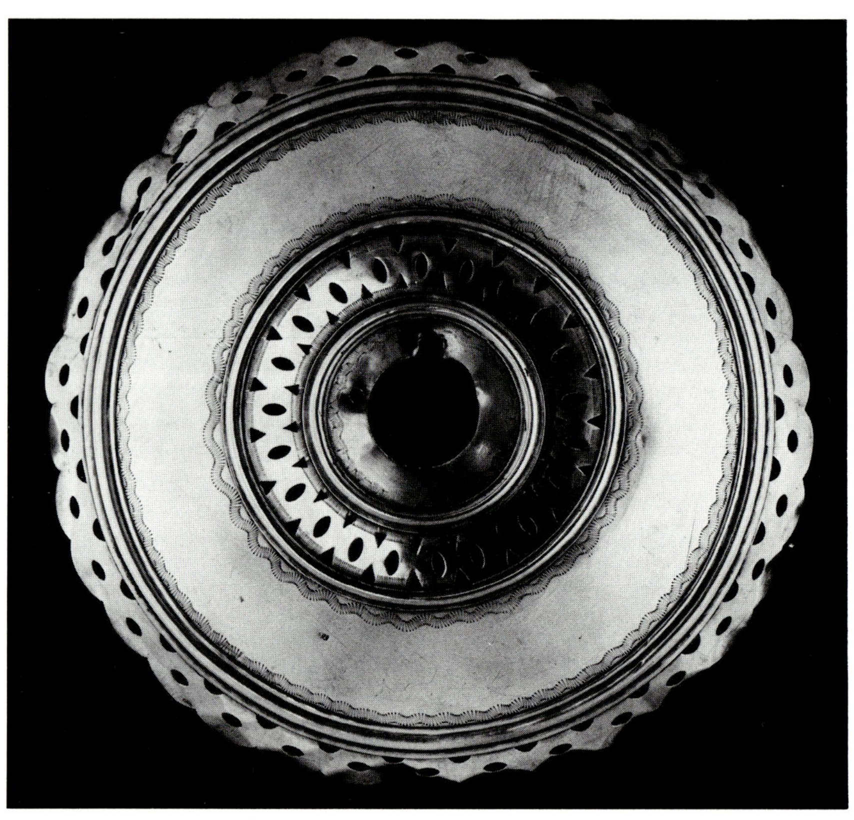

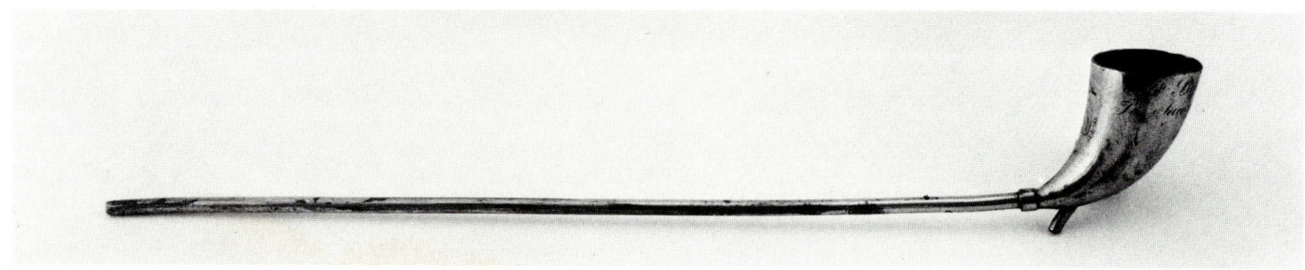

VII / THE VALUE OF SILVER

These two Ottawa chiefs from Lake Huron have dressed in their finest clothing to meet with the representative of the English king. Their prestige is evident in the amount of silver they are wearing. Whereas the fur trader saw the value of a piece of silver in simple monetary terms, the Indians attached to it other social values.

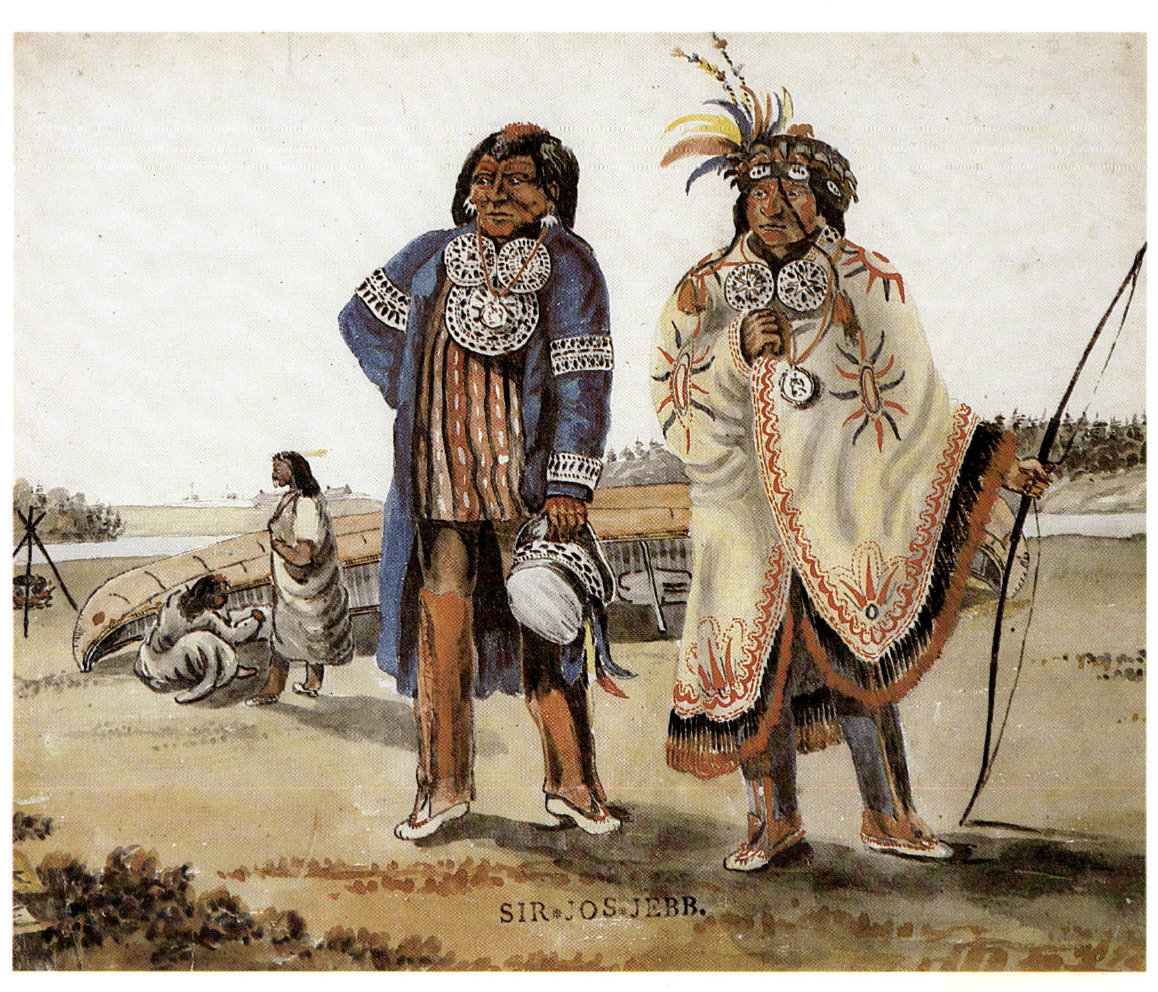

70/British Silver Coins
VALUE: 3 5-shilling coins,
3 2-shilling 6-pence coins,
3 1-shilling coins,
and 1 sixpence
DATE: 1707–46
SIZE: Largest, 3.4 cm diam.
COLL.: Bk Canada

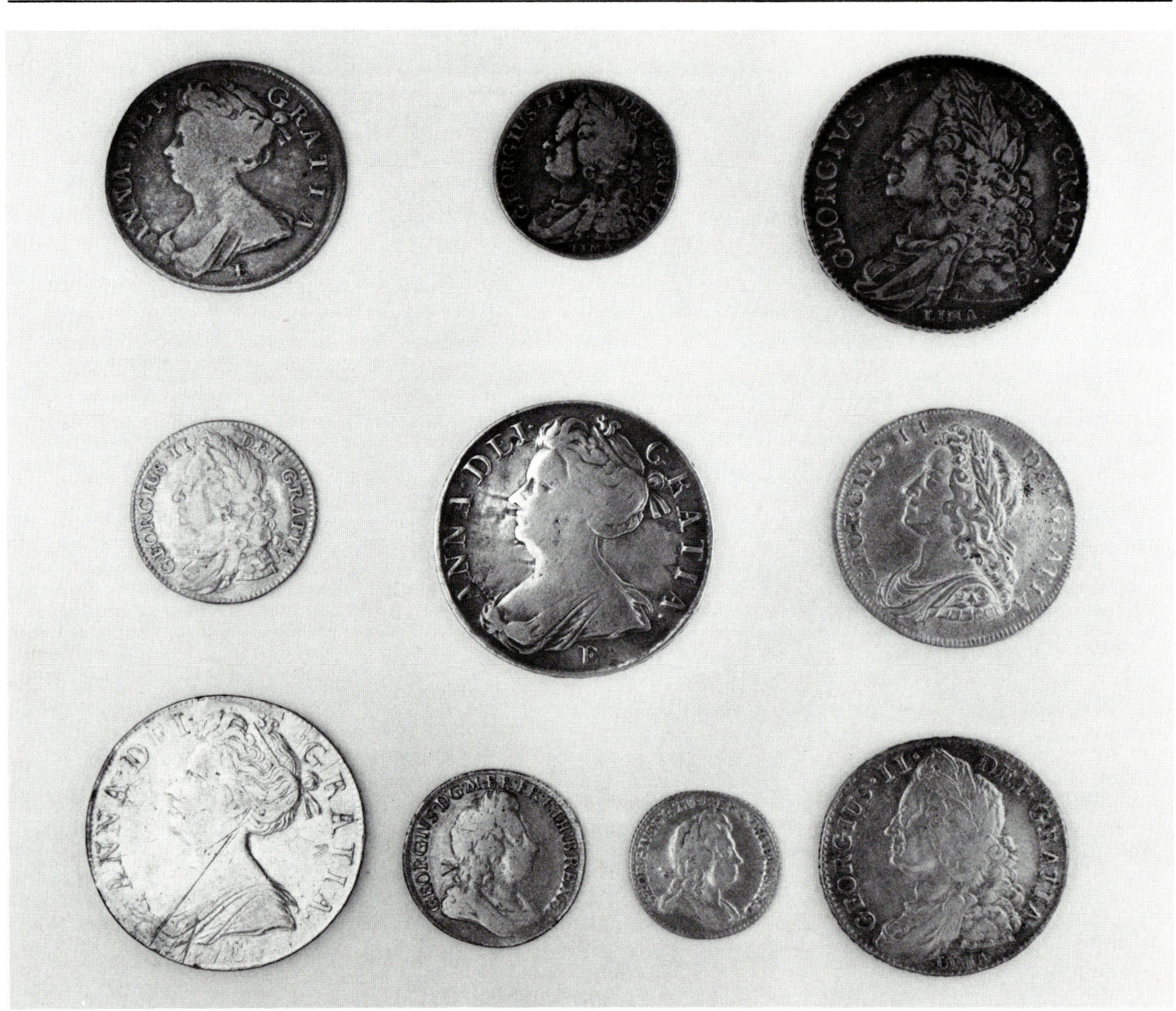

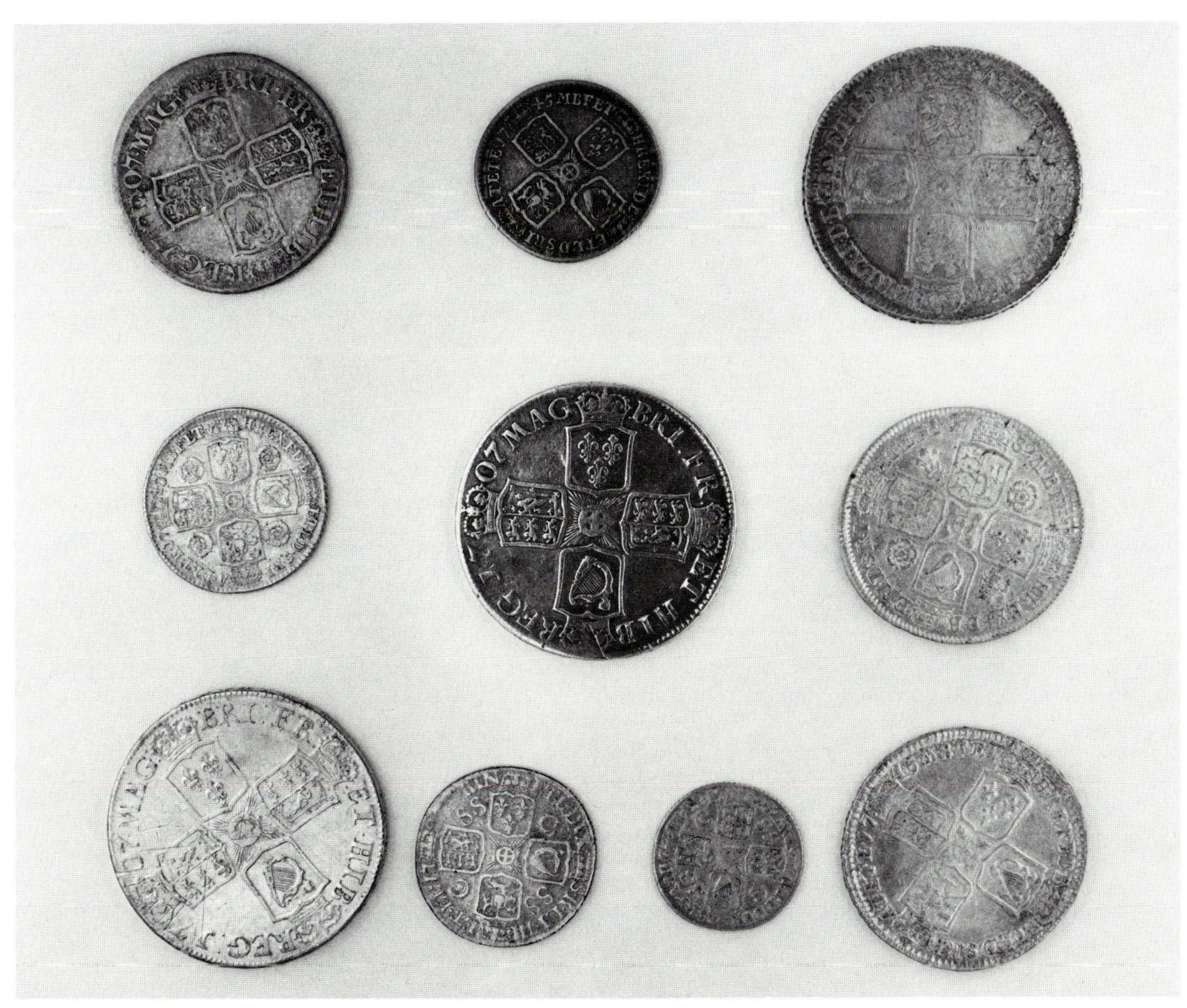

71/Crescent Gorget
MARK: CF (British hallmarks)
MAKER: Crespin Fuller (London, 1813)
SIZE: 12 cm w. × 11 cm h.
COLL.: ROM (HD7809)

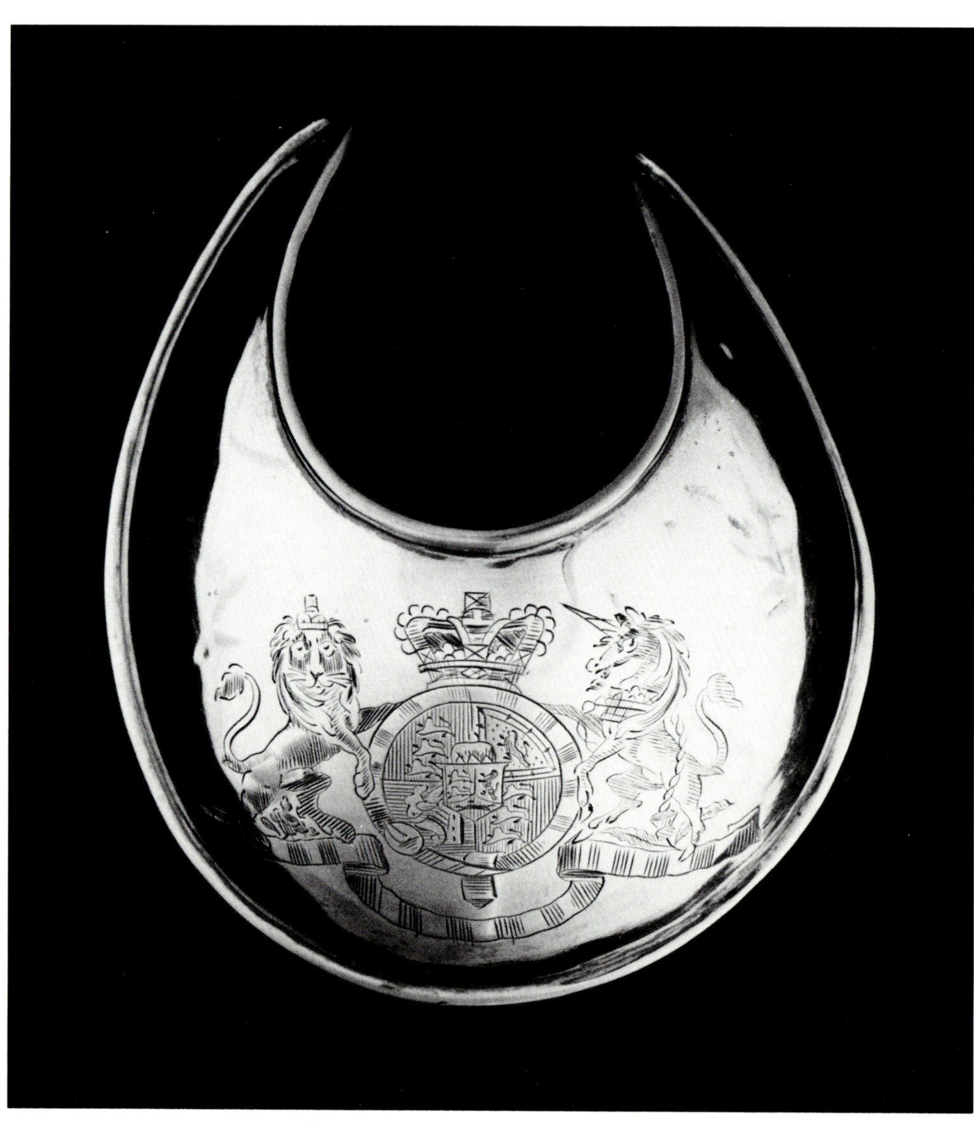

VIII / EUROPEAN ORIGINS

The quantity of silver this Indian woman is wearing on her European-style dress indicates that she was probably the wife or daughter of an influential Iroquois chief or great warrior. Although much trade silver was European in design, the Indians had their own reasons for their choices and often wore their ornaments in unexpected ways.

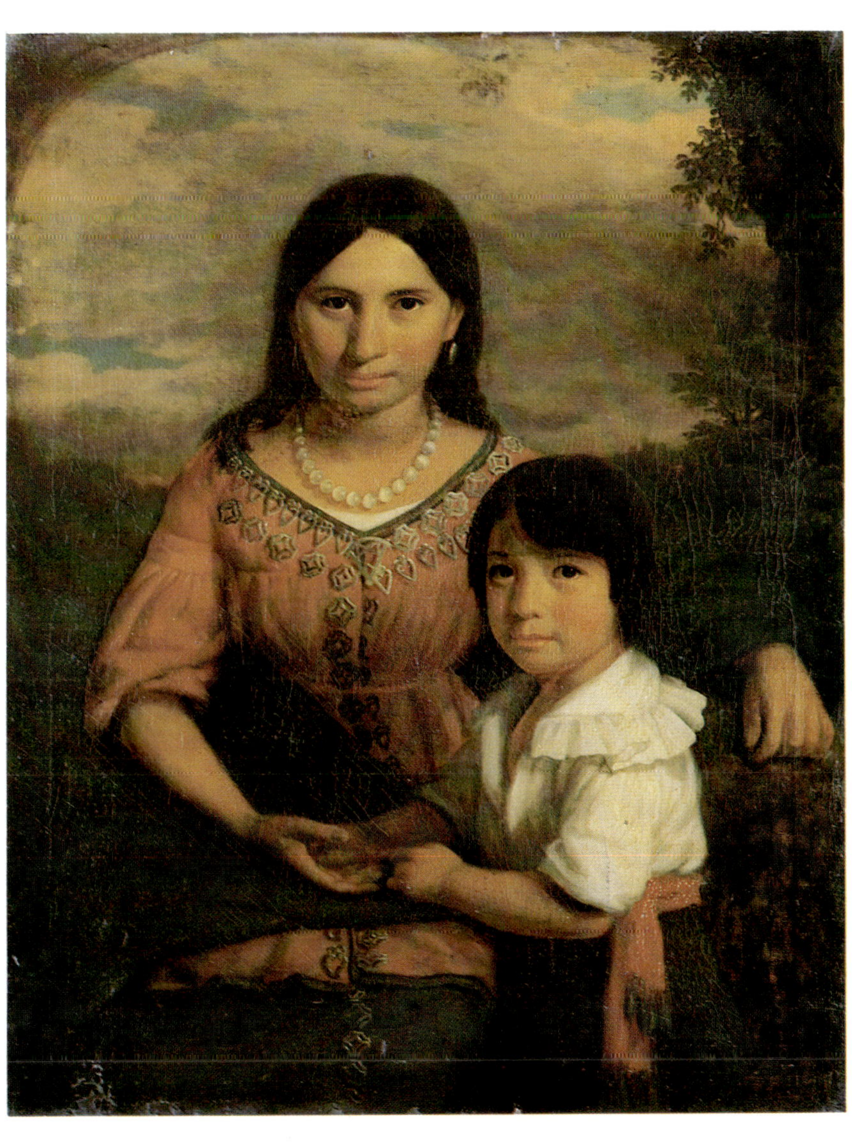

72/British Military Gorget
MATERIALS: Gilded brass
DATE: 1760–1820
SIZE: 11.0 cm w. × 9.3 cm h.
COLL.: Glenbow (R1266.2)

73/French Military Gorget
MATERIALS: Gilded brass; silver cockerel
DATE: c. 1850
SIZE: 14 cm w. × 9 cm h.
COLL.: ROM (HD6315)

74/Crescent Gorget
MARK: BP PJD
MAKER: Unknown
SIZE: 14 cm w. × 6 cm h.
COLL.: ROM (HD6307)

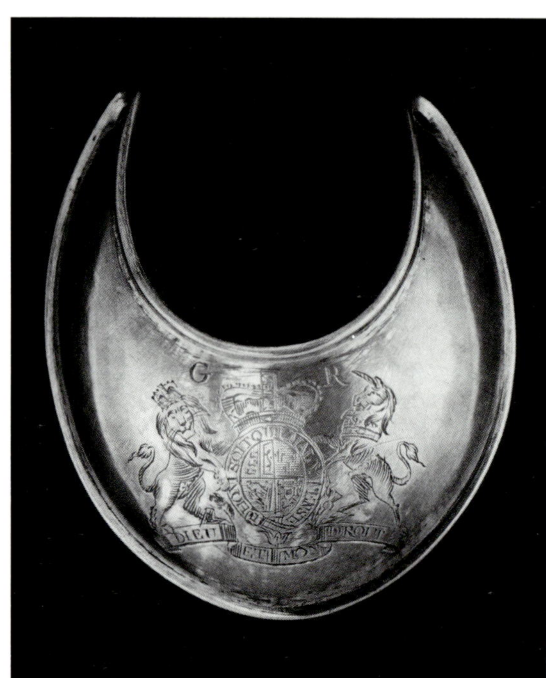

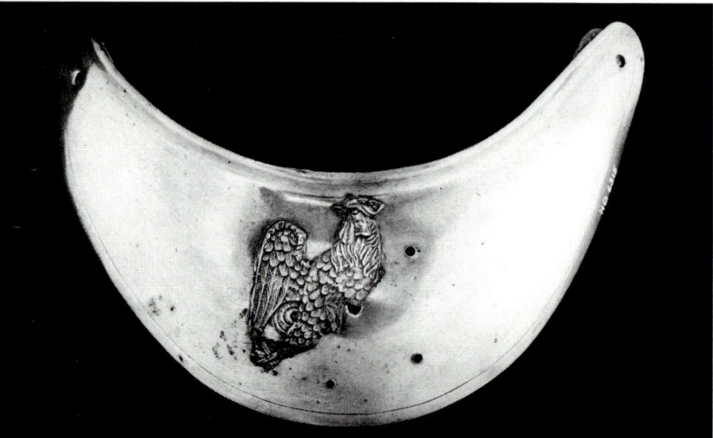

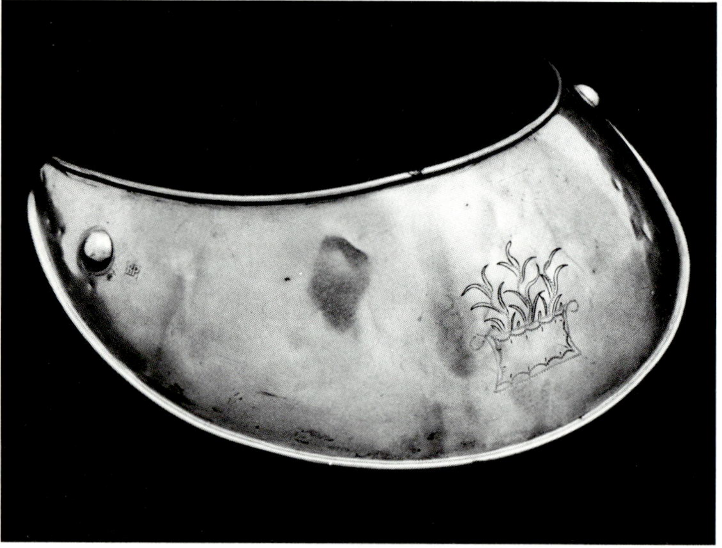

75/Crescent Gorget
MARK: None
MAKER: Unknown
SIZE: 13.0 cm w. × 4.5 cm h.
COLL.: ROM (HD6308)

76/Crescent Gorget
MARK: None
MAKER: Unknown
SIZE: 13.0 cm w. × 4.5 cm h.
COLL.: ROM (HD6318)

77/Crescent Gorget
MARK: None
MAKER: Unknown
SIZE: 13.2 cm w. × 9.5 cm h.
COLL.: Glenbow (R1266.1)

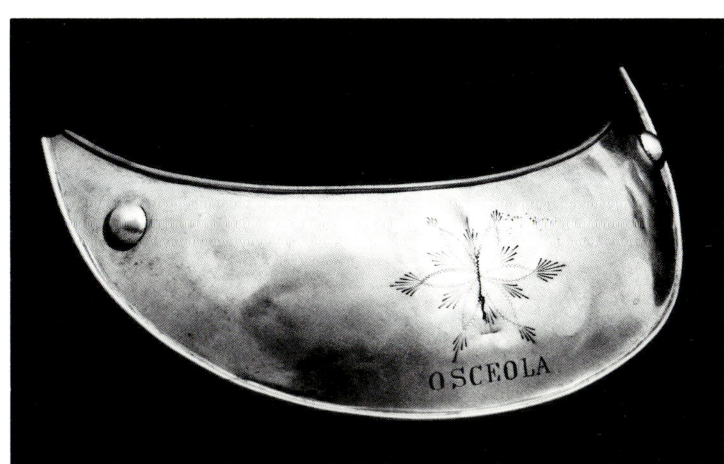

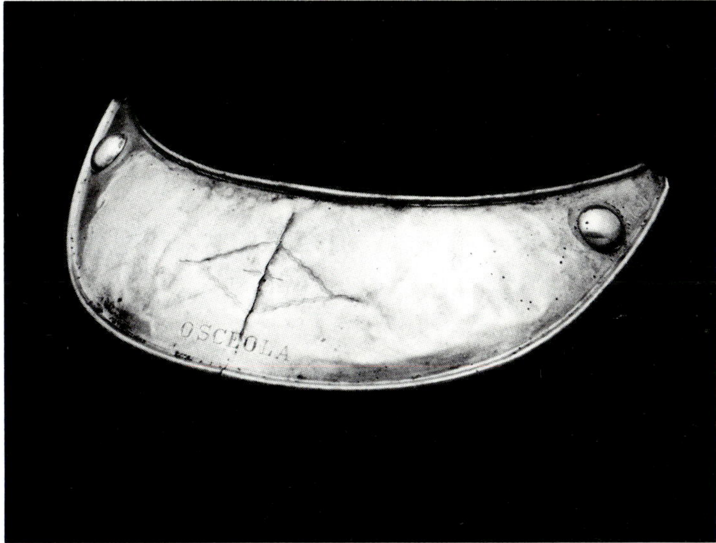

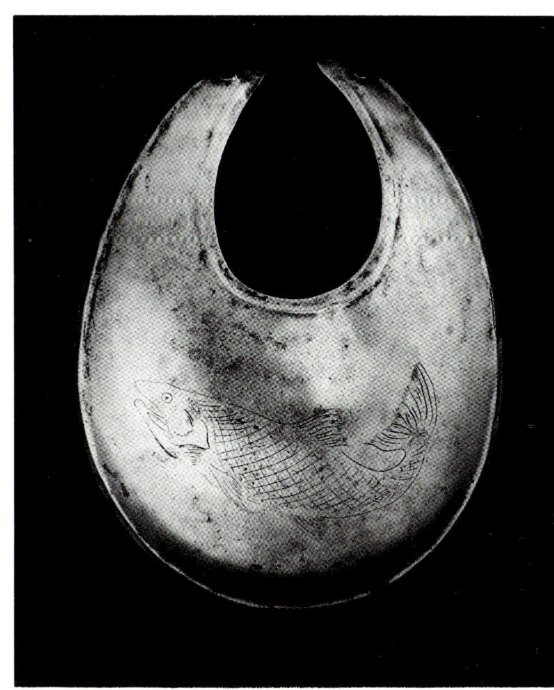

78/Crescent Gorget
MARK: RC
MAKER: Robert Cruickshank
(Boston, Montreal, 1767–1809)
SIZE: 14.0 cm w. × 4.5 cm h.
COLL.: ROM (911.3.33)

79/Crescent Gorget
MARK: None
MAKER: Unknown
SIZE: 5.4 cm w. x 13.5 cm h.
COLL.: Heye (2/8427)

80/Crescent Gorget
MARK: None
MAKER: Unknown
SIZE: 16 cm w. × 5 cm h.
COLL.: Heye (2/6726B)

81/Four Crescent Gorgets
MARK: None
MAKER: Unknown
SIZE: Largest, 16.0 cm w. × 4.5 cm h.; total h., 19.0 cm
COLL.: Heye (2/6725)

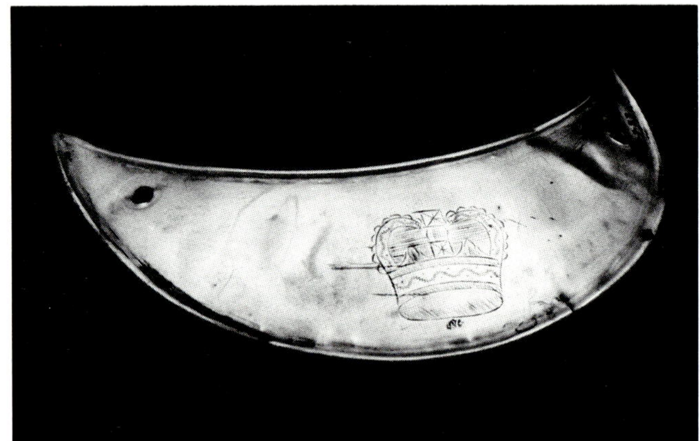

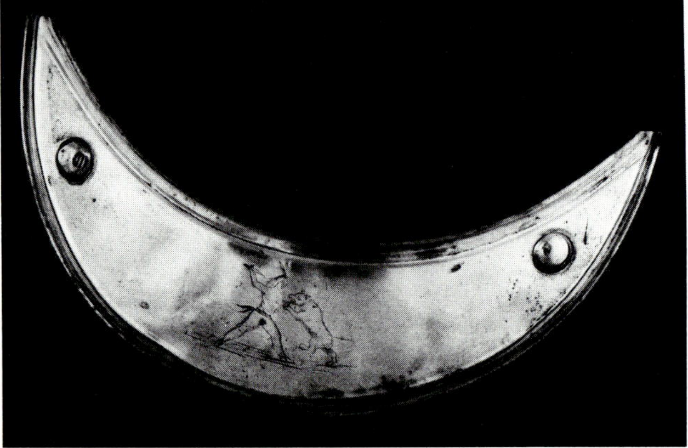

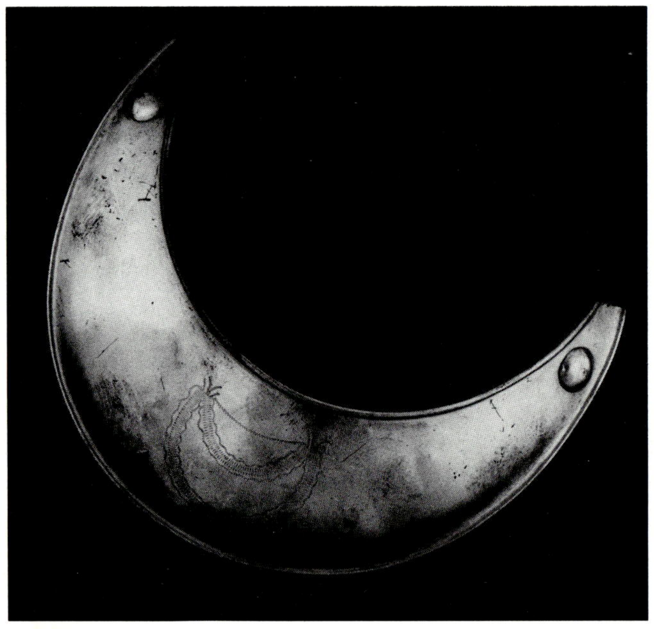

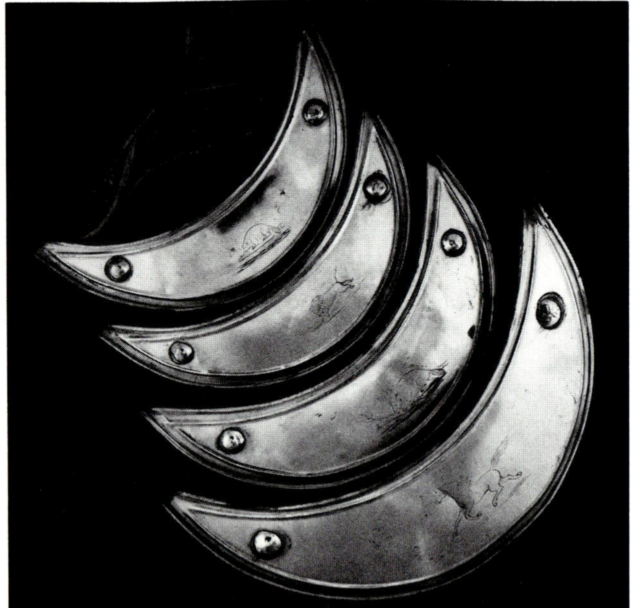

82/American Fur Company Medal
OBV.: PRESIDENT OF THE AMERICAN FUR COMPANY
REV.: FORT UNION U.M.O.
SIZE: 6.6 cm diam.
COLL.: ANS

83/Medal
MARK: RC
MAKER: Robert Cruickshank (Boston, Montreal, 1767–1809)
SIZE: 8.5 cm diam.
COLL.: NGC, Birks (C220)

85/Round Brooch (German silver)
MARK: MONTREAL
MAKER: Unknown
SIZE: 19.5 cm diam.
COLL.: McCord (M19191)

84/British Medal
OBV.: GEORGIVS III DEI GRATIA BRITANNIARVM REX F: D:
REV.: Royal arms of Britain 1814
SIZE: 7.6 cm diam.
COLL.: NMM (III-H-471)

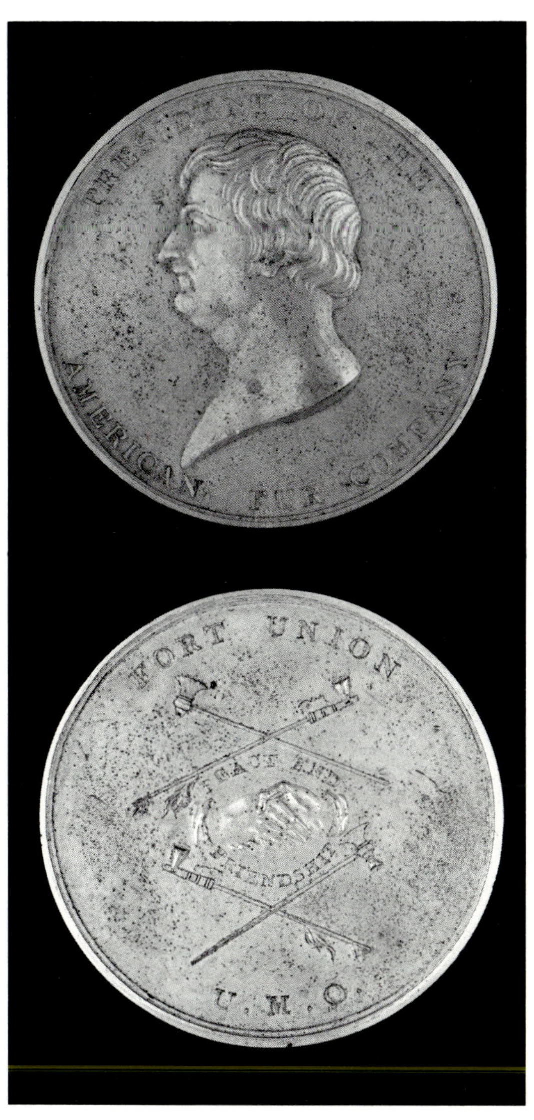

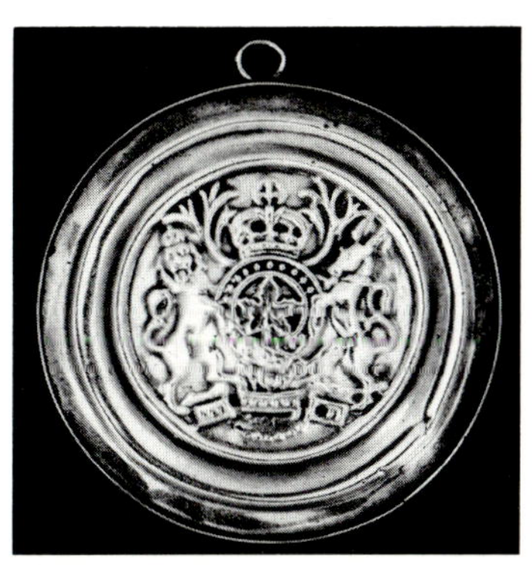

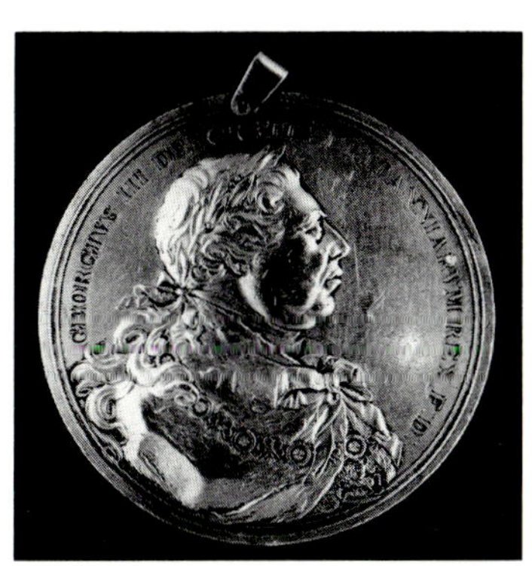

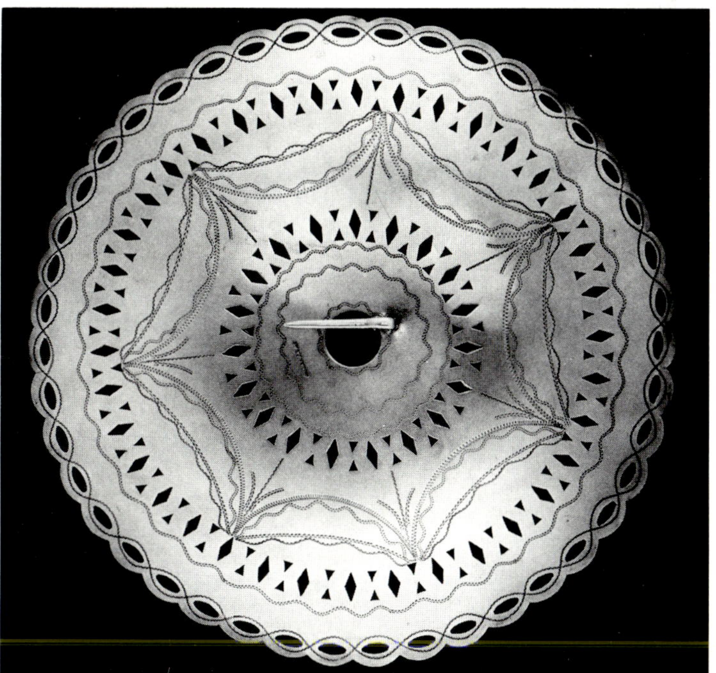

86/Crucifix
MARK: RC
MAKER: Robert Cruickshank
(Boston, Montreal, 1767–1809)
SIZE: 7.7 cm h. × 3.7 cm w.
COLL.: McCord (M198)

87/Latin Cross
MARK: RC
MAKER: Robert Cruickshank
(Boston, Montreal, 1767–1809)
SIZE: 12.0 cm h. × 6.6 cm w.
COLL.: Heye (2/8038)

88/Latin Cross
MARK: CA
MAKER: Charles Arnoldi
(Montreal, 1779–1817)
SIZE: 9.2 cm h. × 4.6 cm w.
COLL.: NMM (III-Q-47)

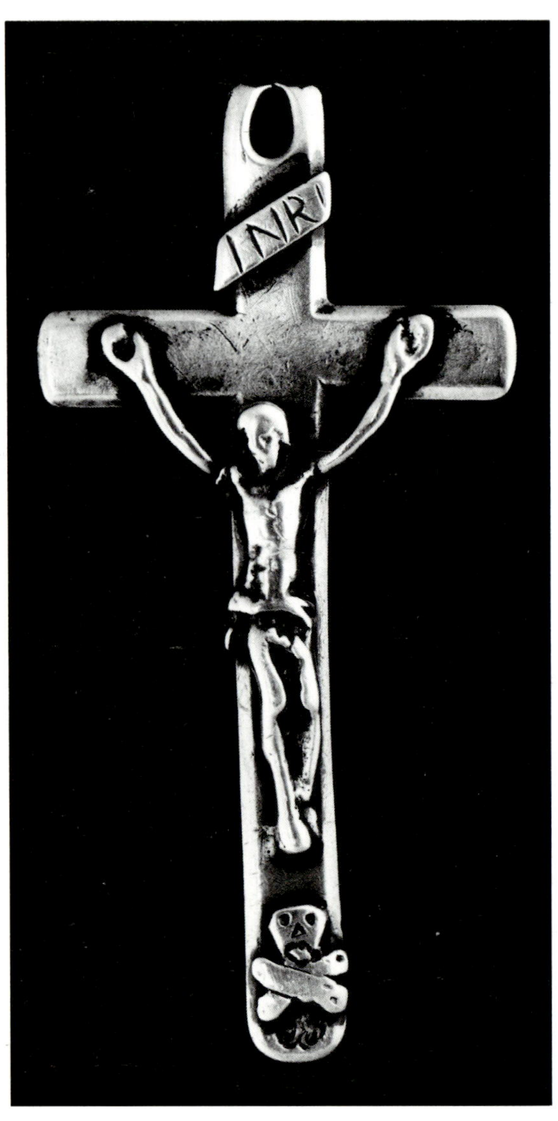

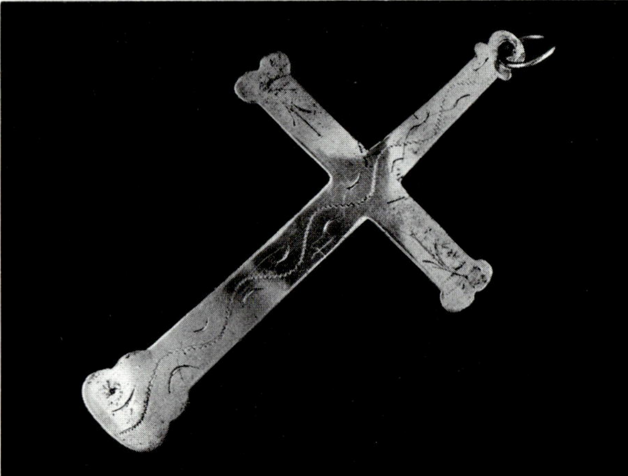

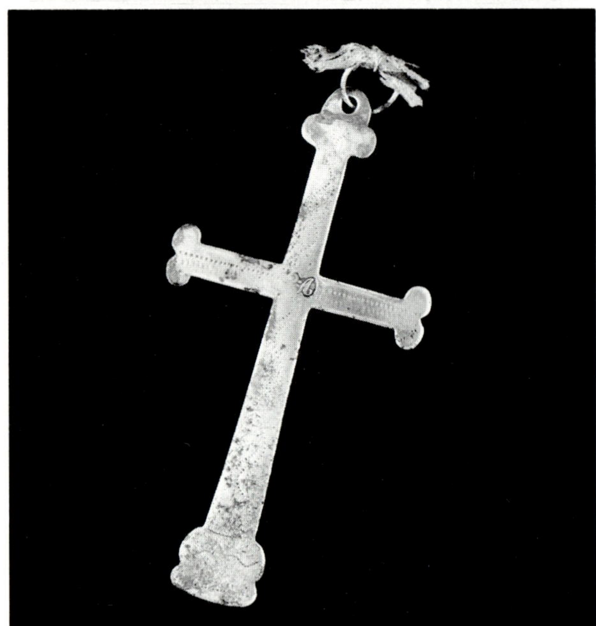

89/Lorraine Cross
MARK: I.W.
MAKER: Unknown
SIZE: 9.5 cm h. × 4.6 cm w.
COLL.: Heye (2/9710)

90/Lorraine Cross
MARK: None
MAKER: Unknown
SIZE: 12.7 cm h. × 6.3 cm w.
COLL.: McCord (M174)

91/Lorraine Cross
MARK: RC
MAKER: Robert Cruickshank
(Boston, Montreal, 1767–1809)
SIZE: 7.6 cm h. × 3.8 cm w.
COLL.: NMM (III-Q-46)

92/Cross
MARK: IK
MAKER: John Kinzie
(Chicago, 1780–1812)
SIZE: 5 cm h. × 4 cm w.
COLL.: Heye (20/7094)

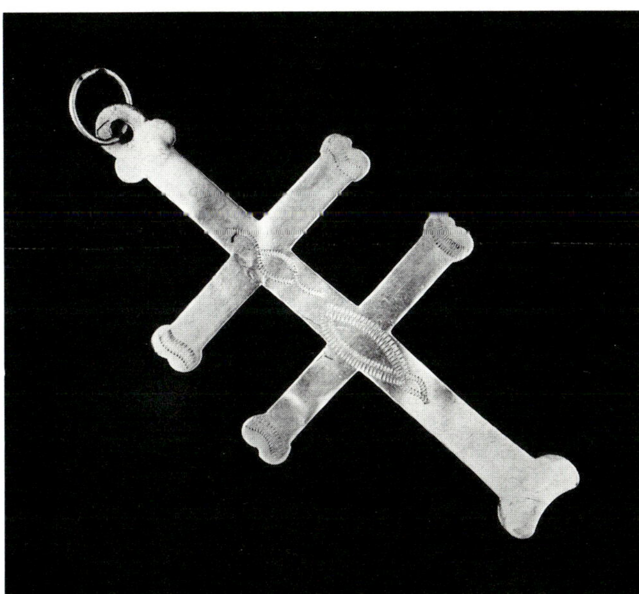

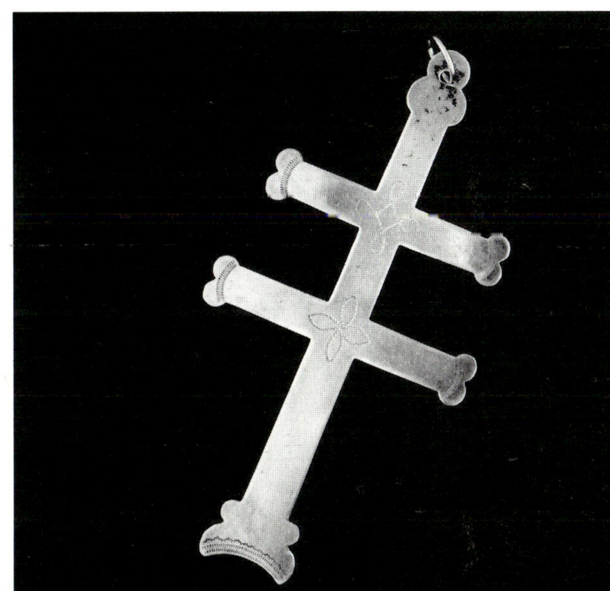

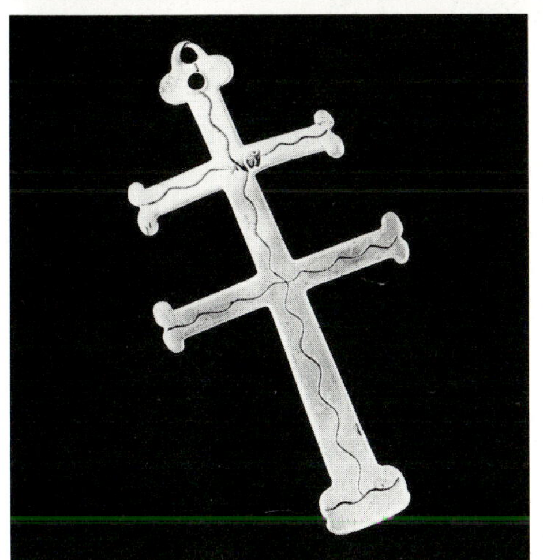

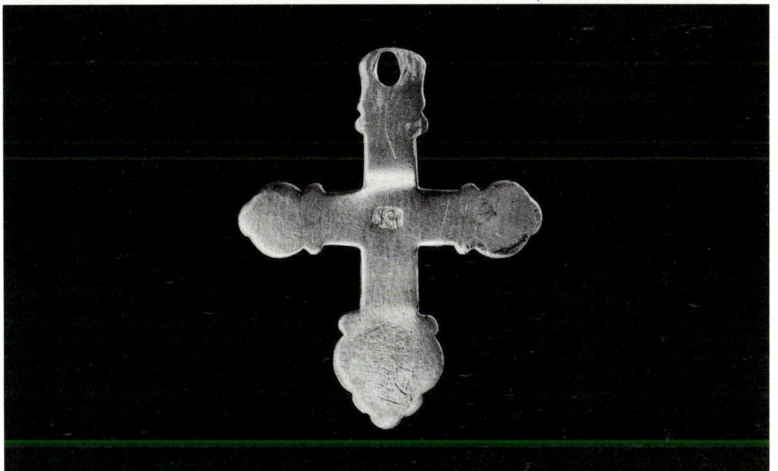

93/Cross with Chain of Glass and Silver Beads
MARK: CA
MAKER: Charles Arnoldi (Montreal, 1779–1817)
SIZE: Cross, 14.5 cm h. × 10.7 cm w.; chain, 91.5 cm l.
COLL.: McCord (M1893.1)

94/Four Crosses
MARK: NR
MAKER: Narcisse Roy (Montreal, 1765–1819)
SIZE: 2.2 cm h. × 1.8 cm w.
COLL.: ROM (890.1.6–9)

95/Necklace of Silver Crosses and Glass Beads
MARK: None
MAKER: Unknown
SIZE: 35 cm l.
COLL.: NGC, Birks (C292B)

98/Scottish Luckenbooth Heart Brooch
DATE: 1820–50
SIZE: 7.7 cm h. × 5.4 cm w.
COLL.: NMAS (NGB-38)

99/Scottish Luckenbooth Heart Brooch
DATE: c. 1775
SIZE: 3.4 cm h. x 2.4 cm w.
COLL.: NMAS (NGA-201)

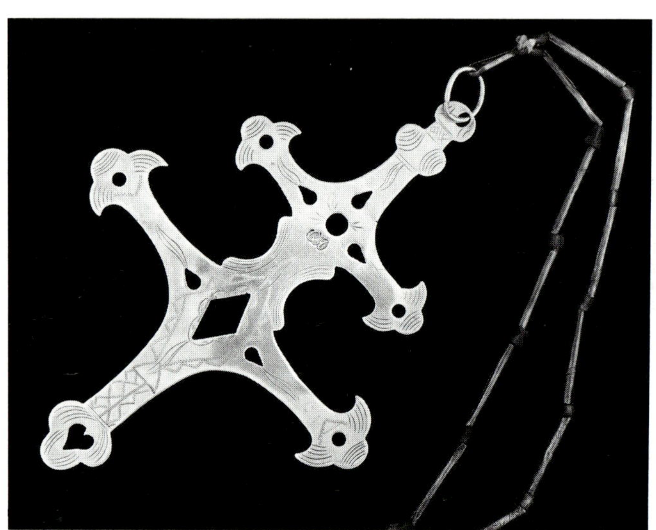

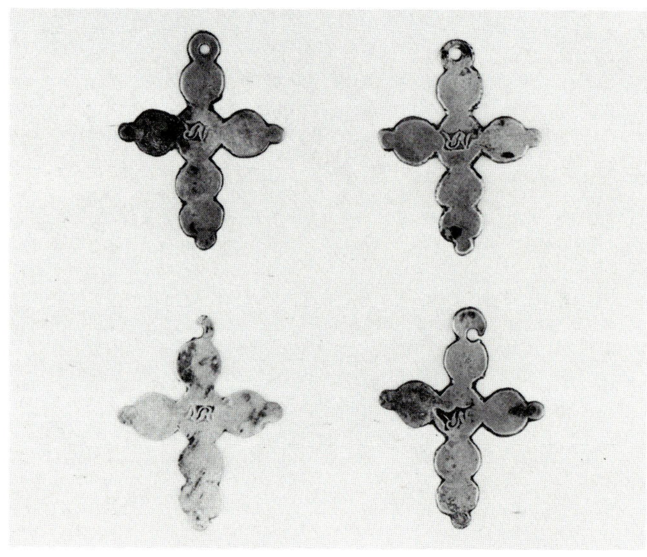

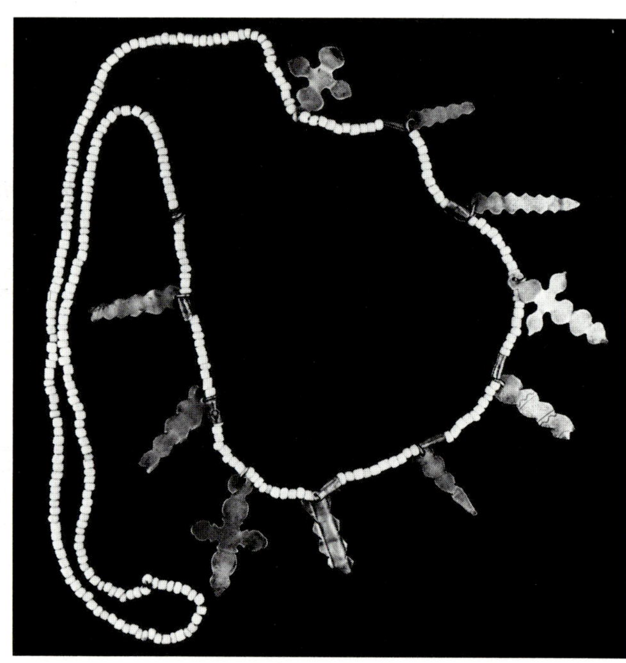

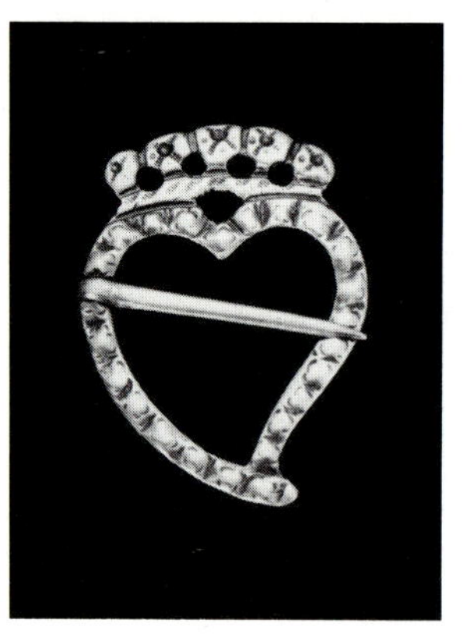

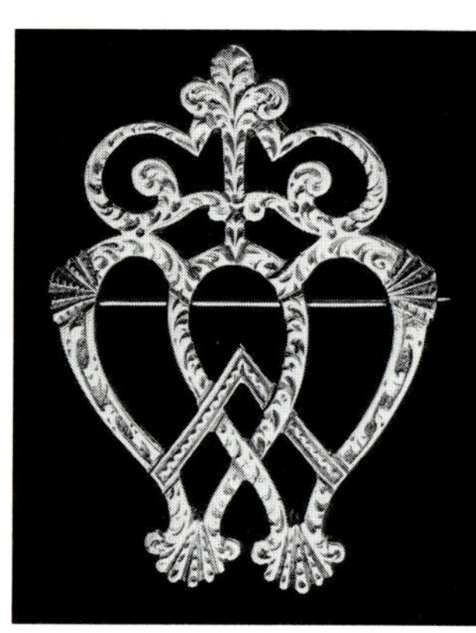

96/Cross
MARK: (Lion) M (cipher)
MAKER: Unknown
SIZE: 7.3 cm h. × 4.7 cm w.
COLL.: NGC, Birks (U127)

97/Cross
MARK: PH
MAKER: Pierre Huguet *dit* Latour, Sr. or Jr. (Montreal, 1771–1829)
SIZE: 29.5 cm h. × 20.0 cm w.
COLL.: Heye (14/5981)

100/Plain Heart Brooch
MARK: None
MAKER: Unknown
SIZE: 2.8 cm h. × 2.2 cm w.
COLL.: Heye (8291)

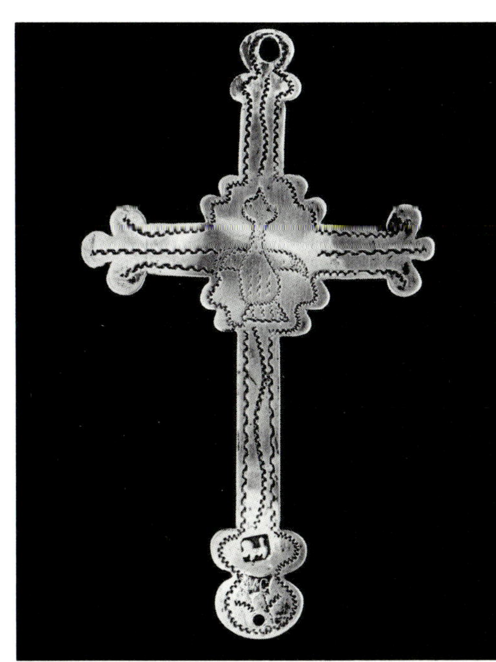

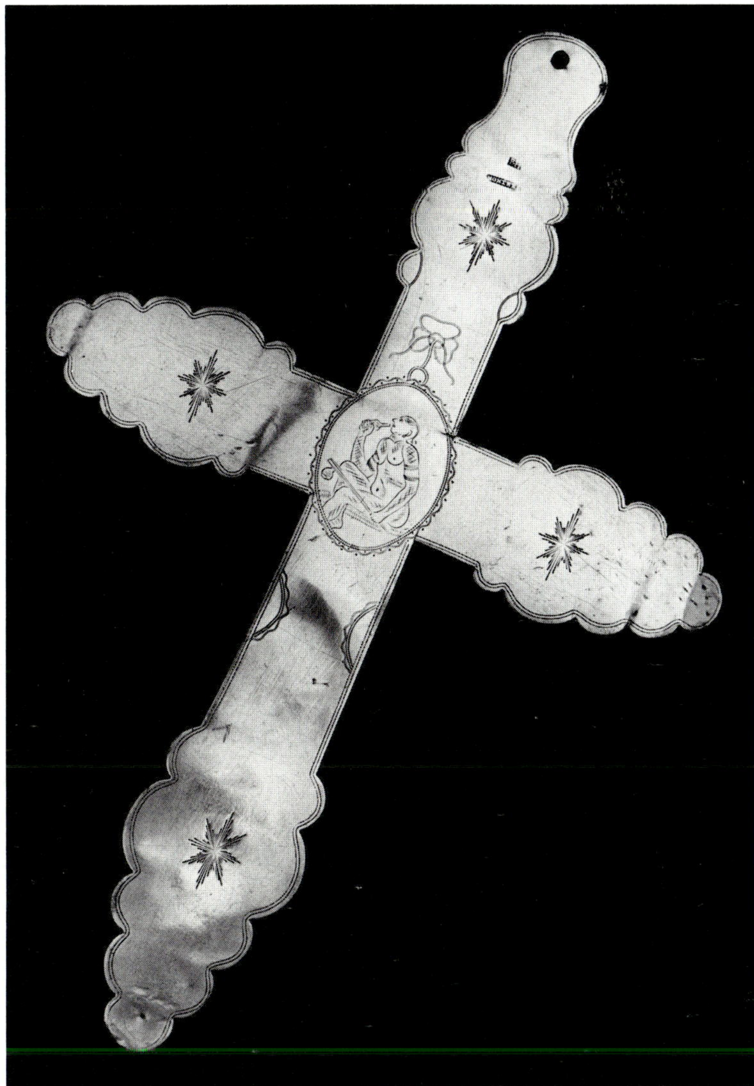

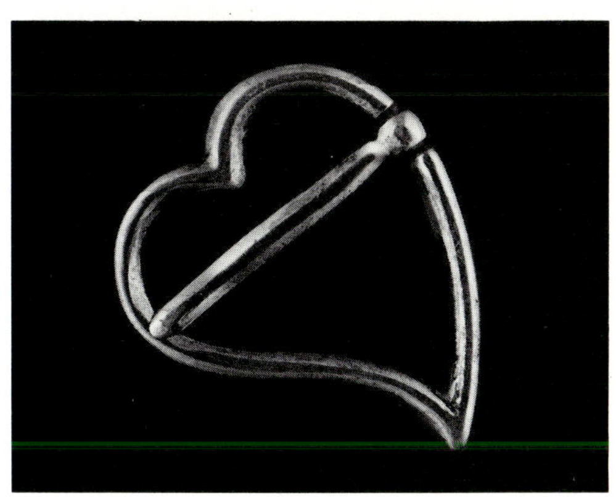

101/Heart Brooch
MARK: None
MAKER: Unknown
SIZE: 2.9 cm h. × 2.0 cm w.
COLL.: NMM (III-I-690)

102/Heart Brooch
MARK: None
MAKER: Unknown
SIZE: 3.4 cm h. × 2.0 cm w.
COLL.: NMM (III-I-695)

103/Heart Brooch
MARK: NR
MAKER: Narcisse Roy (Montreal, 1779–1817)
SIZE: 3.2 cm h. × 1.3 cm w.
COLL.: Heye (20/1871)

104/Heart Brooch
MARK: RC
MAKER: Robert Cruickshank (Boston, Montreal, 1767–1809)
SIZE: 3.0 cm h. × 2.1 cm w.
COLL.: NMM (III-Q-43)

105/Double-Heart Brooch
MARK: HB
MAKER: Unknown
SIZE: 2.0 cm h. × 1.7 cm w.
COLL.: NGC, Birks (U176)

106/Double-Heart Brooch
MARK: None
MAKER: Unknown
SIZE: 2.7 cm h. × 2.1 cm w.
COLL.: NMM (III-I-163)

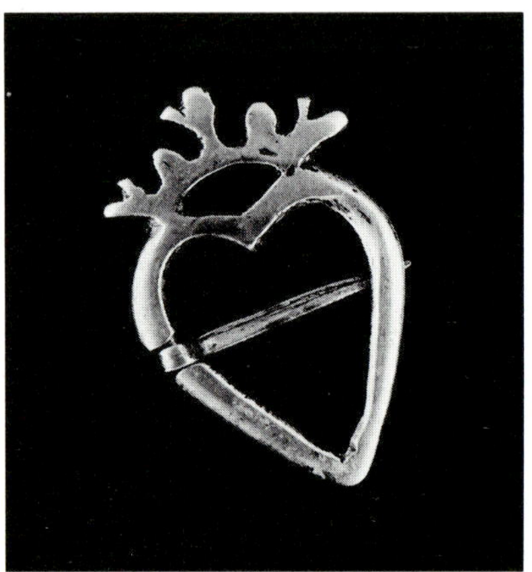

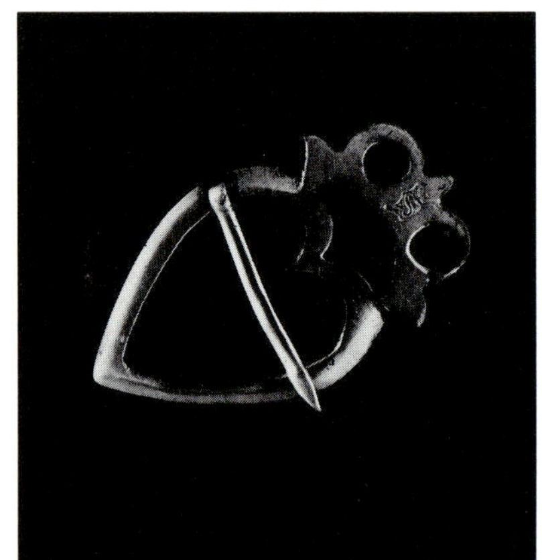

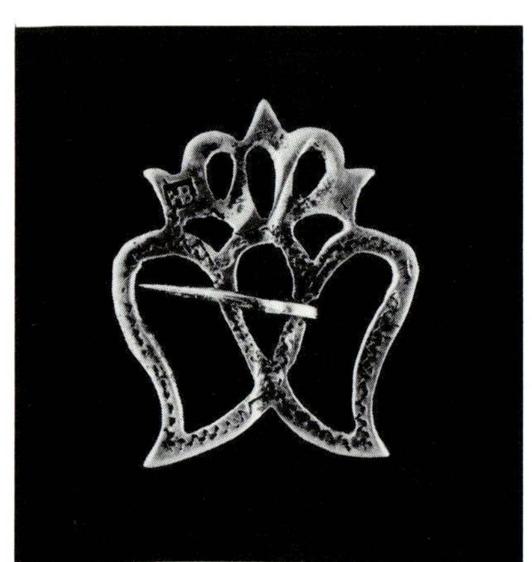

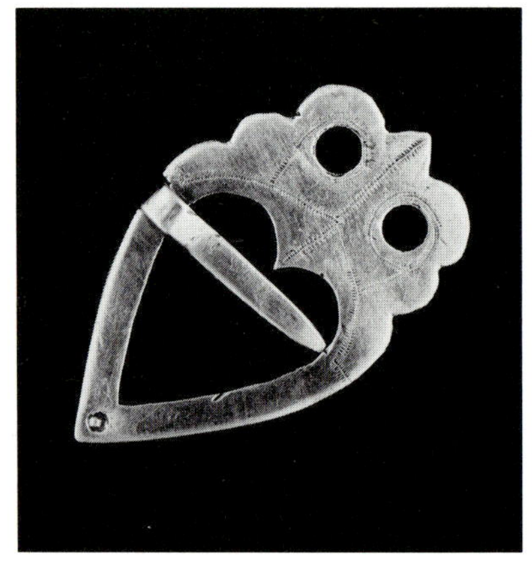

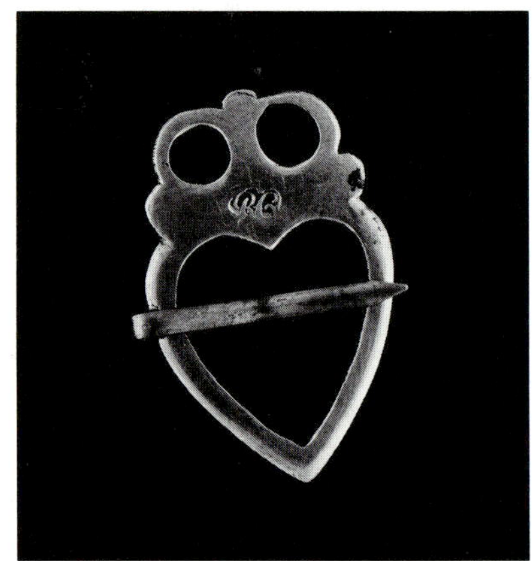

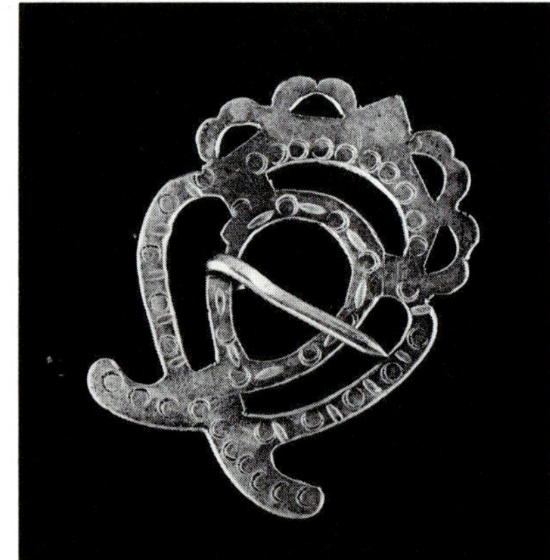

107/Double-Heart Brooch
MARK: None
MAKER: Unknown
SIZE: 2.5 cm h. × 2.1 cm w.
COLL.: NMM (III-I-408)

108/Double-Heart Brooch
MARK: None
MAKER: Unknown
SIZE: 2.7 cm h. × 2.1 cm w.
COLL.: NMM (III-I-160)

109/Double-Heart Brooch
MARK: None
MAKER: Unknown
SIZE: 4 cm h. × 3 cm w.
COLL.: Heye (2/9711)

110/Double-Heart Brooch
MARK: None
MAKER: Unknown
SIZE: 4 cm h. × 3 cm w.
COLL.: Heye (2/9711)

111/Double-Heart Brooch
MARK: None
MAKER: Unknown
SIZE: 3.5 cm h. × 3.0 cm w.
COLL.: Heye (1/1603)

112/Double-Heart Brooch
MARK: None
MAKER: Unknown
SIZE: 3.5 cm h. × 2.5 cm w.
COLL.: NMM (III-I-1254)

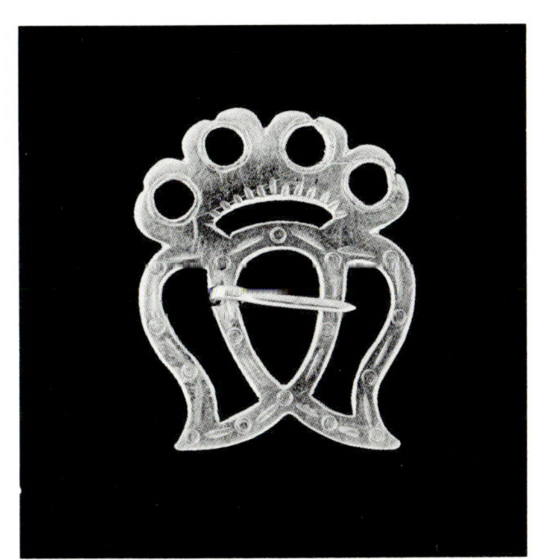

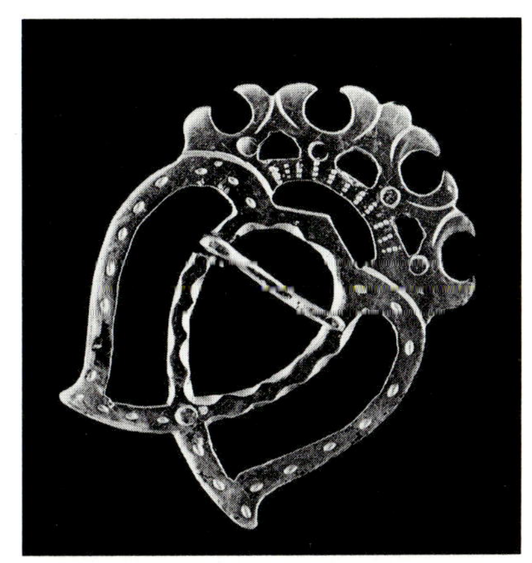

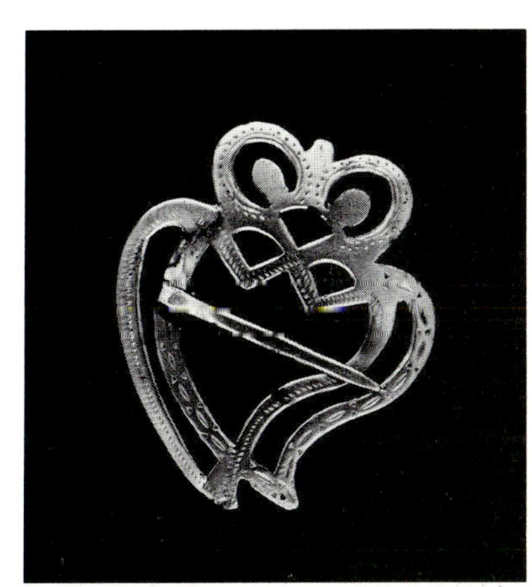

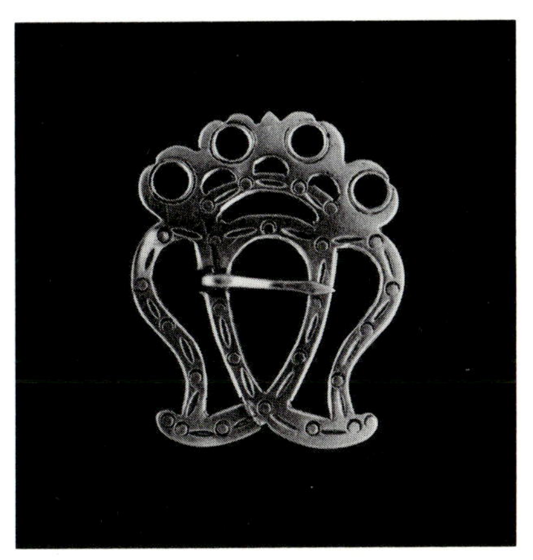

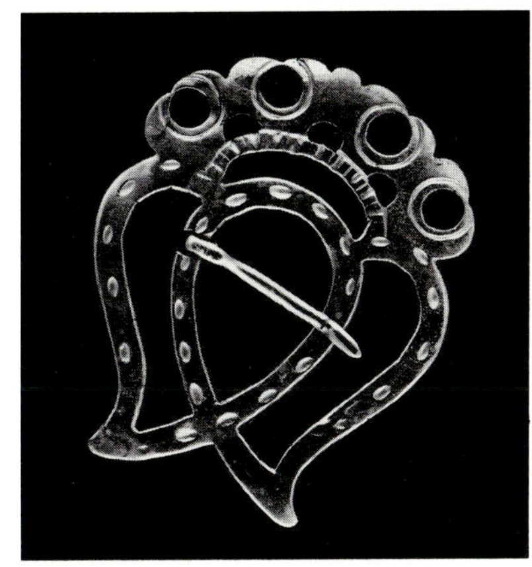

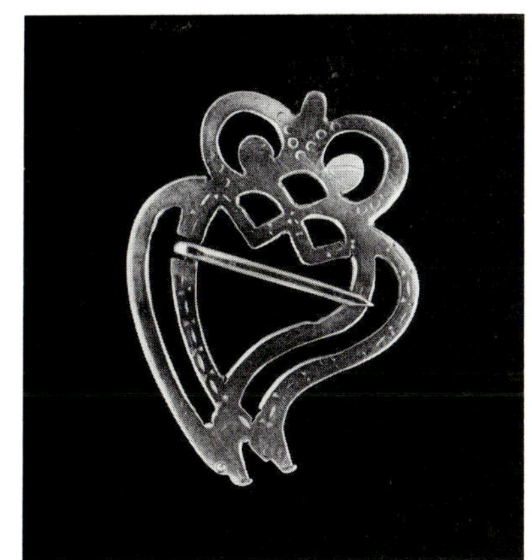

113/Double-Heart Brooch
MARK: None
MAKER: Unknown
SIZE: 4.3 cm h. × 3.0 cm w.
COLL.: McCord

114/Heart-shaped Gorget
MARK: PC (British hallmarks)
MAKER: Unknown
SIZE: 11.5 cm h. × 10.9 cm w.
COLL.: MMFA (953.Ds.13)

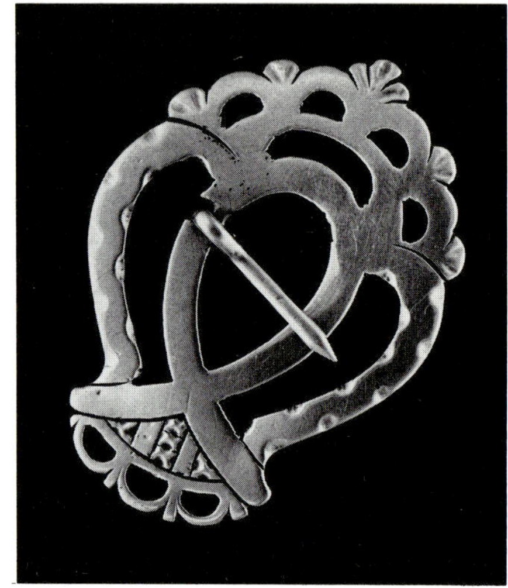

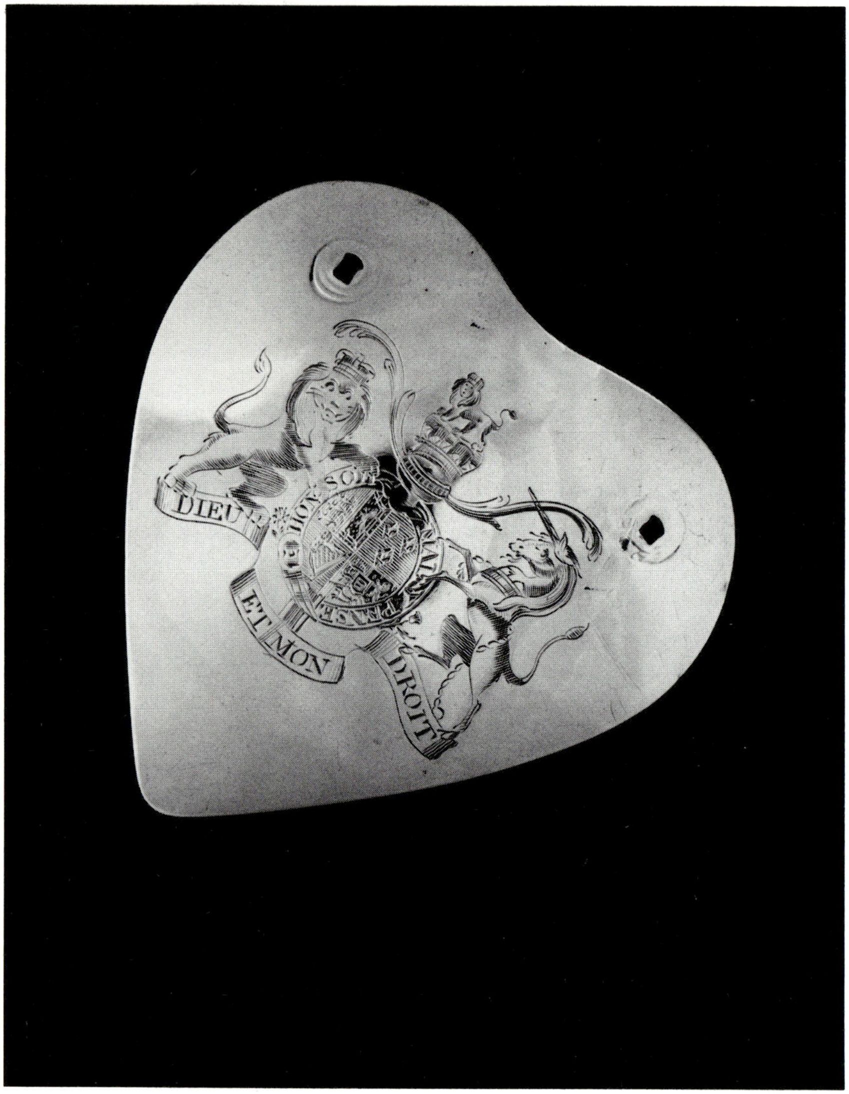

115/Masonic Jewel
MATERIALS: Brass
DATE: 20th century
SIZE: 5.7 cm h. × 3.8 cm w.
COLL.: OMC

116/Masonic-Style Brooch
MARK: MUNRO
MAKER: Possibly Alex Munro (Saint John, N.B., 1754–1828)
SIZE: 4.0 cm h. × 4.1 cm w.
COLL.: NGC, Birks (M188)

117/Masonic-Style Brooch
MARK: None
MAKER: Unknown
SIZE: 5.5 cm h. × 4.3 cm w.
COLL.: Heye (10/4197)

118/Masonic-Style Brooch
MARK: None
MAKER: Unknown
SIZE: 5.9 cm h. × 4.9 cm w.
COLL.: NMM (III-I-684)

119/Masonic-Style Brooch
MARK: None
MAKER: Unknown
SIZE: 4.8 cm h. × 3.8 cm w.
COLL.: NMM (III-I-701)

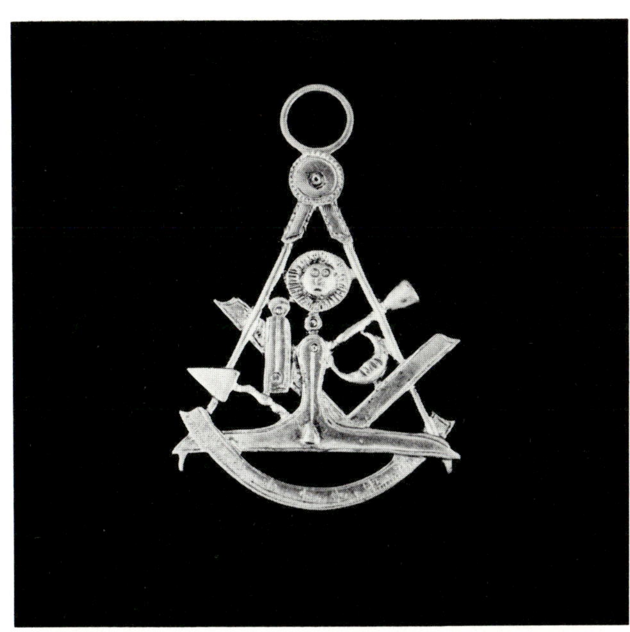

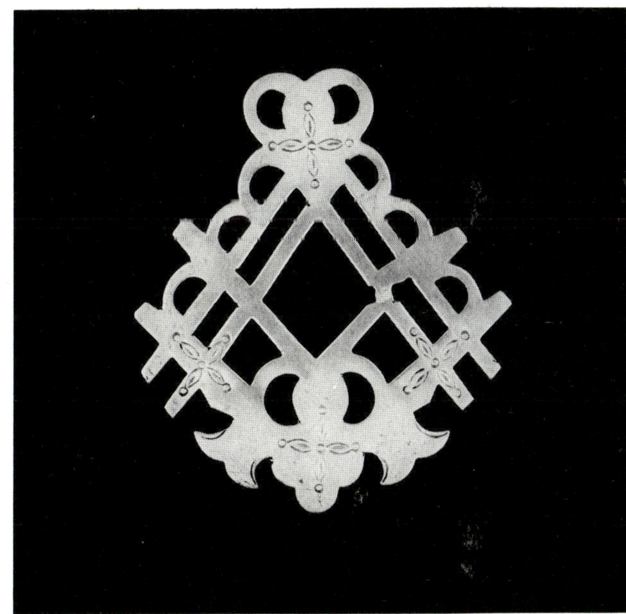

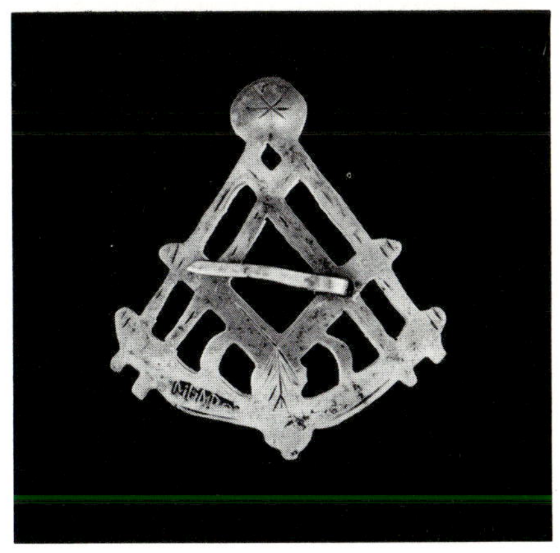

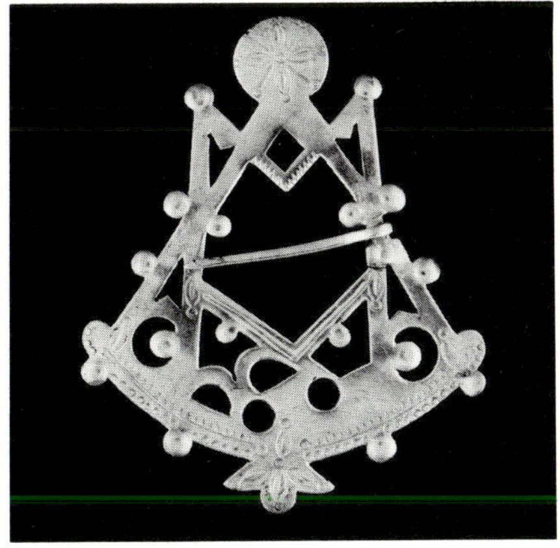

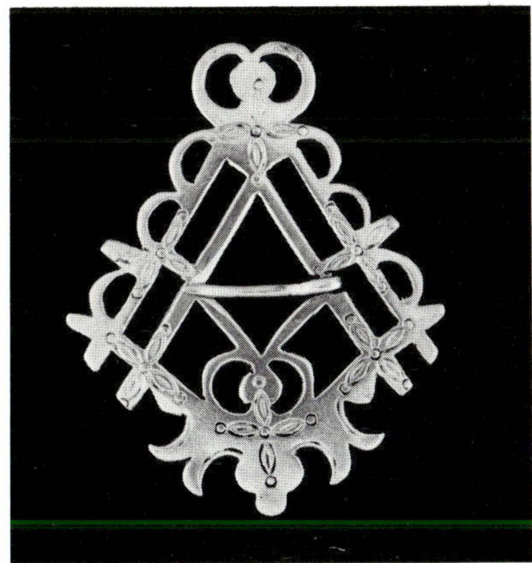

120/Council Square Brooch
MARK: None
MAKER: Unknown
SIZE: 2.3 cm square
COLL.: Heye (2/9711)

121/Council Square Brooches
MARK: None
MAKER: Unknown
SIZE: 2.5 cm square
COLL.: Heye (2/9711)

122/Ring Brooch
MARK: None
MAKER: Unknown
SIZE: 2.4 cm diam.
COLL.: NMM (III-I-110)

123/Ring Brooch
MARK: None
MAKER: Unknown
SIZE: 2.4 cm diam.
COLL.: NMM (III-I-800)

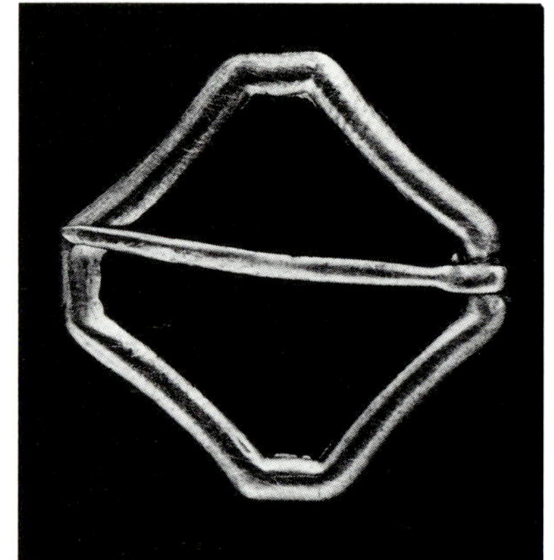

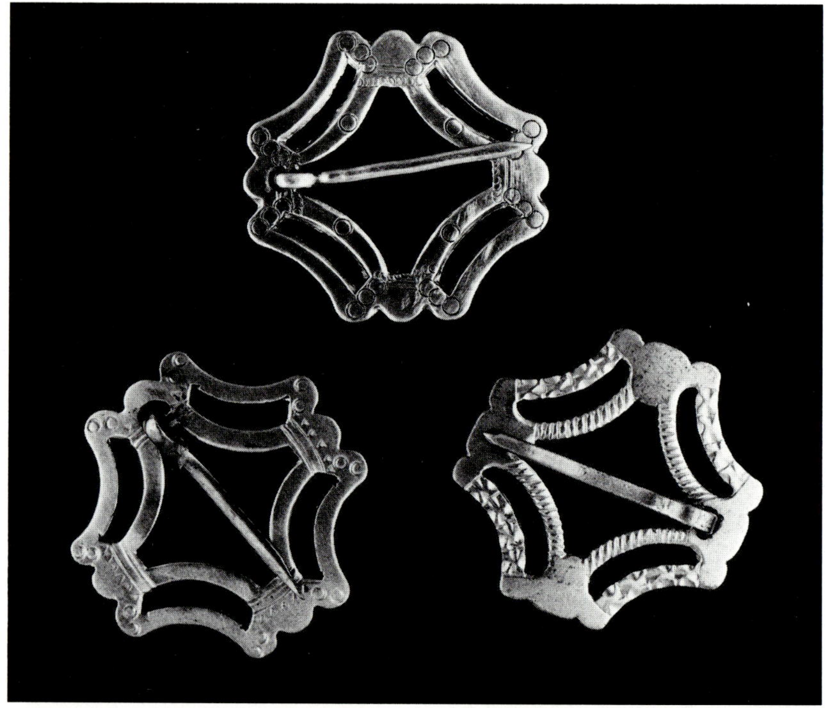

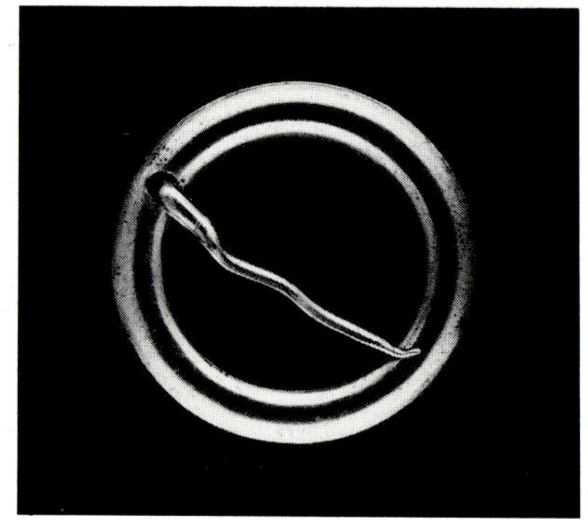

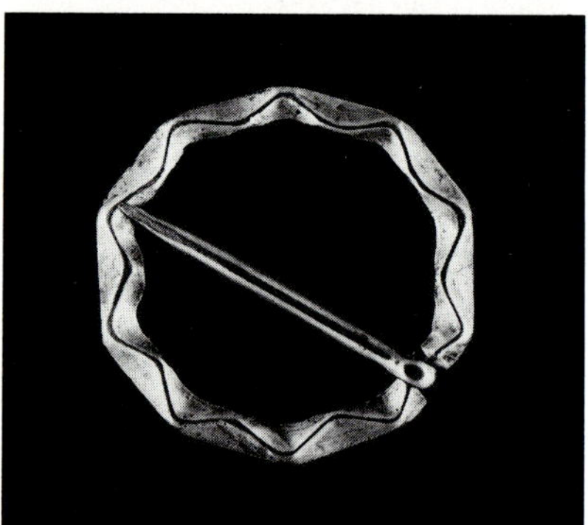

124/Round Brooch
MARK: W
MAKER: Unknown
SIZE: 9.7 cm diam.
COLL.: Heye (24/959)

125/Round Brooch
MARK: None
MAKER: Unknown
SIZE: 9.4 cm diam.
COLL.: Heye (20/1236)

126/Round Brooch
MARK: None
MAKER: Unknown
SIZE: 8.7 cm diam.
COLL.: Heye (3/2401)

127/Round Brooch
MARK: None
MAKER: Unknown
SIZE: 4.3 cm diam.
COLL.: NMM (III-I-324)

128/Round Brooch
MARK: None
MAKER: Unknown
SIZE: 3.5 cm diam.
COLL.: NMM (III-I-53)

129/Round Brooch
MARK: None
MAKER: Unknown
SIZE: 3 cm diam.
COLL.: NMM (III-I-803)

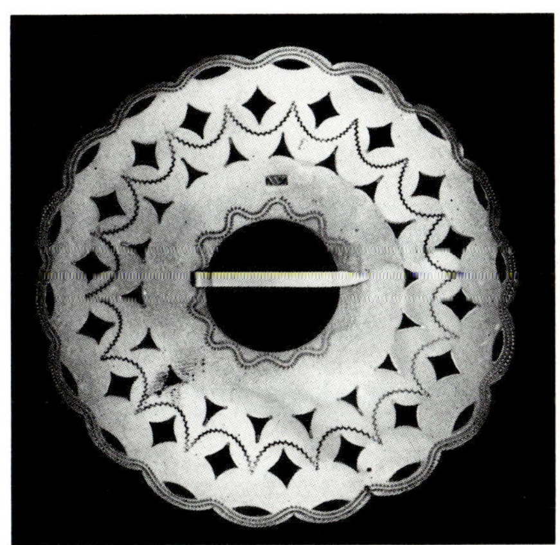

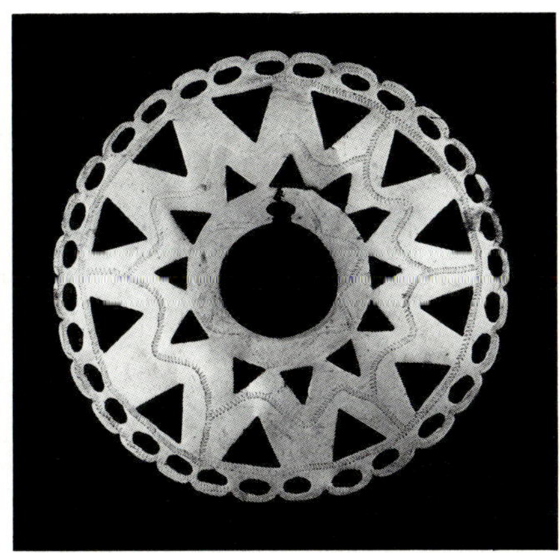

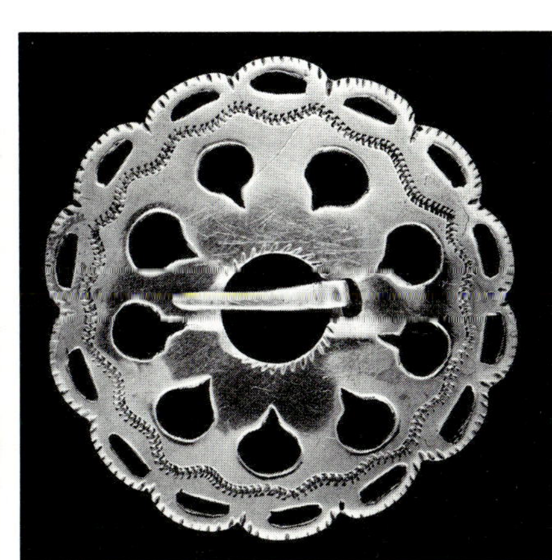

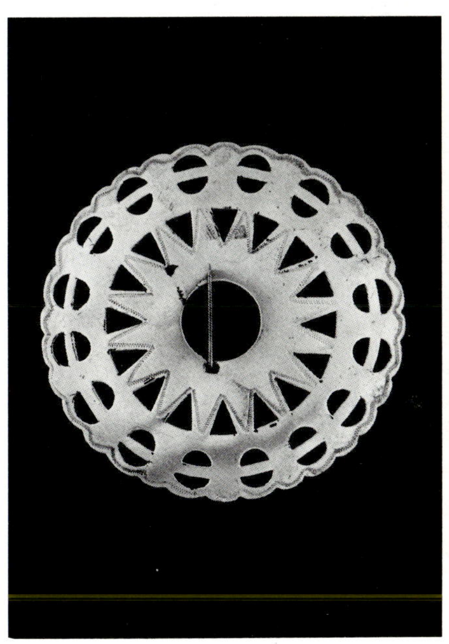

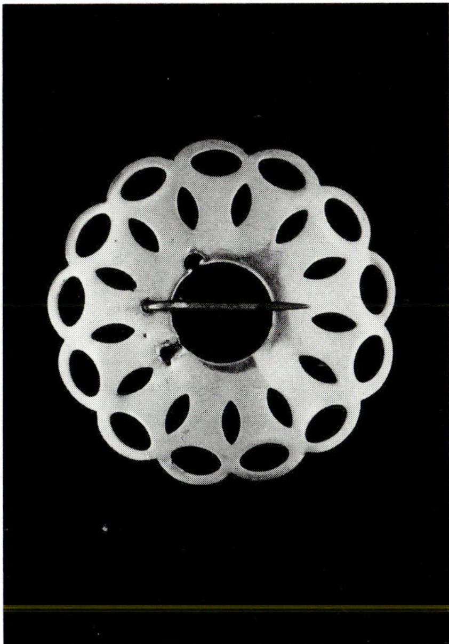

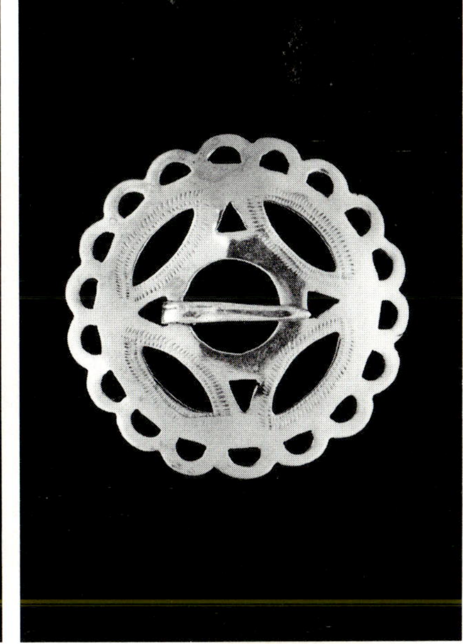

130/Round Brooch
MARK: None
MAKER: Unknown
SIZE: 3 cm diam.
COLL.: NMM (III-I-804)

131/Round Brooch
MARK: None
MAKER: Unknown
SIZE: 2.7 cm diam.
COLL.: NMM (III-I-777)

133/Round Star-Brooch
MARK: None
MAKER: Unknown
SIZE: 2.7 cm diam.
COLL.: NMM (III-I-776)

132/Round Brooch
MARK: None
MAKER: Unknown
SIZE: 1.4 cm diam.
COLL.: NMM (III-I-811)

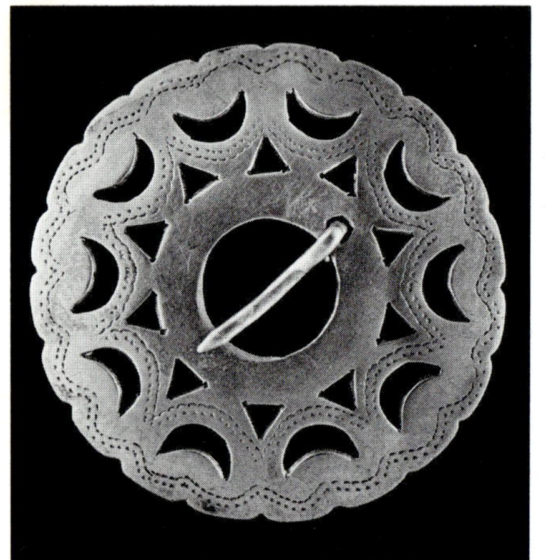

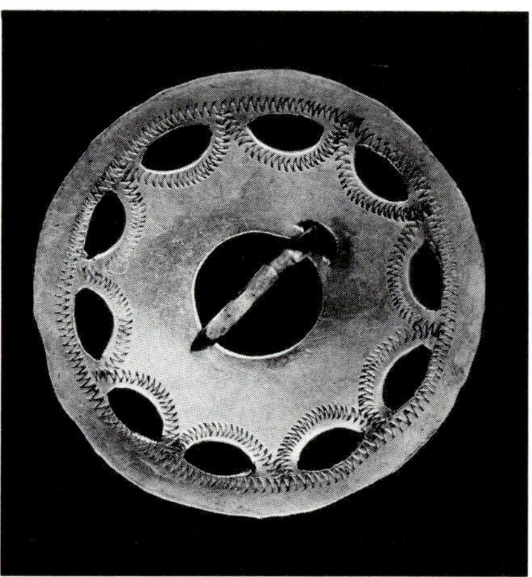

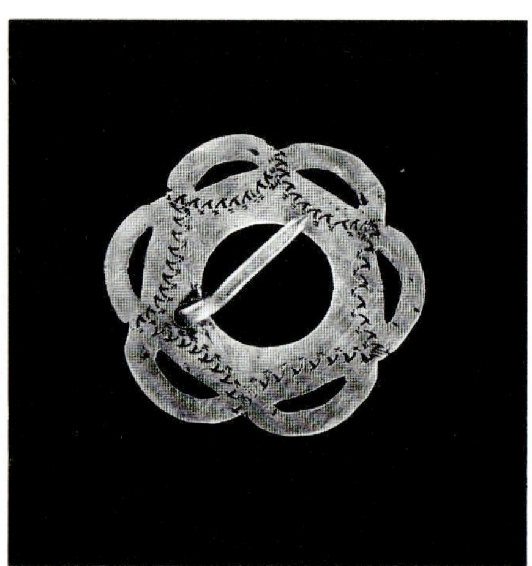

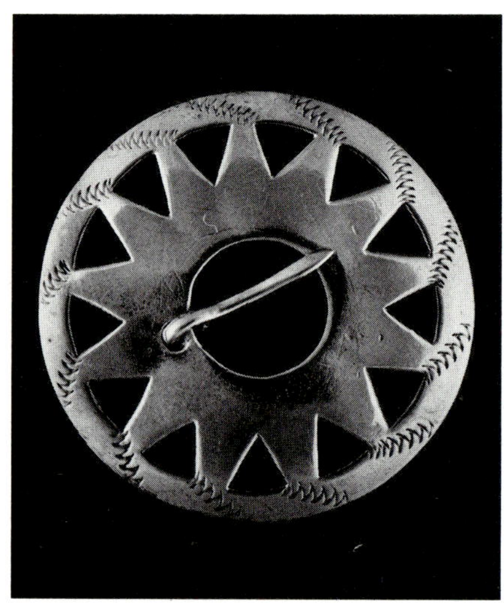

134/Star Brooch
MARK: None
MAKER: Unknown
SIZE: 2.9 cm diam.
COLL.: NMM (III-I-515)

135/Star Brooch
MARK: None
MAKER: Unknown
SIZE: 5.5 cm diam.
COLL.: ROM (892.1.22)

137/Star Brooch
MARK: None
MAKER: Unknown
SIZE: 4.3 cm diam.
COLL.: Heye (2/14)

136/Star Brooch
MARK: None
MAKER: Unknown
SIZE: 3 cm diam.
COLL.: NMM (III-I-698)

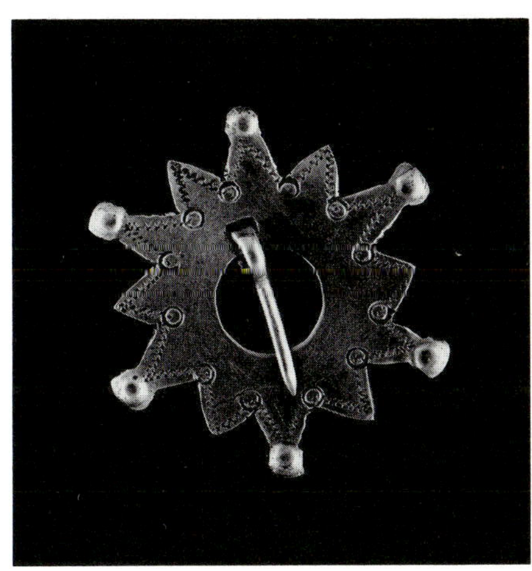

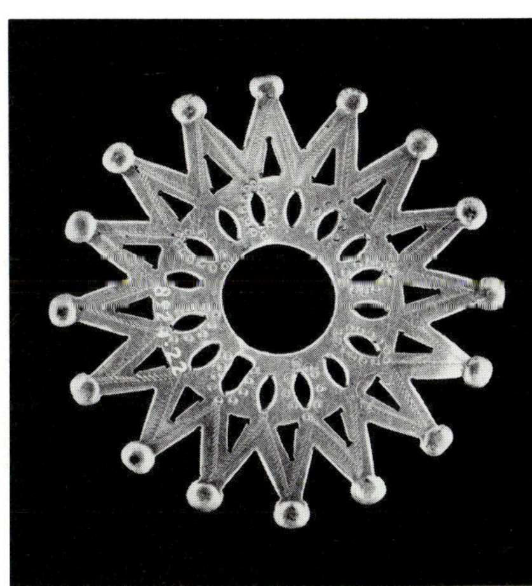

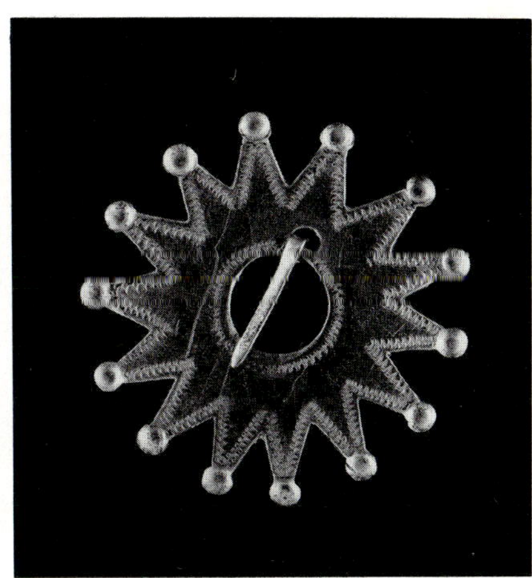

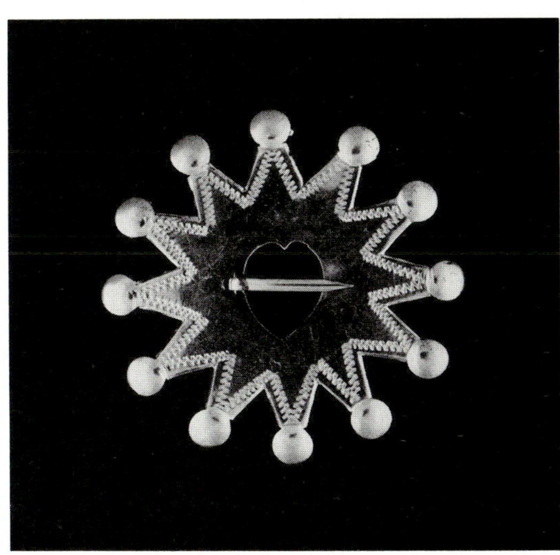

138/Head-Scarf
MATERIALS: Silk, silver ornaments
DATE: c. 1780
SIZE: 82 cm diagonally
COLL.: NMM (III-X-245)

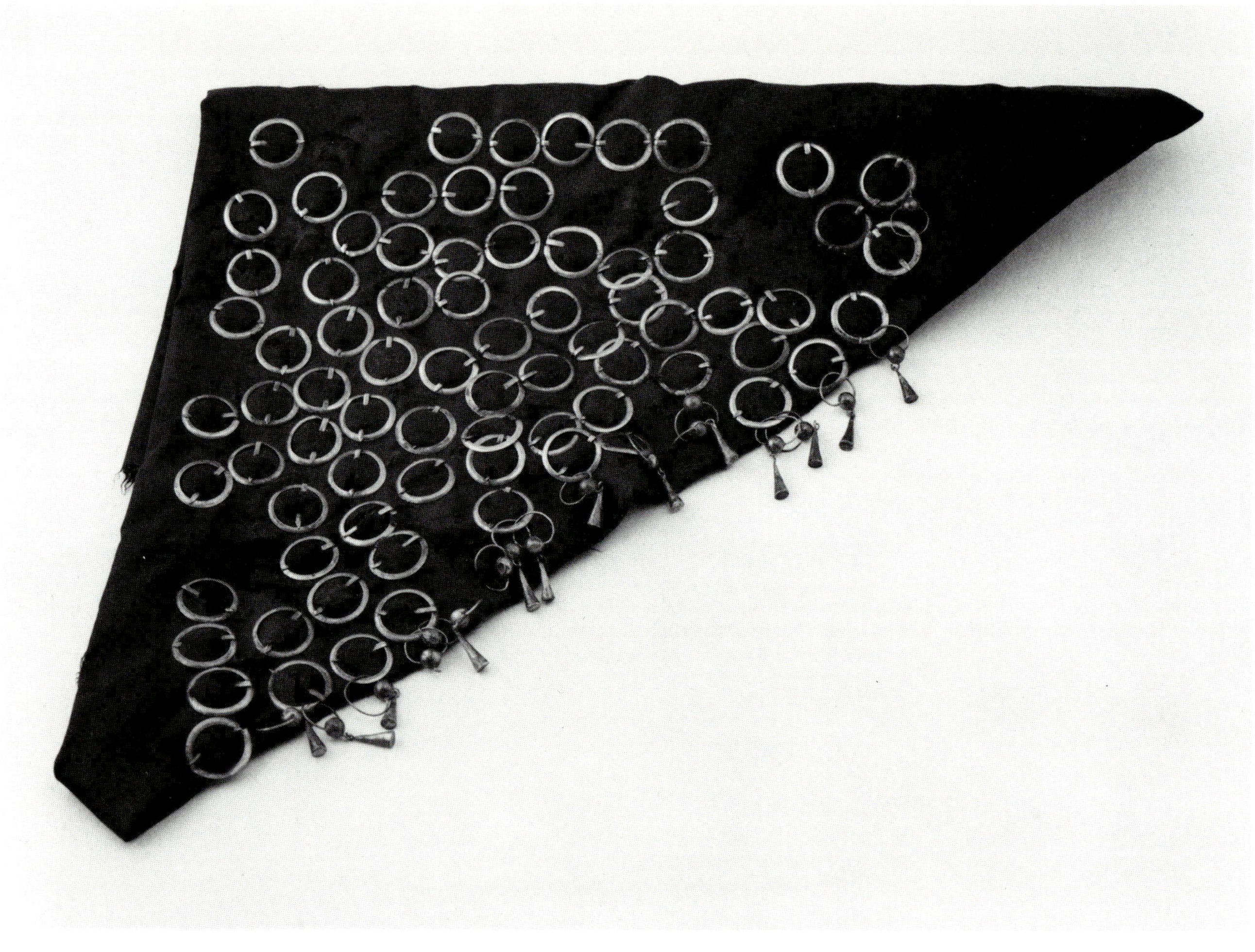

IX / INDIAN DESIGNS

Many types of trade silver copied earlier Indian ornaments made in other materials, such as bark, leather, shell or stone. For example, headbands and armbands were originally made from skins, and hair-pipes from shells, before they were reproduced in silver. In this portrait by Paul Kane, an Ojibwa Indian wears clothes of European style. However, the series of crescent gorgets suspended from his neck, his silver wristbands, and the legbands serving as garters are distinctively Indian in inspiration.

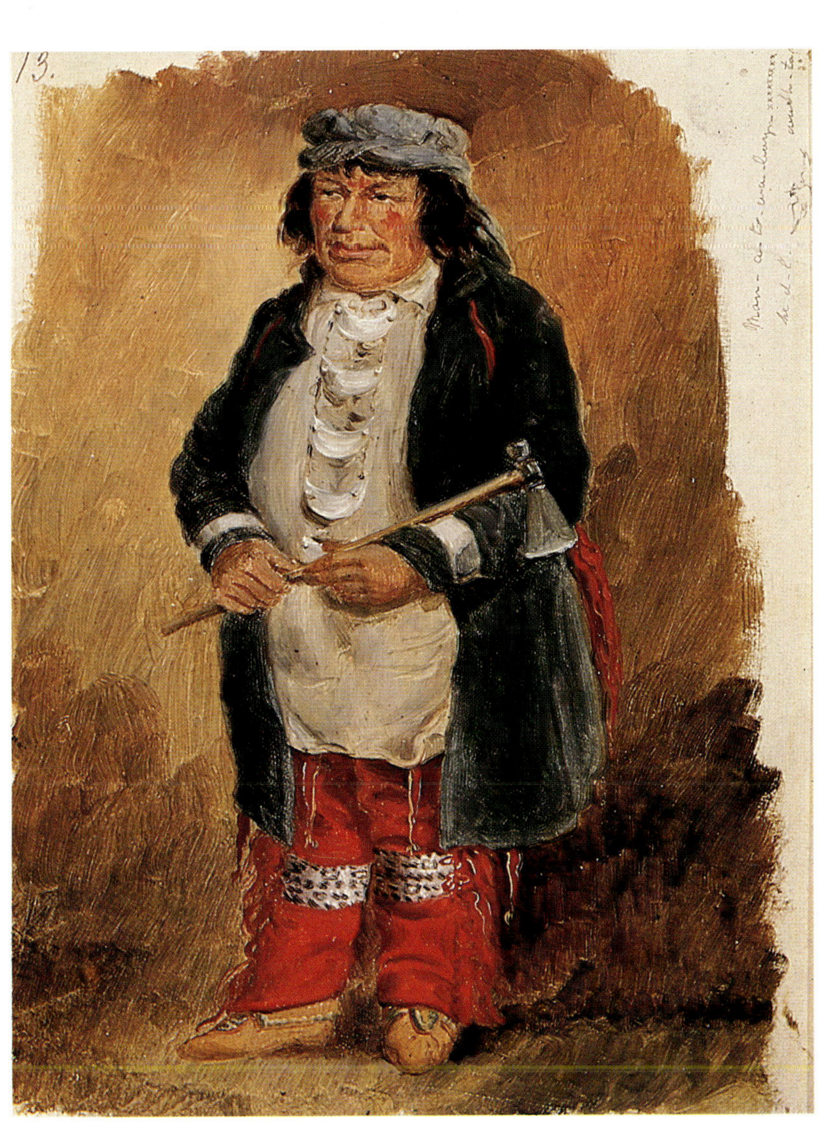

139/Shell Pendant
MATERIALS: Cast of original
DATE: 1600–50
SIZE: 10.5 cm diam.
COLL.: NMM (VIII-F-14134c)

140/Round Gorget
MARK: None
MAKER: Unknown
SIZE: 7 cm diam.
COLL.: ROM (HD7520)

141/Round Gorget
MARK: None
MAKER: Unknown
SIZE: 8.5 cm diam.
COLL.: Heye (19/4568)

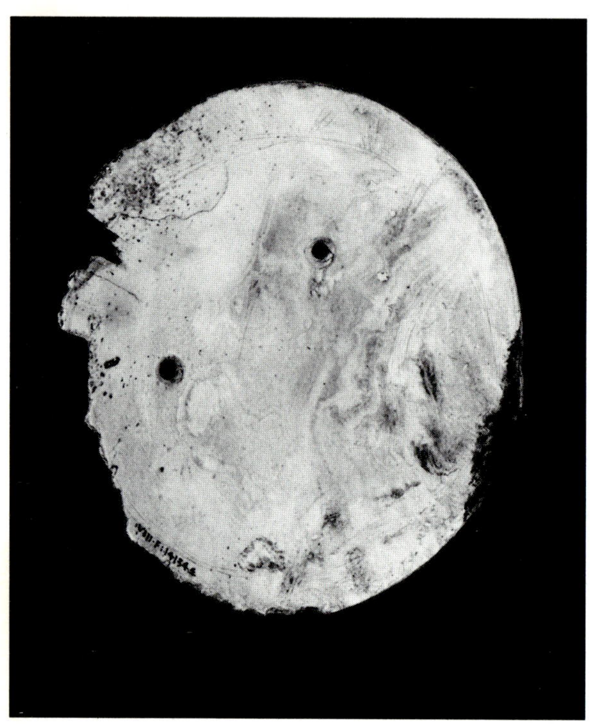

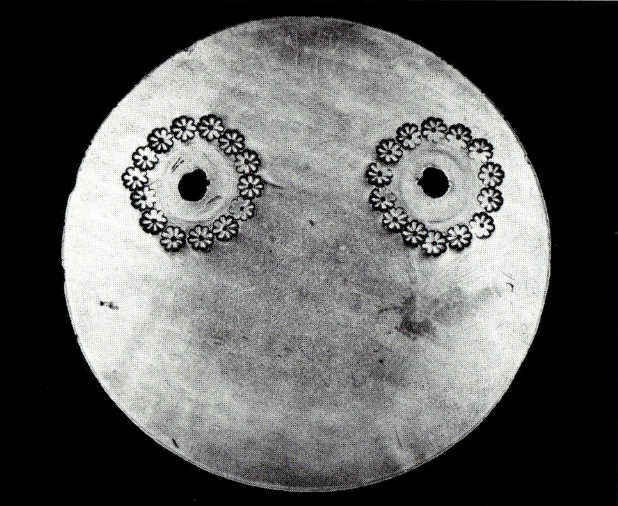

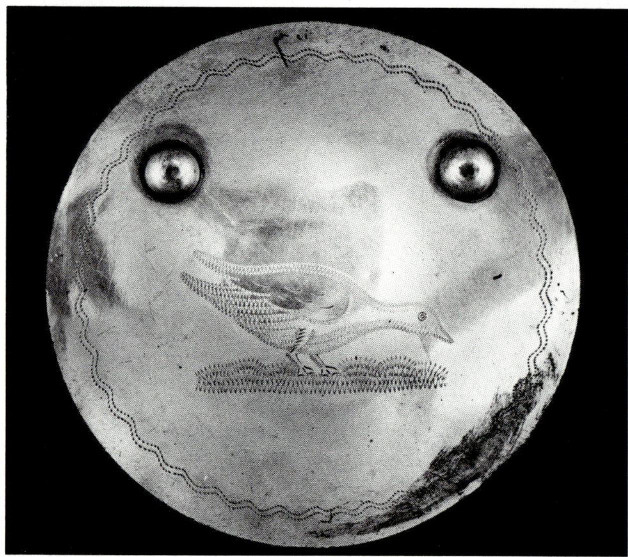

142/Conch-Shell and Silver Gorget
MARK: None
MAKER: Unknown
SIZE: 9 cm diam.
COLL.: ROM (HD6627)

143/Hair-Plate (German silver)
MARK: None
MAKER: Unknown
SIZE: 7.3 cm diam.
COLL.: NMM (III-H-227)

146/Ear-Bobs
MARK: None
MAKER: Unknown
SIZE: 4.2 cm l.
COLL.: Glenbow (AX28)

144/Earrings
MARK: RC
MAKER: Robert Cruickshank (Boston, Montreal, 1767–1809)
SIZE: 3.7 cm l.
COLL.: U. Sask. (FfMj-1001-4)

145/Earrings
MARK: None
MAKER: Unknown
SIZE: 2.8 cm l.
COLL.: NMM (III-I-325a, b)

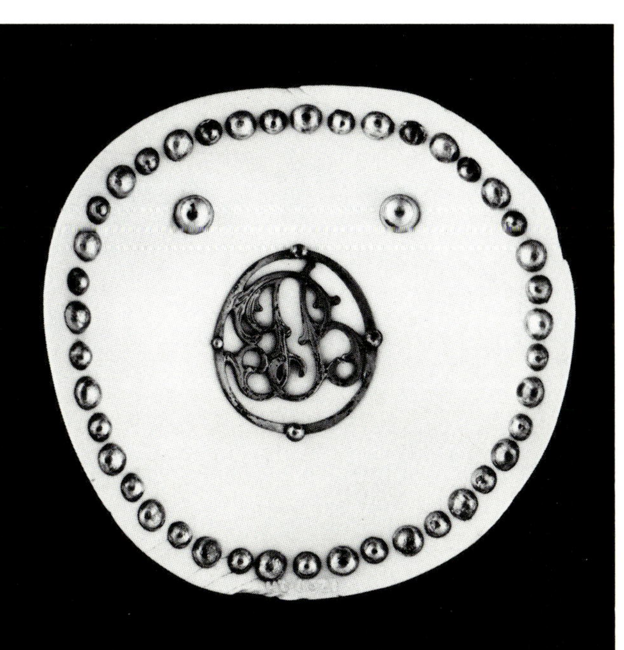

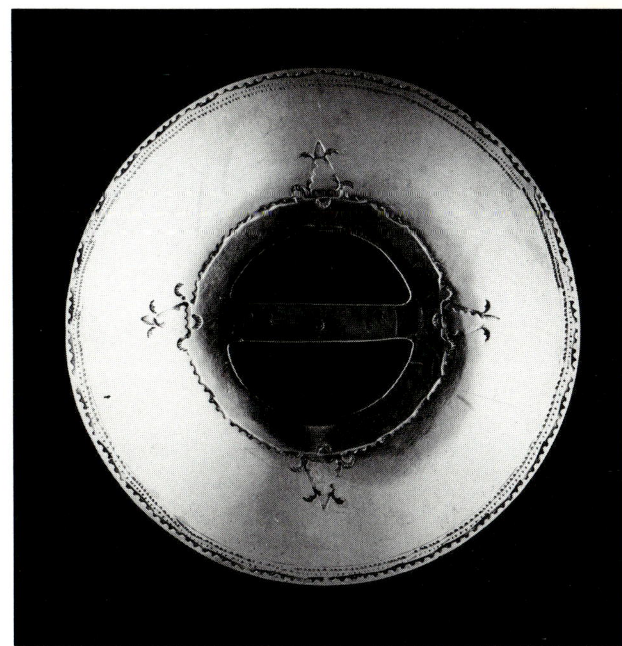

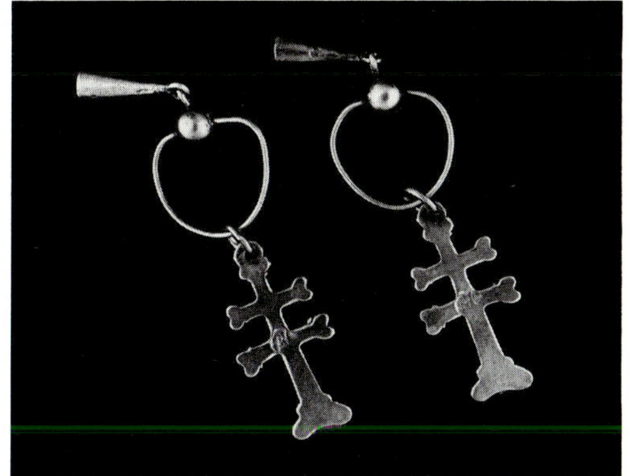

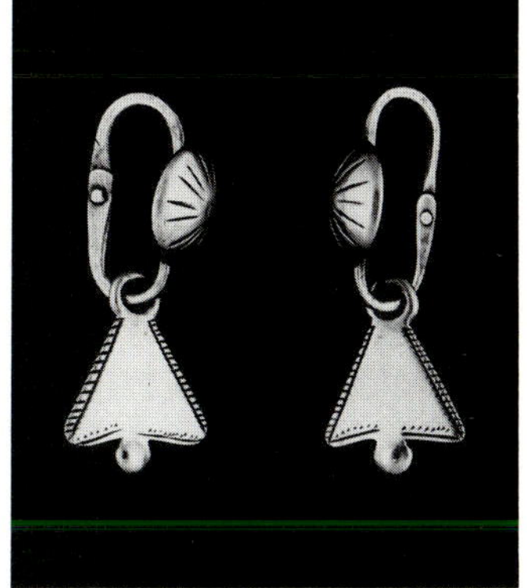

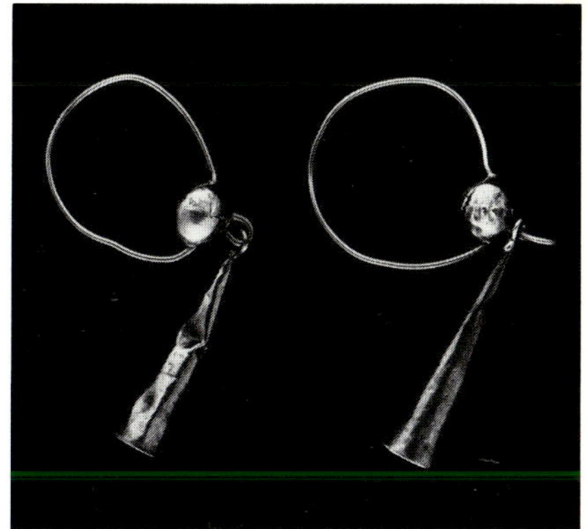

147/Ear-Wheels
MARK: 2 marked IS;
3 marked RC
MAKERS: Jonas or
"Widow" Schindler
(Quebec, Montreal,
1760–1823);
Robert Cruickshank
(Boston, Montreal,
1767–1809)
SIZE: 5.8 cm diam.
COLL.: NMM (III-X-246)

148/Nose Ornaments
MARK: None
MAKER: Unknown
SIZE: 3 cm l.
COLL.: NMM (III-X-274a, b)

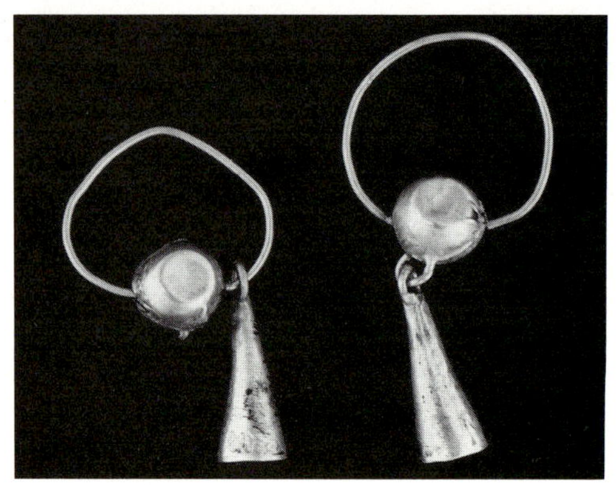

149/Ear-Wheel or Pendant (fragments)
MARK: MONTREAL
MAKER: Unknown
SIZE: 6.8 cm diam.
COLL.: Putnam (AR14737A–D)

150/Headband or Hatband
MARK: None
MAKER: Unknown
SIZE: 57 cm l. × 1 cm w.
COLL.: NMM (III-I-681)

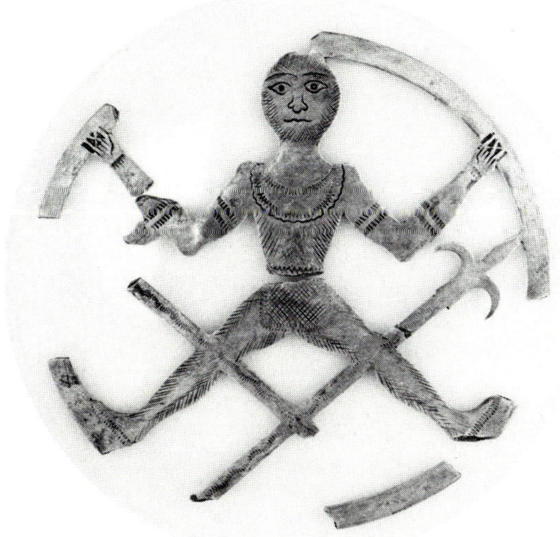

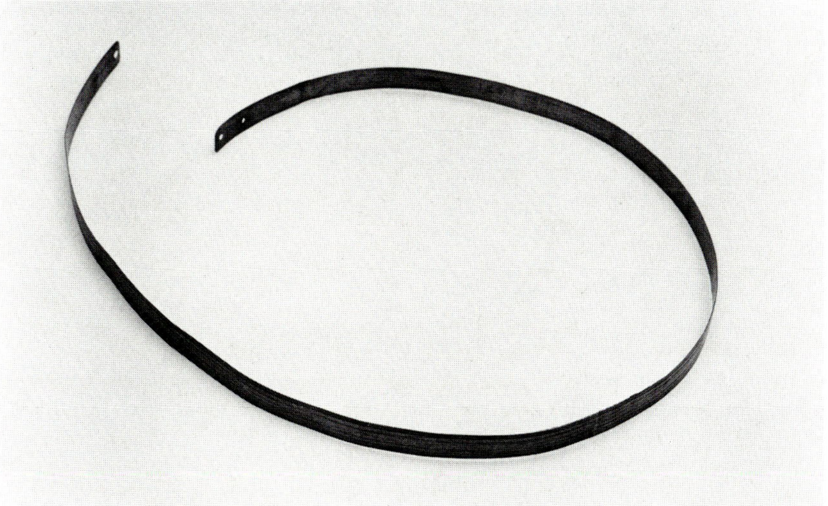

151/Armband
MARK: SF (British hallmarks)
MAKER: Unknown
SIZE: 26.3 cm l. × 6.2 cm w.
COLL.: ROM (921.10.2)

152/Armband
MARK: PB WB
MAKER: Peter and William Bateman
(London, late 18th century)
SIZE: 26.7 cm l. × 6.0 cm w.
COLL.: ROM (HD6422)

153/Wristband
MARK: IS
MAKER: Jonas or "Widow" Schindler
(Quebec, Montreal, 1760–1823)
SIZE: 15.3 cm l. × 2.0 cm w.
COLL.: McCord (M1885.2)

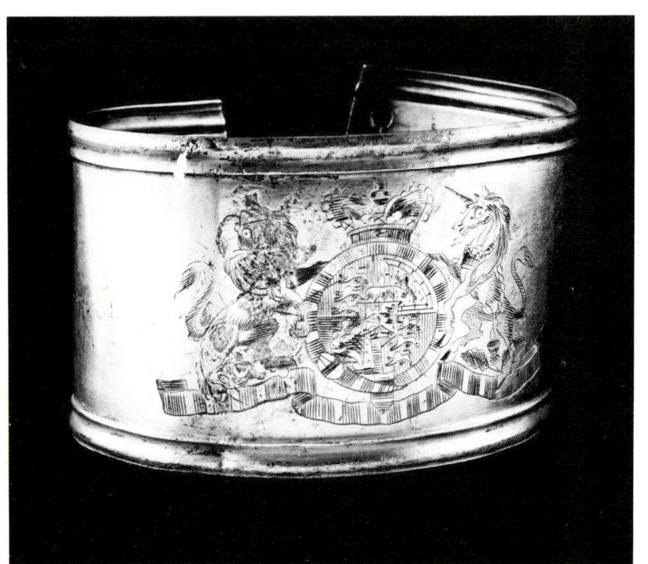

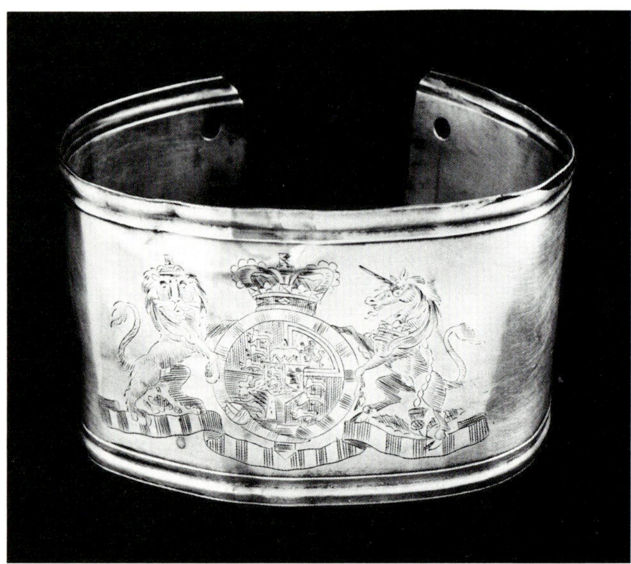

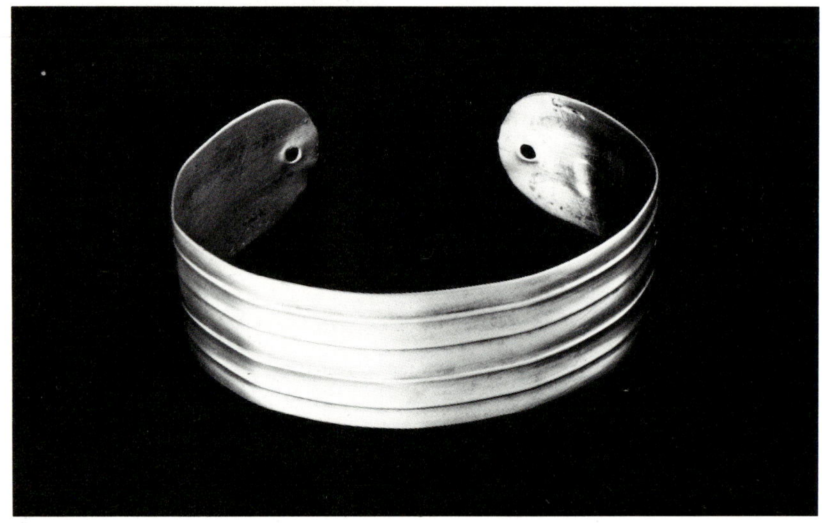

X / MARKS OF OWNERSHIP

Only rarely is it possible to identify the Indian owner of a piece of trade silver. Although some pieces carry personalized marks, such as totem engravings, these cannot be traced to their owners. However, the possessions of a few famous Indians have been preserved by their descendants. Such was the case with Joseph Brant, who became prominent among the Mohawks after Britain recognized his assistance to the British forces during the American Revolution. They gave Captain Brant several military decorations, including a medal, silver armbands and a gorget. The latter is on display at the Joseph Brant Museum in Burlington, Ontario.

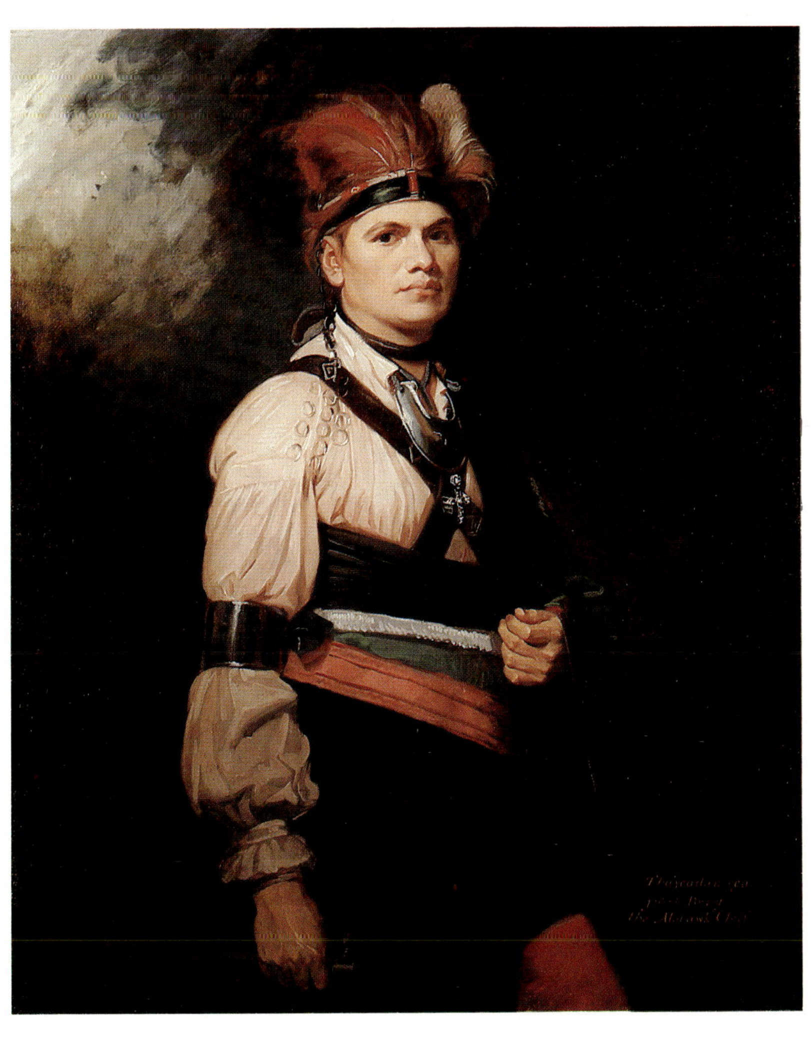

154/Round Gorget
MARK: JT
MAKER: Jonathan Tyler
(Montreal, 1817–28)
SIZE: 15 cm diam.
COLL.: McCord (M410)

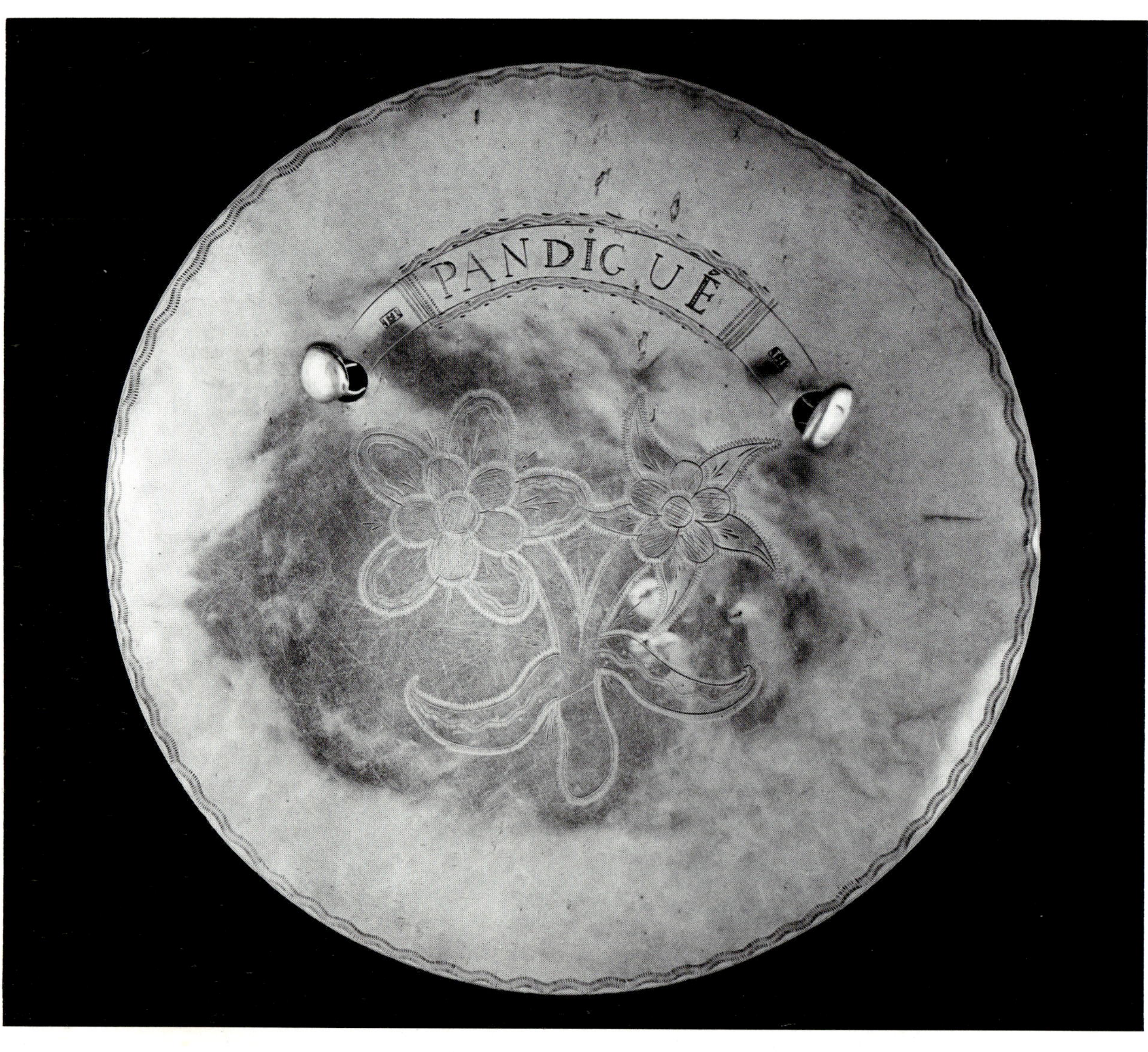

155/Crescent Gorget
MARK: CF (British hallmarks)
MAKER: Crespin Fuller (London, 1813)
SIZE: 11 cm w. × 12 cm h.
COLL.: ROM (HD6313)

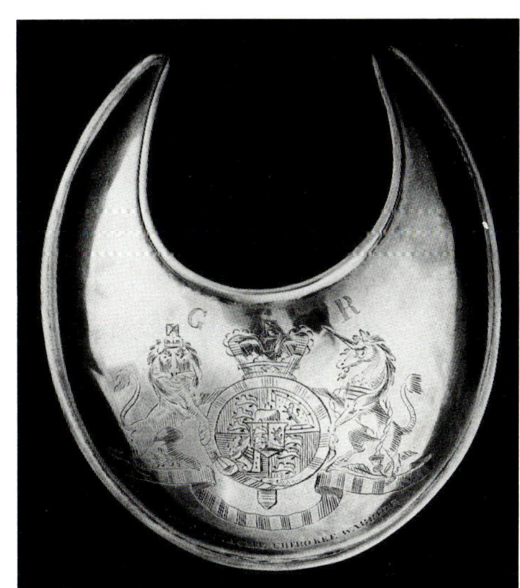

156/Cross
MARK: JD
MAKER: Possibly John Dupuy (Philadelphia, 1769–1803)
SIZE: 31.5 cm h. × 22.0 cm w.
COLL.: Heye (1/2140)

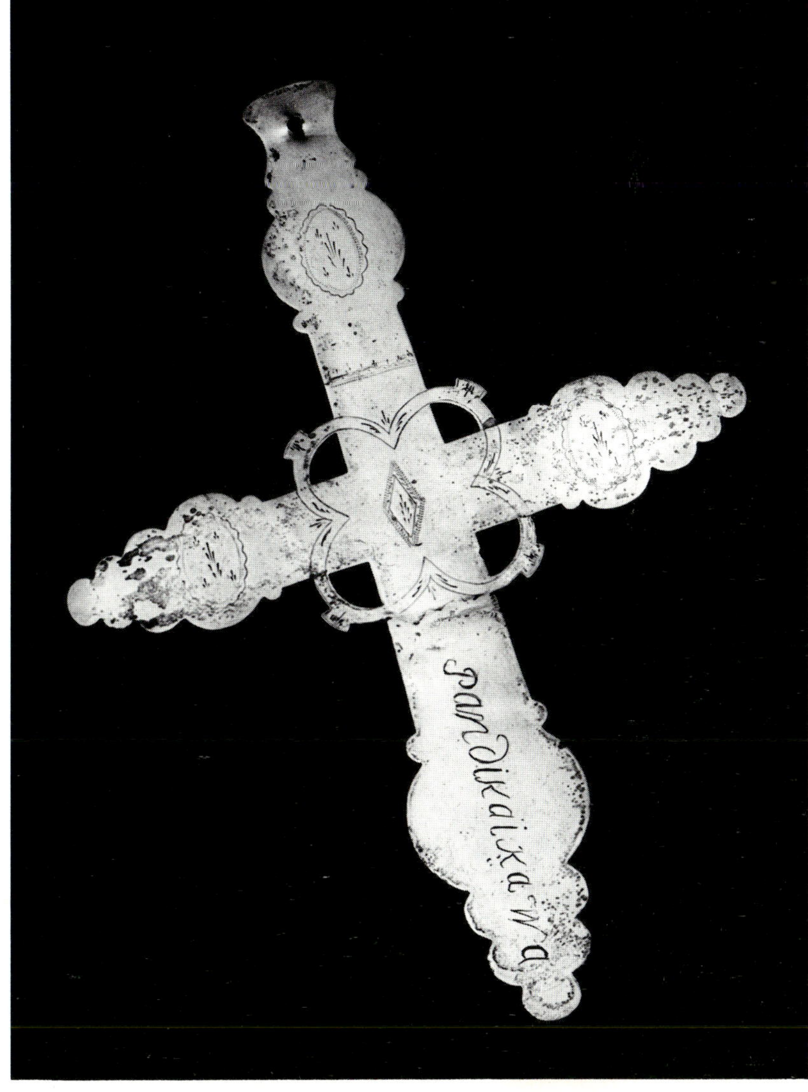

157/Round Gorget
MARK: (Lion) A
MAKER: Unknown
SIZE: 9.3 cm diam.
COLL.: NBM (979.130.4)

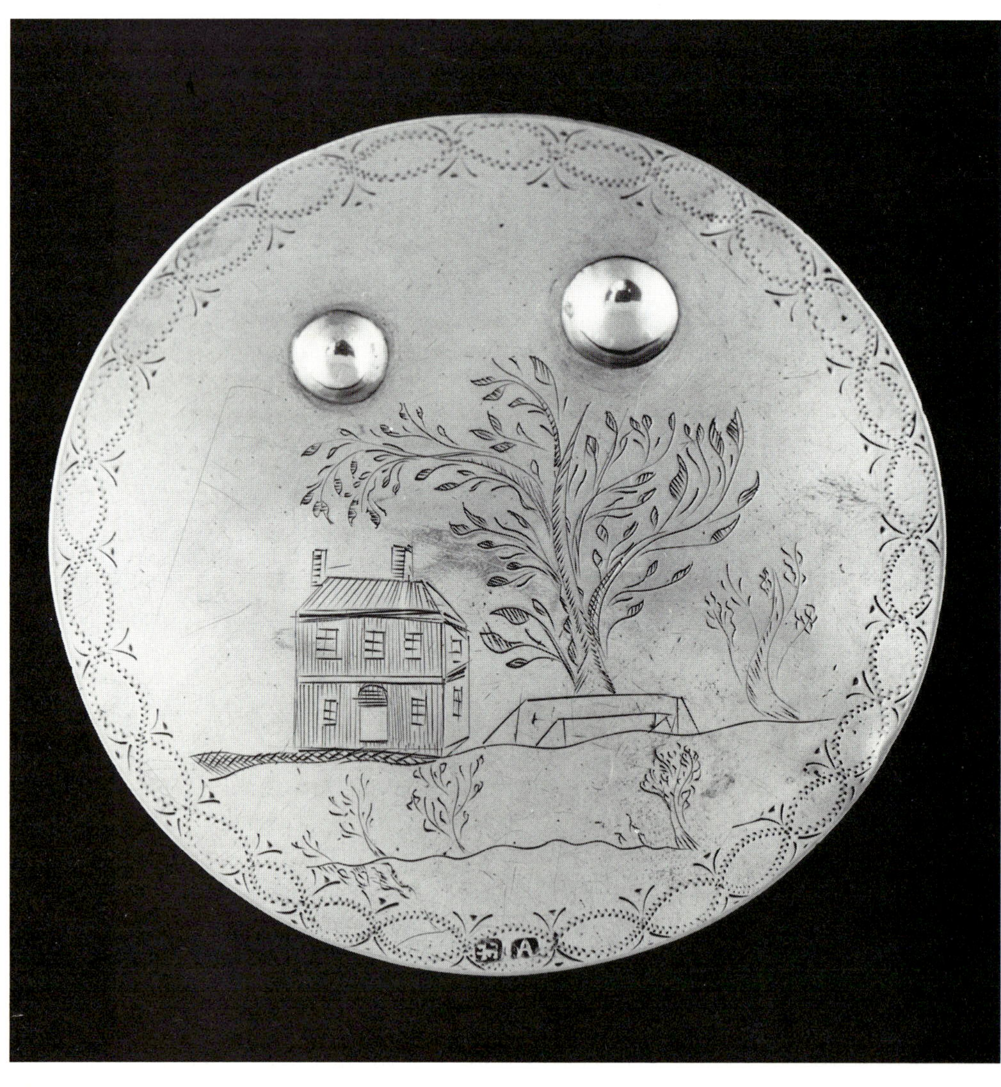

158/Armband
MARK: JT
MAKER: Jonathan Tyler (Montreal, 1817–28)
SIZE: 16.4 cm l. × 4.5 cm w.
COLL.: McCord (M1883)

159/Silver Arrow
MARK: None
MAKER: Unknown
SIZE: 9.5 cm l. × 2.5 cm w.
COLL.: McCord (M12682)

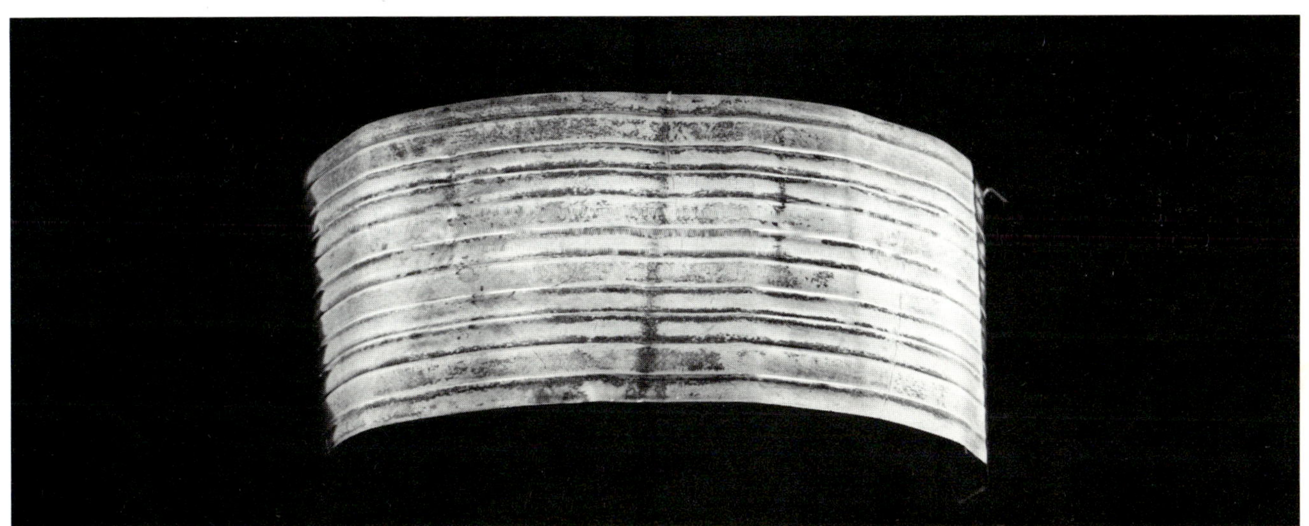

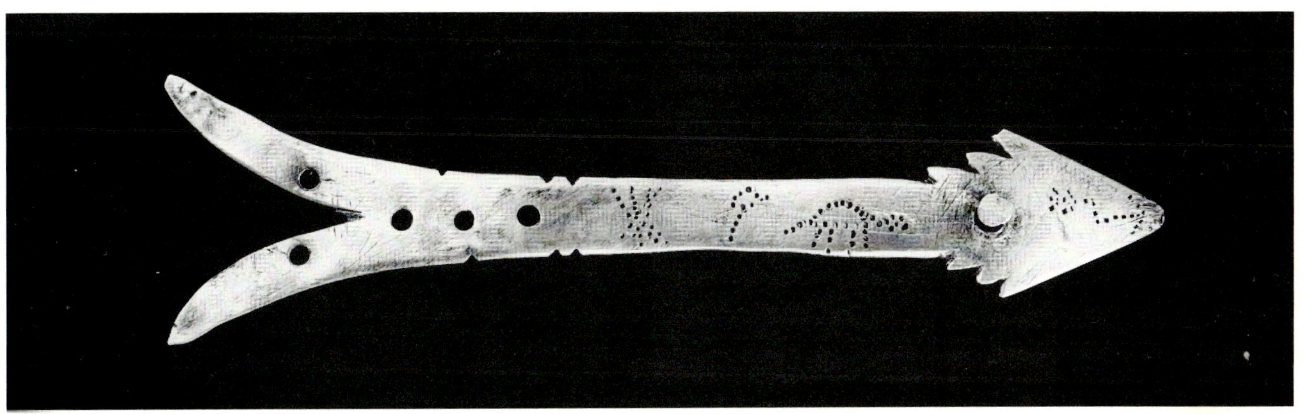

160/Crescent Gorgets
MARK: RC
MAKER: Robert Cruickshank
(Boston, Montreal, 1767–1809)
SIZE: 12.5 cm w. × 5.3 cm h.;
total h., 41.0 cm
COLL.: NMM (III-X-247)

161/Armband
MARK: CA MONTREAL
MAKER: Charles Arnoldi
(Montreal, 1779–1817)
SIZE: 24.8 cm l. × 7.6 cm w.
COLL.: NGC, Birks (C485)

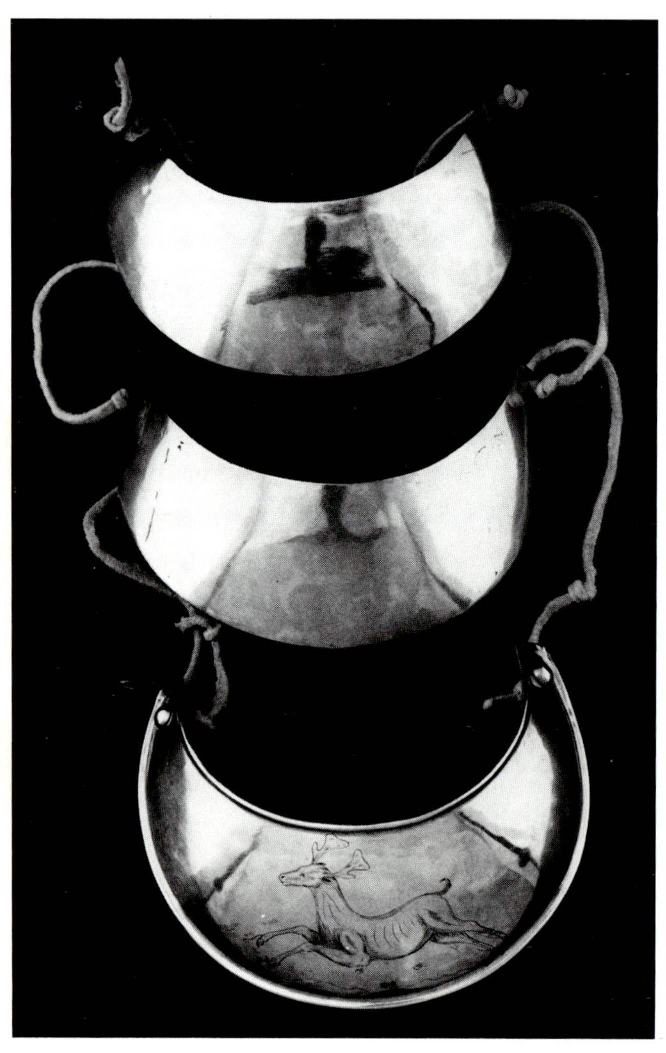

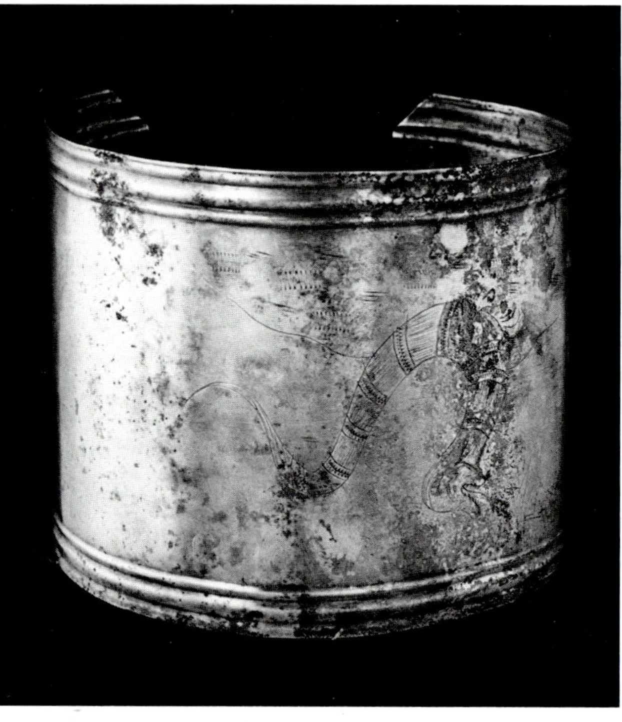

162/Crescent Gorget
MARK: None
MAKER: Unknown
SIZE: 11.5 cm w. × 4.5 cm h.
COLL.: ROM (911.3.34)

163/Crescent Gorget
MARK: JR
MAKER: Unknown
SIZE: 12.7 cm w. × 4.7 cm h.
COLL.: Heye (2/8427)

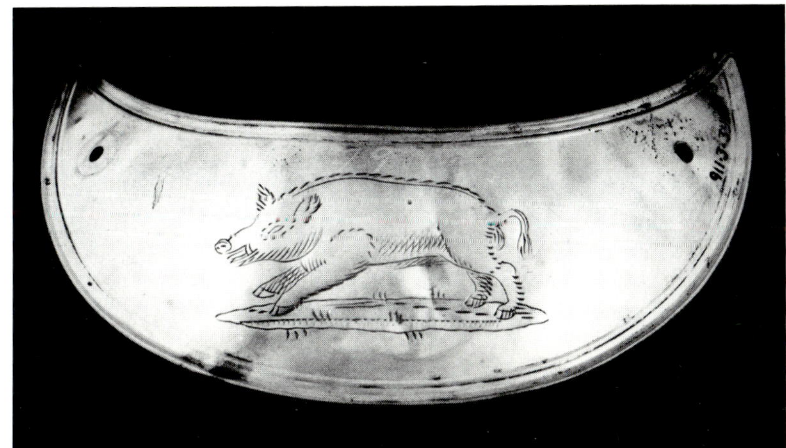

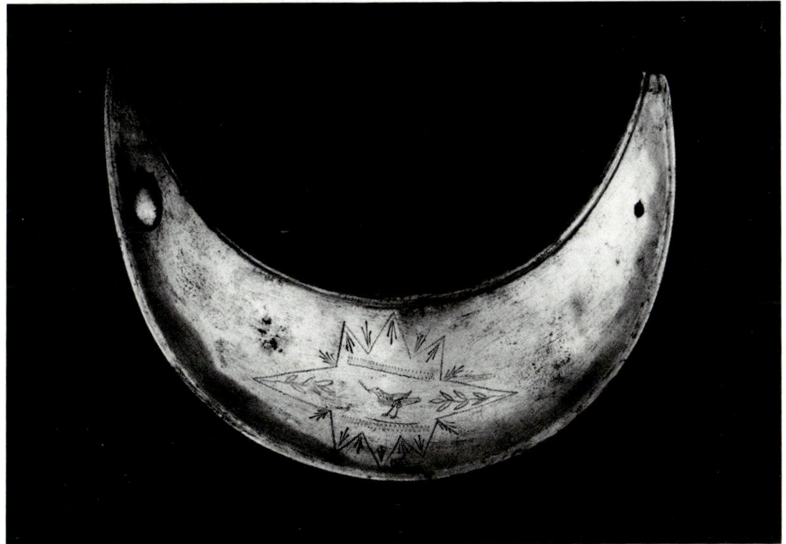

164/Crescent Gorget
MARK: JB
MAKER: Unknown
SIZE: 12.7 cm w. × 4.5 cm h.
COLL.: Heye (2/8427)

165/Crescent Gorget
MARK: None
MAKER: Unknown
SIZE: 12.0 cm w. × 4.8 cm h.
COLL.: Heye (17/9768)

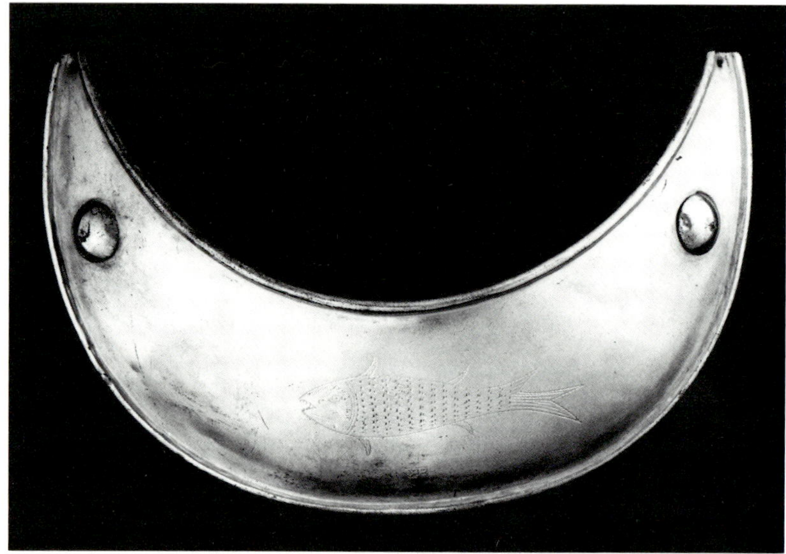

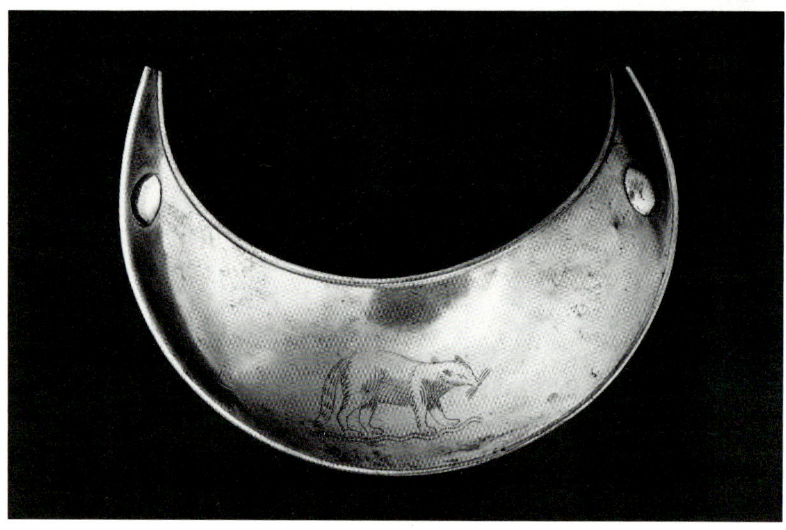

XI / WEARING THE SILVER

Most Indian trade silver was worn as jewellery, but a few unusual uses have been observed. This portrait by George Catlin shows two round brooches hanging from the top of a cradleboard in the same way as baubles are often hung above a modern crib to amuse an infant. The reason may have been the same, or perhaps the brooches served as charms. The woman is wearing silver earrings in the fashion popular among Indians at the time; they hang not only from the lobe but around the rim of the ear as well.

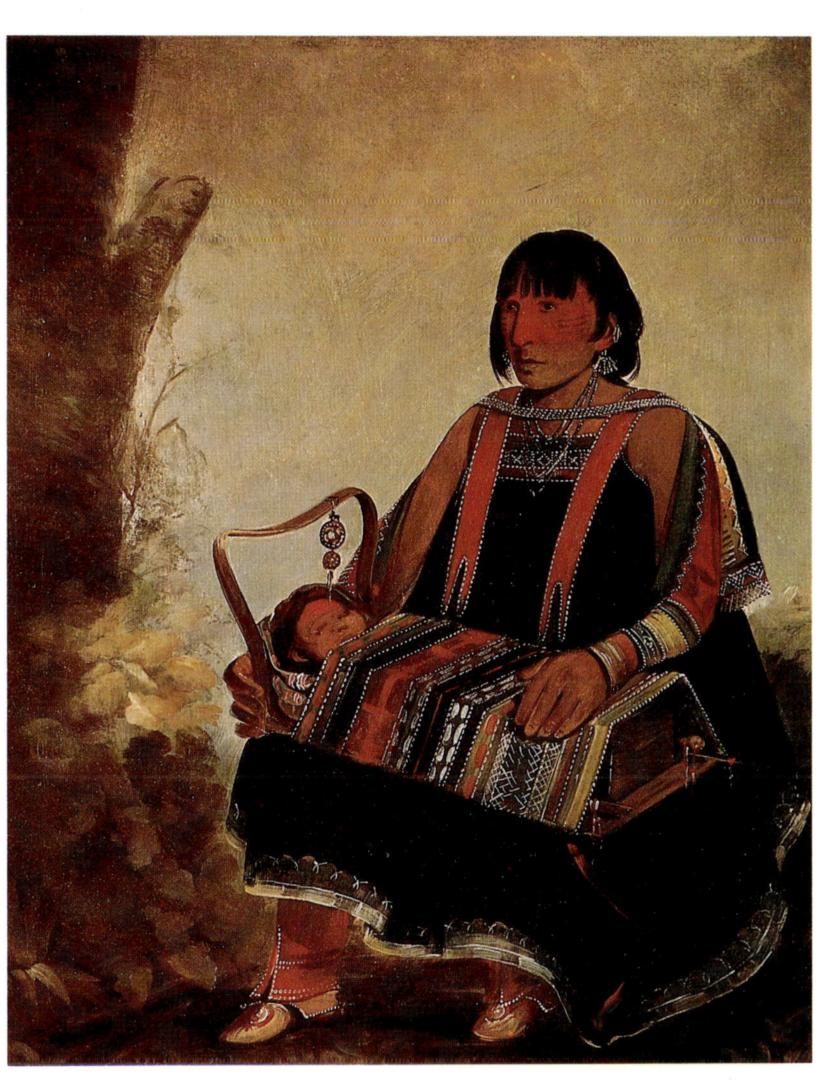

166/Headband
MARK: FD JR
MAKER: Unknown
SIZE: 57.7 cm l. × 6.3 cm w.
COLL.: NMM (III-E-63)

167/Ear-Bobs
MARK: None
MAKER: Unknown
SIZE: 4.4 cm l.
COLL.: Glenbow (AX15)

168/Earrings
MARK: None
MAKER: Unknown
SIZE: 4.5 cm l.
COLL.: NMM (III-I-705a, b)

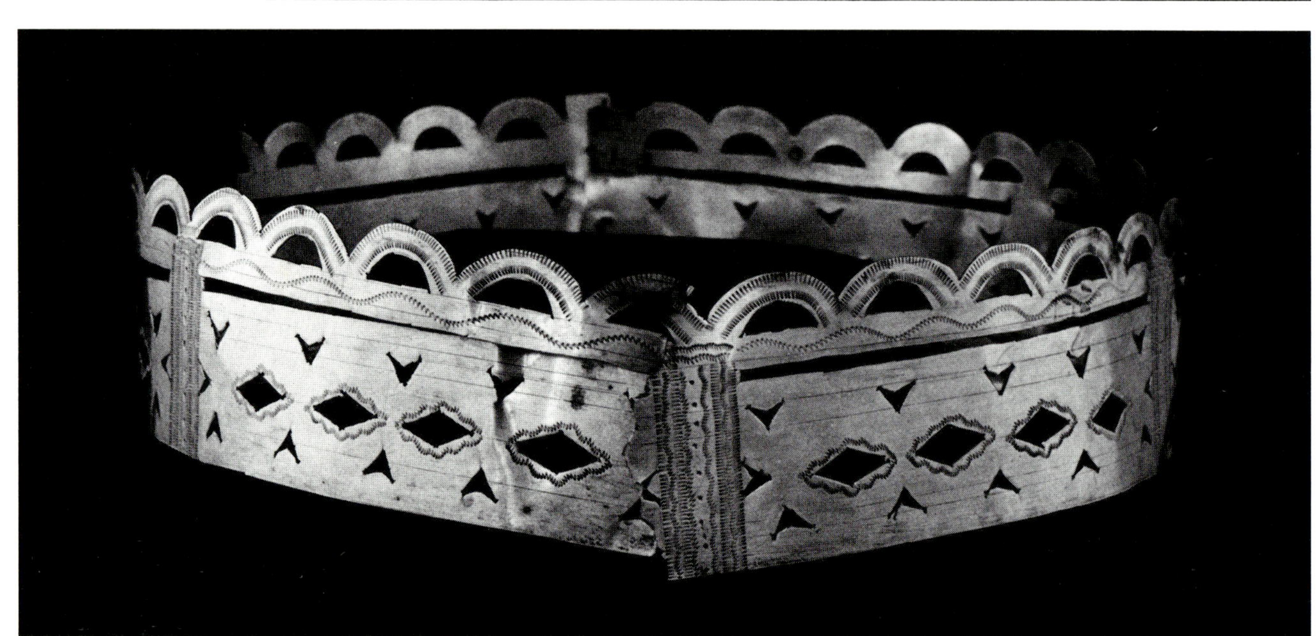

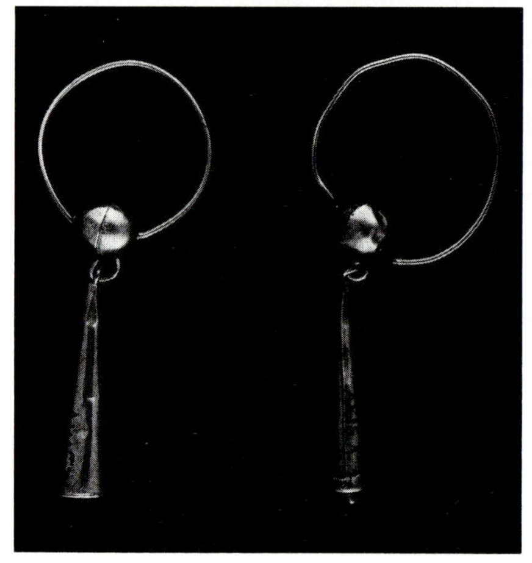

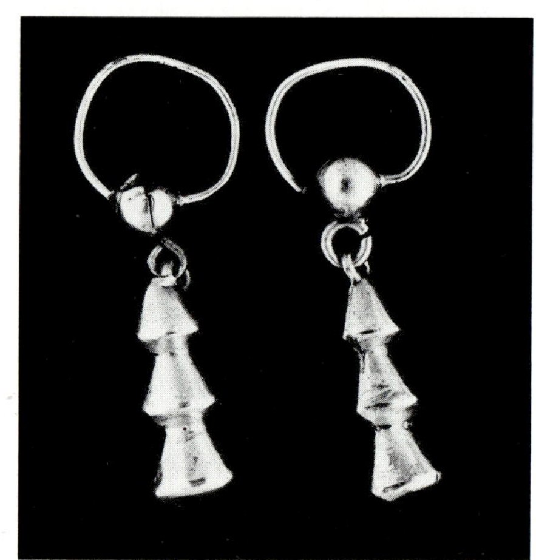

169/Pair of Armbands
MARK: JT
MAKER: Jonathan Tyler
(Montreal, 1817–28)
SIZE: 36 cm l. × 8 cm w.
COLL.: NMM (III-L-16a, b)

170/Round Brooch
MARK: None
MAKER: Unknown
SIZE: 20.2 cm diam.
COLL.: Heye (11/9344)

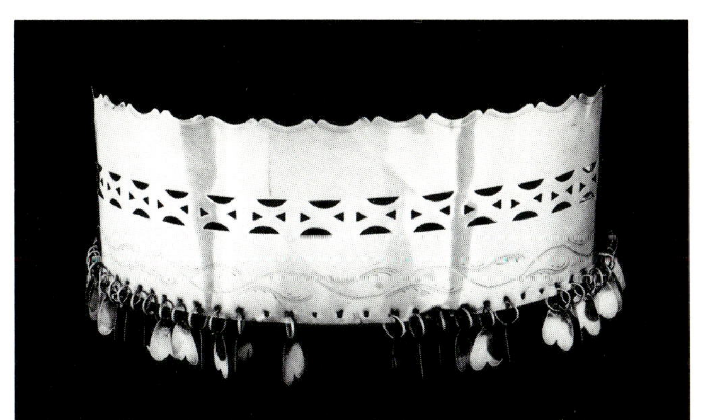

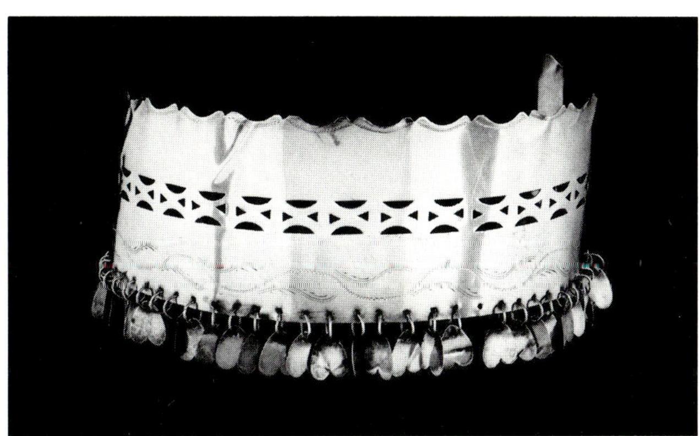

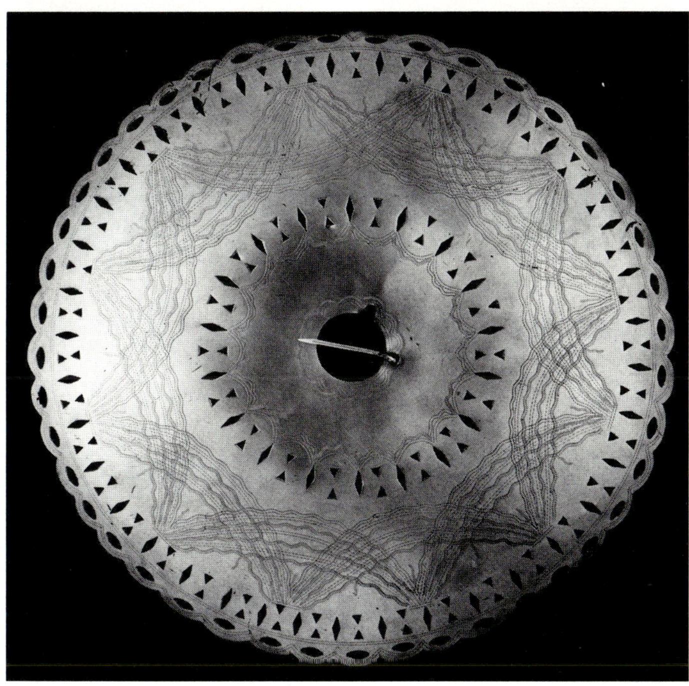

171/Wristband
MARK: RC
MAKER: Robert Cruickshank
(Boston, Montreal, 1767–1809)
SIZE: 16.2 cm l. × 2.2 cm w.
COLL.: NGC, Birks (C214)

172/Thunderbird Pouch
MATERIALS: Wool and linen cloth, quillwork, sheet-silver insets
MARK: CA MONTREAL
MAKER: Charles Arnoldi
(Montreal, 1779–1817)
SIZE: Pouch, 34.0 cm l. × 15.5 cm w.; silver insets, 16.2 cm w. × 3.2 cm h.
COLL.: McCord (M740)

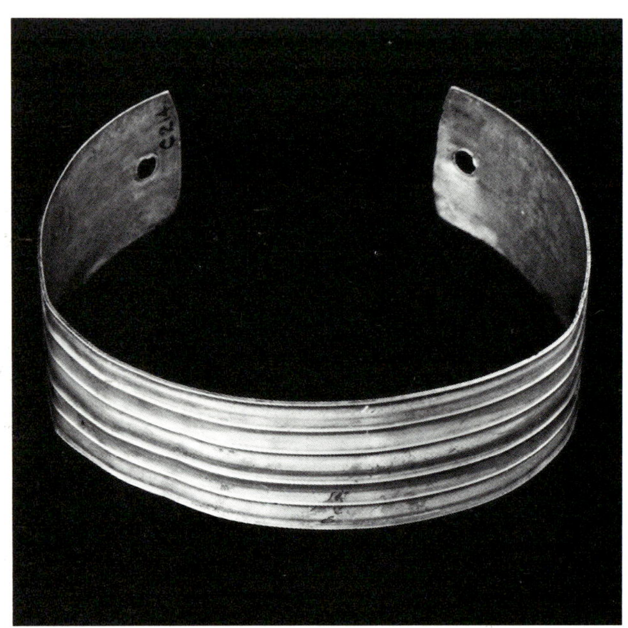

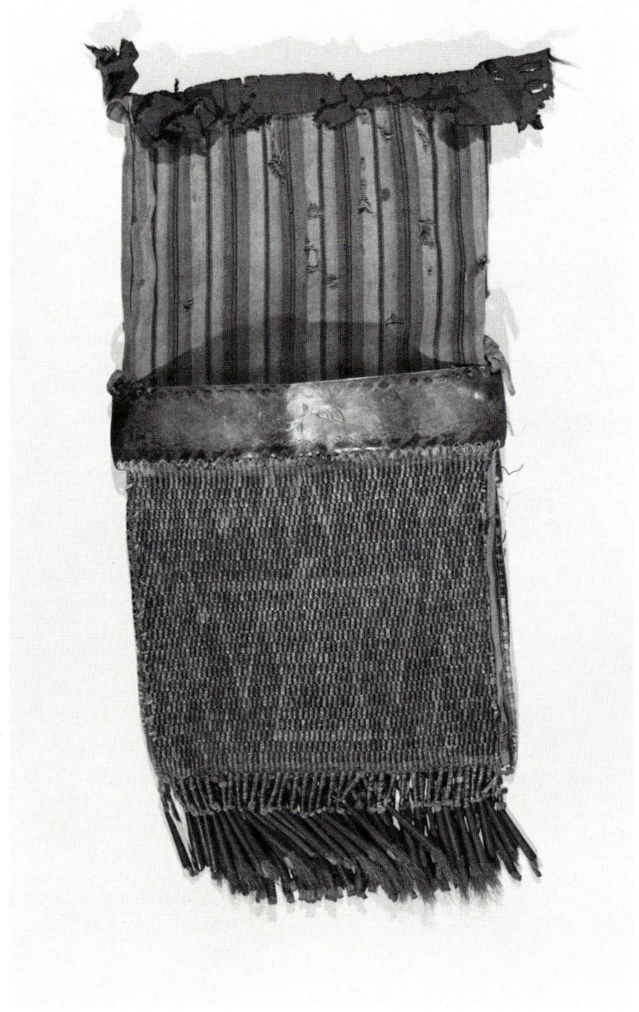

173/Ring Brooches
MARK: None
MAKER: Unknown
SIZE: 2.3 cm diam.
COLL.: McCord

174/Headband
MARK: None
MAKER: Unknown
SIZE: 60.0 cm l. × 3.7 cm w.
COLL.: ROM (HD6515)

175/Earrings
MARK: None
MAKER: Unknown
SIZE: 7 cm l.
COLL.: NMM (III-I-158a, b)

176/Council Square Brooch
MARK: None
MAKER: Unknown
SIZE: 2.3 cm square
COLL.: NMM (III-I-54)

178/Council Square Brooch
MARK: None
MAKER: Unknown
SIZE: 2.2 cm square
COLL.: NMM (III-I-697)

177/Council Square Brooch
MARK: None
MAKER: Unknown
SIZE: 2.4 cm square
COLL.: NMM (III-I-517)

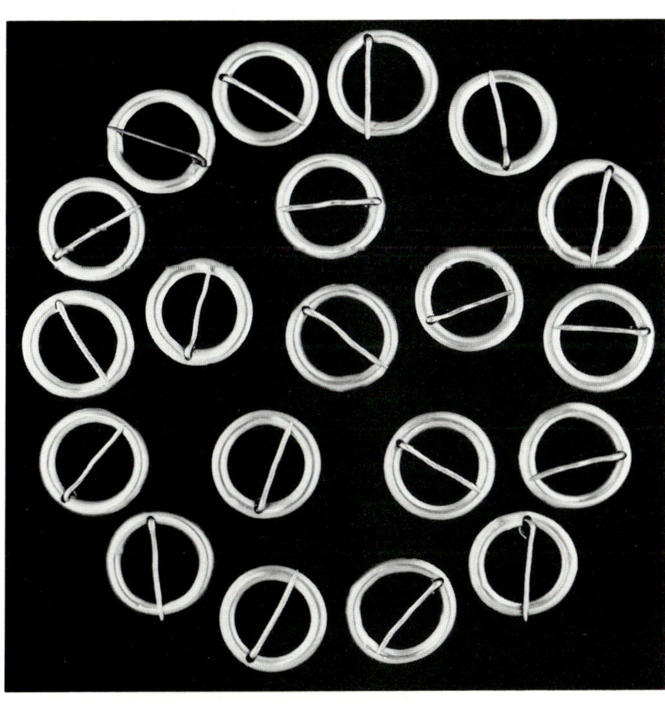

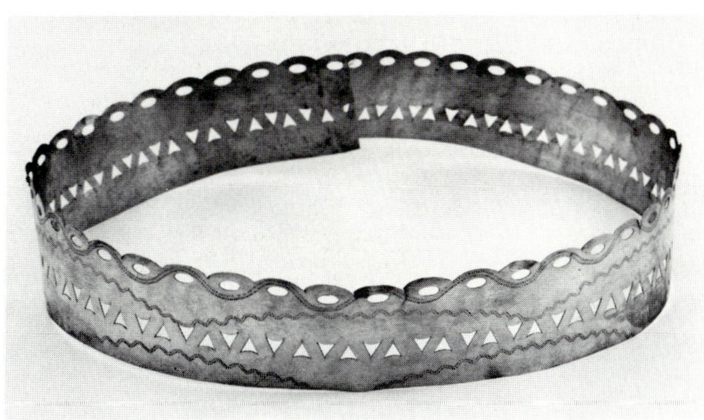

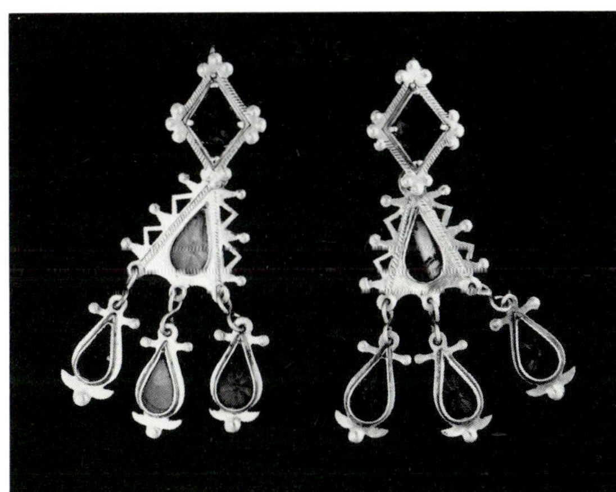

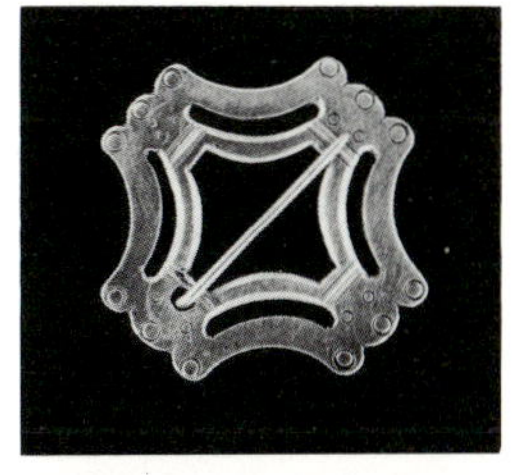

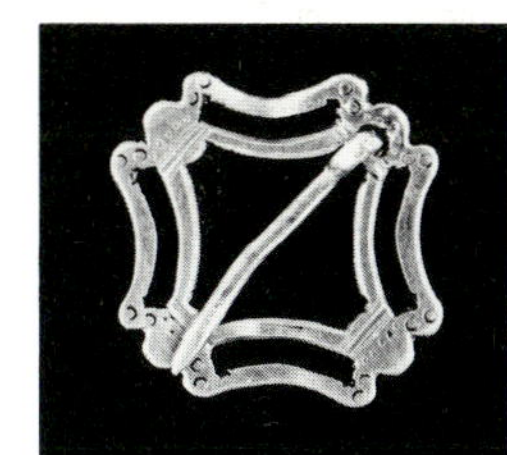

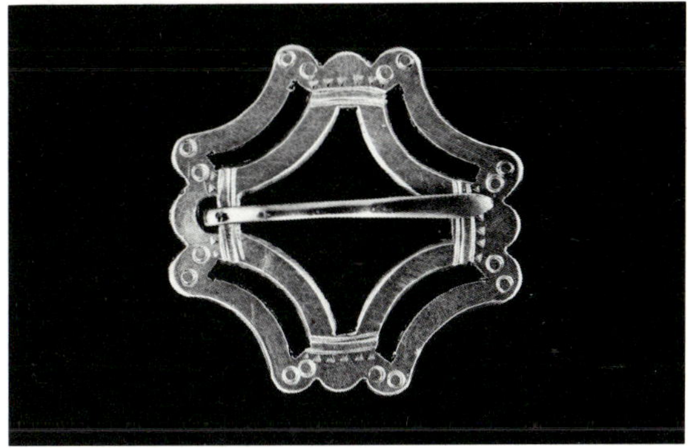

179/Heart Brooch
MARK: None
MAKER: Unknown
SIZE: 3.7 cm h. × 2.6 cm w.
COLL.: NMM (III-I-814)

180/Heart Brooch
MARK: None
MAKER: Unknown
SIZE: 2.7 cm h. × 2.1 cm w.
COLL.: NMM (III-I-407)

181/Star Brooch
MARK: None
MAKER: Unknown
SIZE: 4.1 cm diam.
COLL.: NMM (III-I-806)

182/Wristband
MARK: RC MONTREAL
MAKER: Robert Cruickshank (Boston, Montreal, 1767–1809)
SIZE: 15.2 cm l. × 2.1 cm w.
COLL.: McCord (M1885.1)

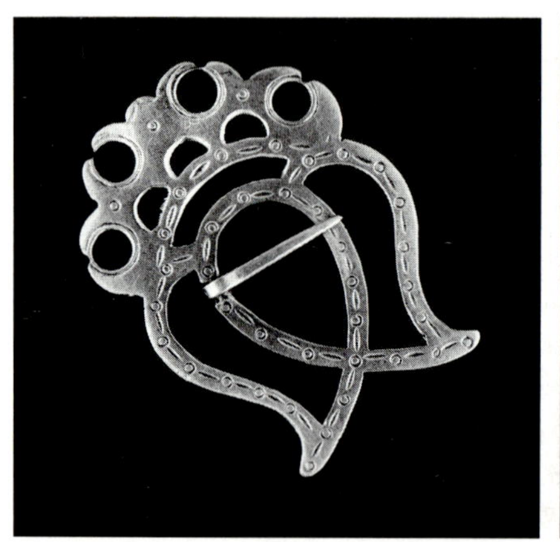

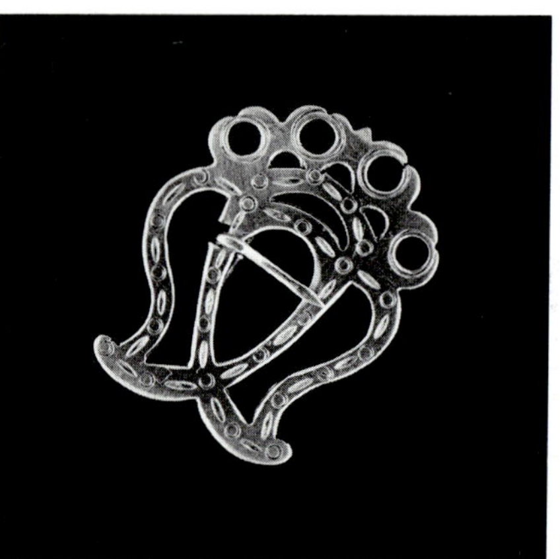

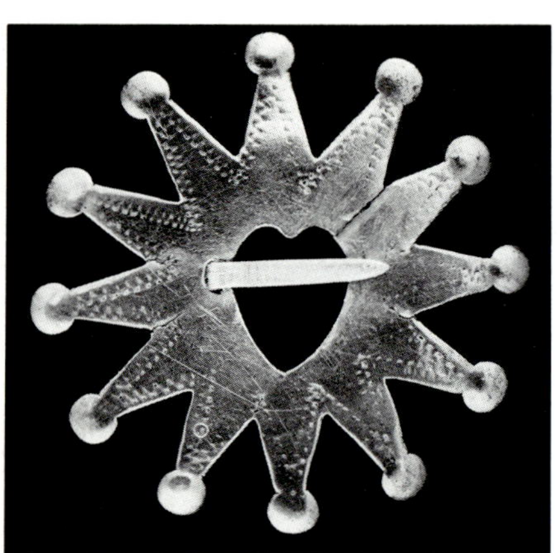

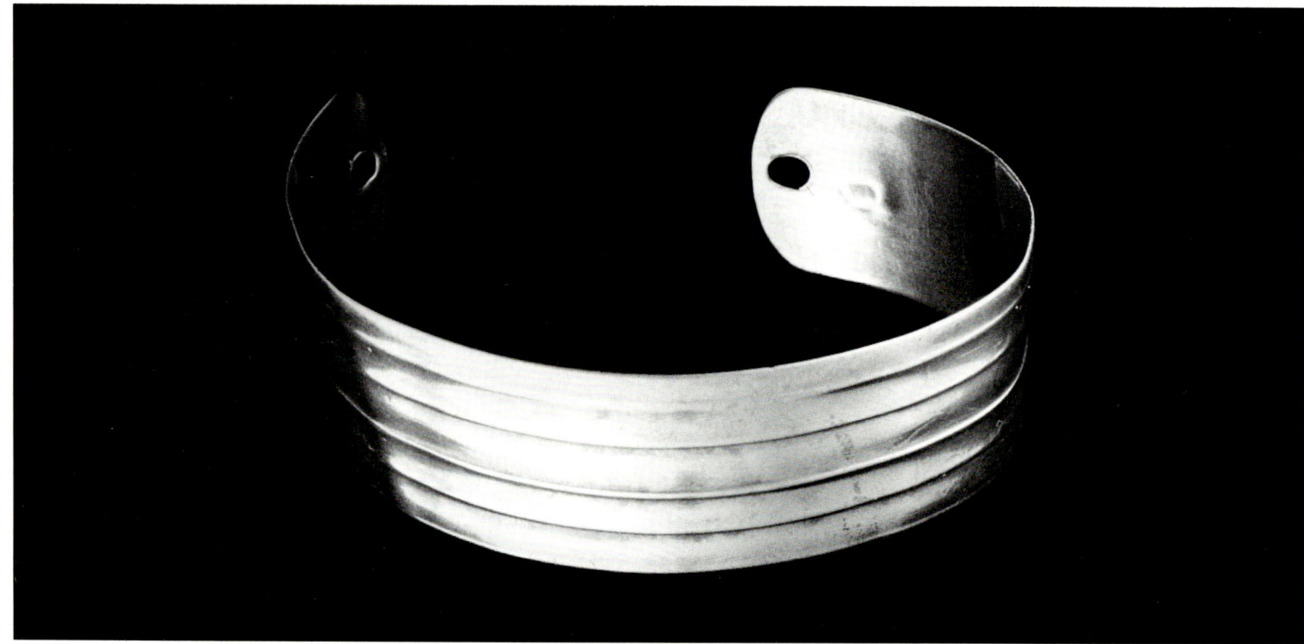

183/Cradleboard Cover
MARK: PH MONTREAL
MAKER: Pierre Huguet *dit* Latour, Sr. or Jr. (Montreal, 1771–1829)
SIZE: 30.5 cm h. × 36.8 cm w.
COLL.: NMM (III-L-196)

186/Star Brooch
MARK: None
MAKER: Unknown
SIZE: 5.1 cm diam.
COLL.: NMM (III-I-805)

184/Cradle Shade
MATERIALS: Wool and silk ribbons, beadwork, silver brooches and appliqués
DATE: Late 19th century
SIZE: 58.5 cm l. × 45.5 cm w. (w/o ribbons)
COLL.: McCord

185/Round Brooch
MARK: None
MAKER: Unknown
SIZE: 2 cm diam.
COLL.: NMM (III-I-866)

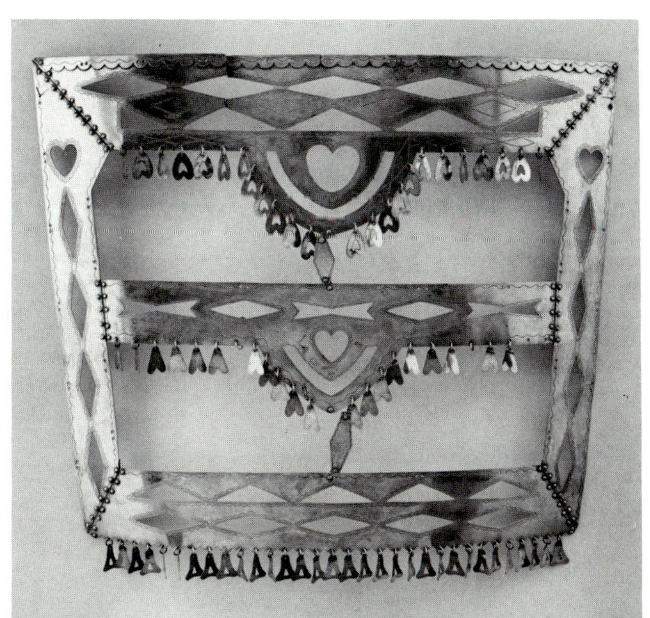

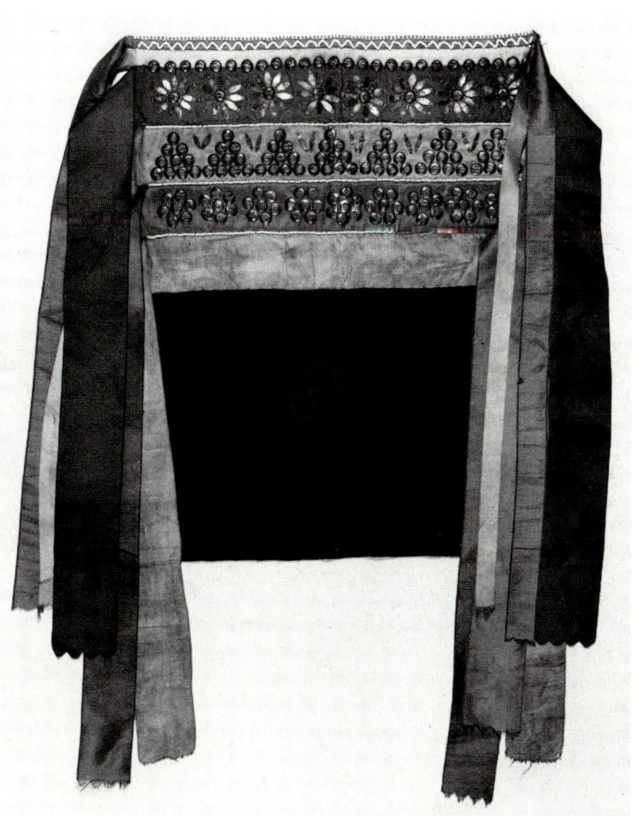

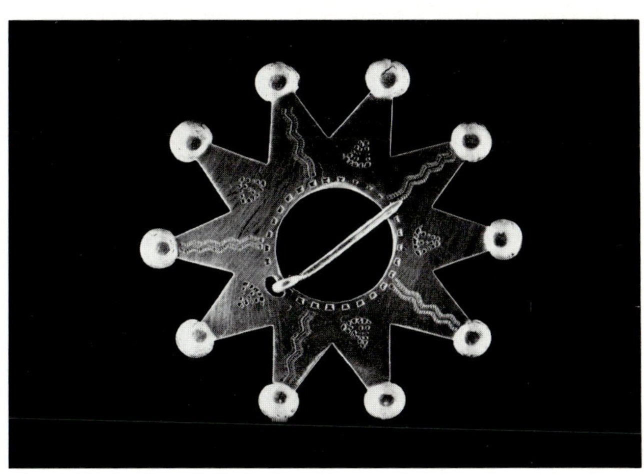

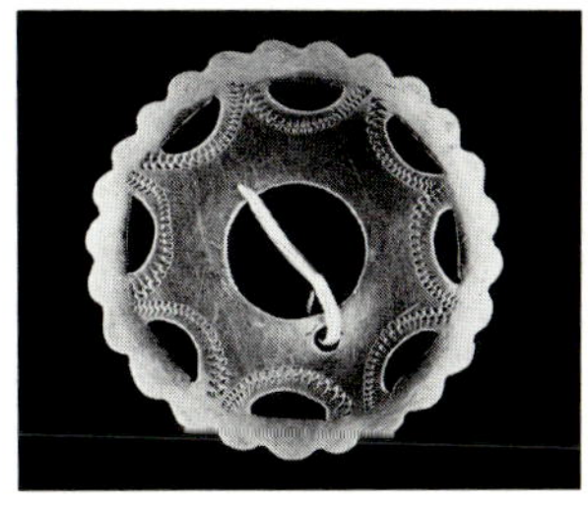

187/Pendant
MARK: None
MAKER: Unknown
SIZE: 11.2 cm h. × 3.2 cm w.
COLL.: Parks (16R-7G3-2)

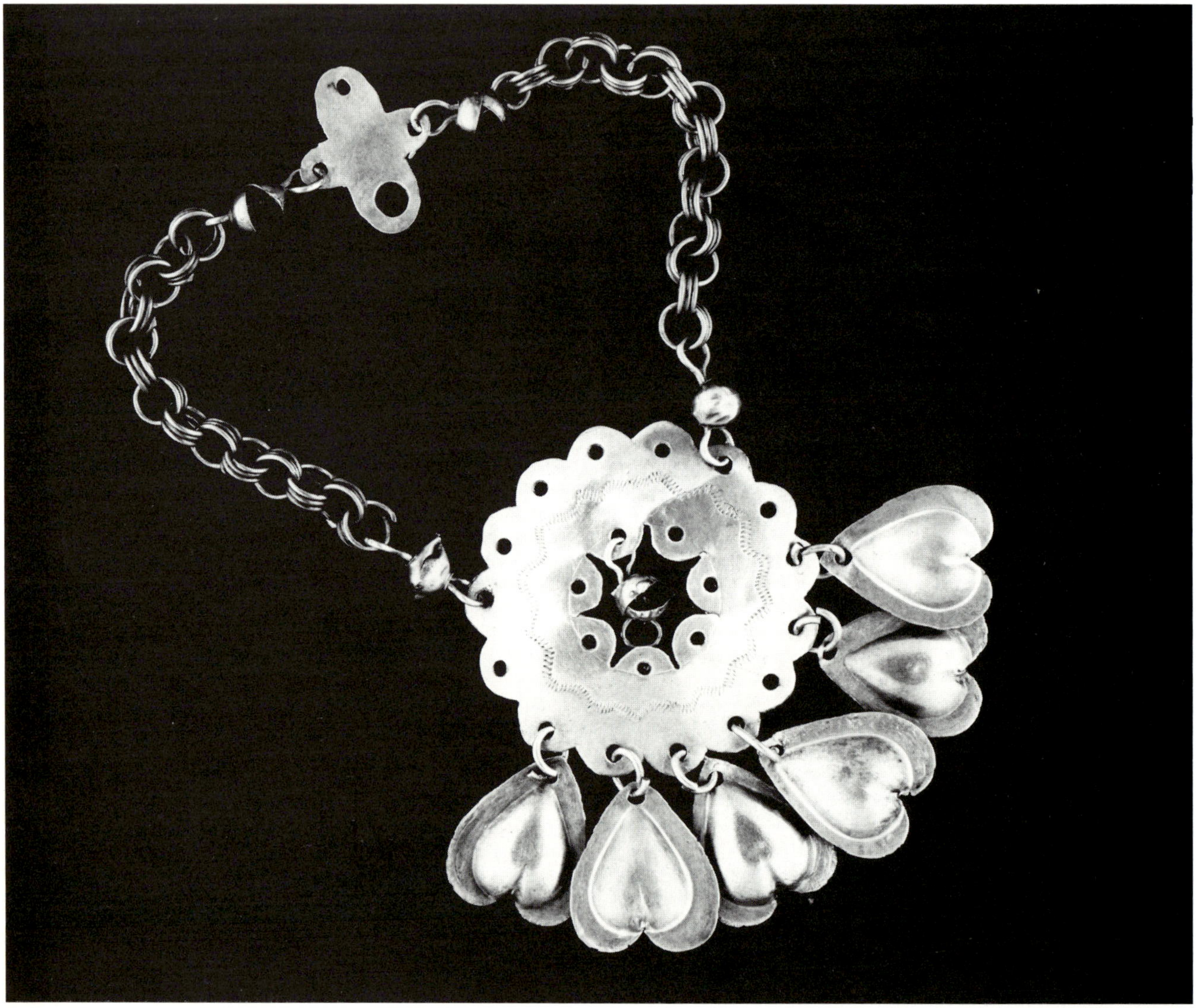

XII / MODERN IROQUOIS SILVERSMITHS

Arthur Powless, an Onondaga living on the Six Nations Reserve in southern Ontario, is one of several Iroquois silversmiths who have revived the art of making trade silver. He fashions a variety of brooches, pendants and rings in the familiar heart, star and Masonic patterns. But, in addition to these copies and adaptations of traditional forms, modern Iroquois silversmiths also make pieces in their own original designs.

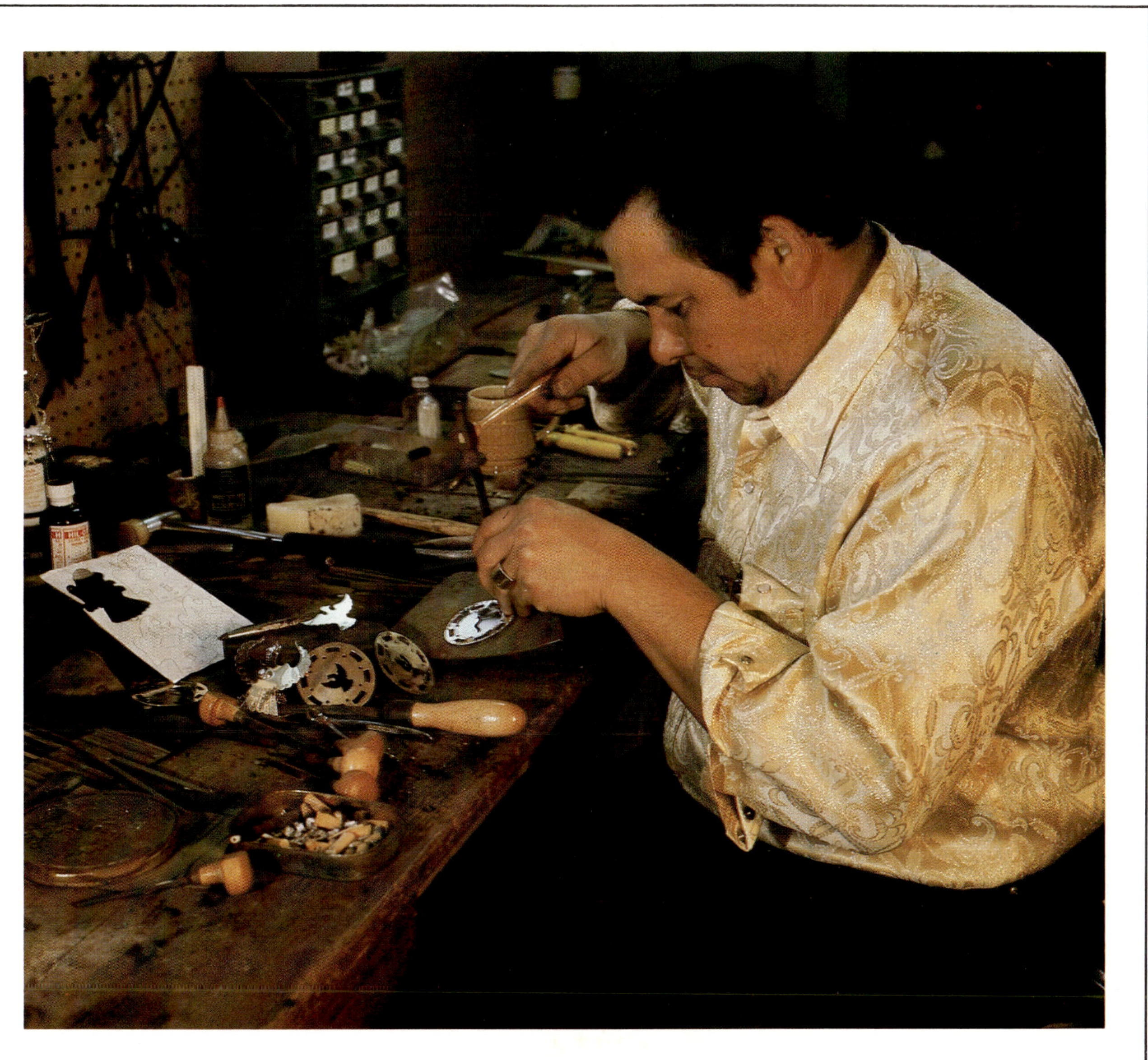

188/Pair of Armbands (modern)
MARK: Eel
MAKER: Arthur Powless (Ohsweken, Ont.)
SIZE: 28.3 cm l. × 6.4 cm w.
COLL.: NMM (III-I-1532a, b)

189/Heart Pendant (modern)
MARK: Eel
MAKER: Arthur Powless (Ohsweken, Ont.)
SIZE: 2.7 cm h. × 2.0 cm w.
COLL.: NMM (III-I-1538)

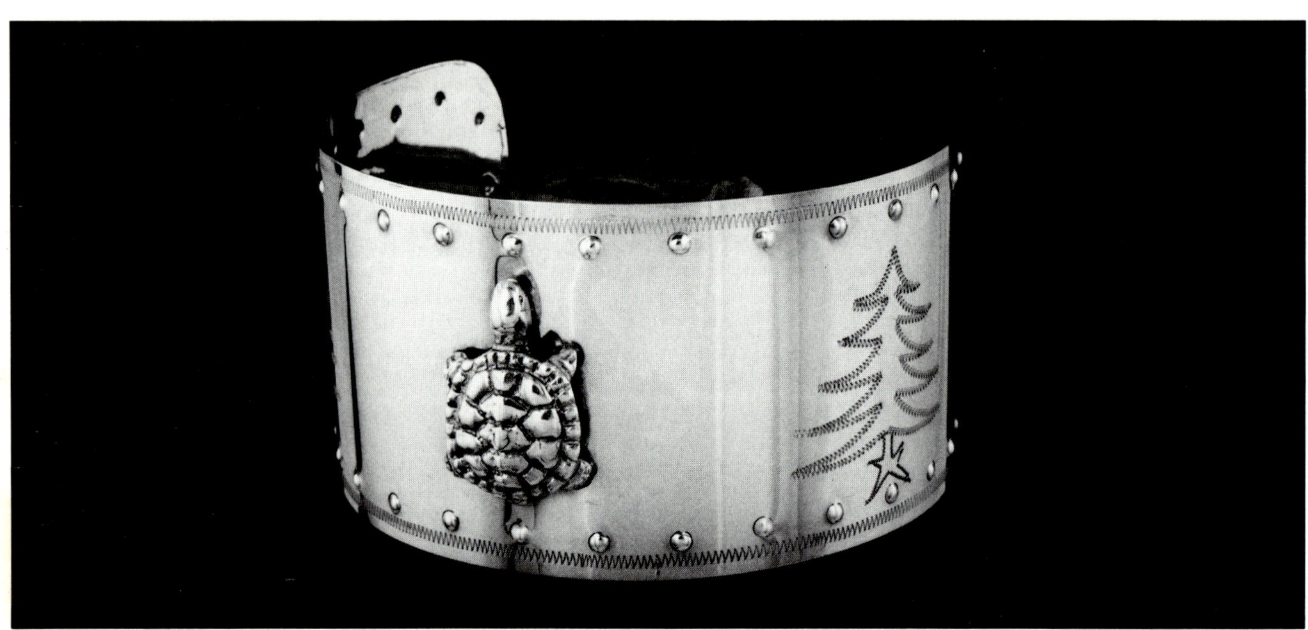

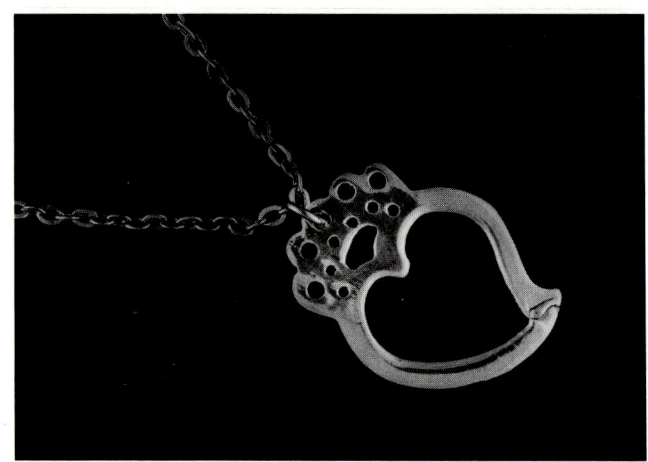

190/Heart Pendant (modern)
MARK: Eel
MAKER: Arthur Powless (Ohsweken, Ont.)
SIZE: 3 cm h. × 2 cm w.
COLL.: NMM (III-I-1539)

191/Council Fire Pendant (modern)
MARK: Eel
MAKER: Arthur Powless (Ohsweken, Ont.)
SIZE: 4.8 cm h. × 4.0 cm w.
COLL.: NMM (III-I-1536)

192/Council Fire Pendant (modern)
MARK: Eel
MAKER: Arthur Powless (Ohsweken, Ont.)
SIZE: 4.1 cm h. × 3.5 cm w.
COLL.: NMM (III-I-1537)

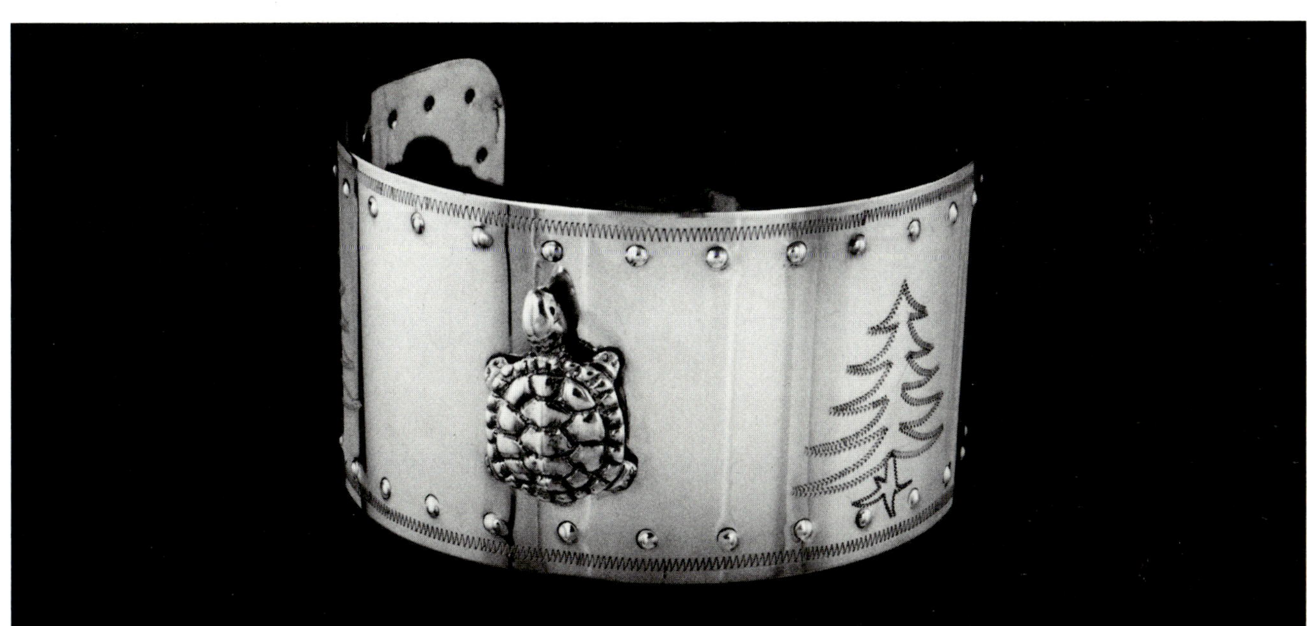

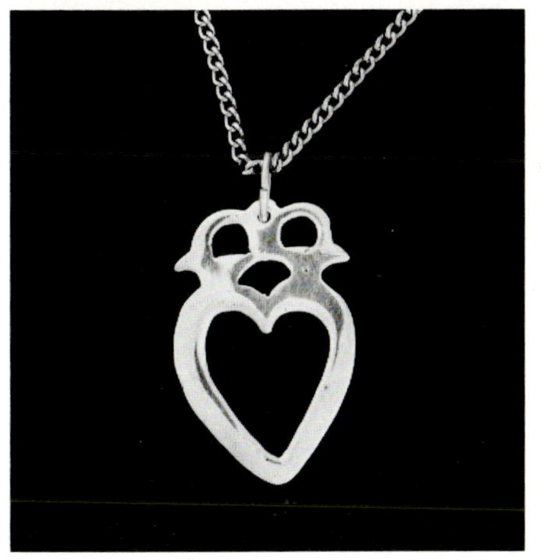

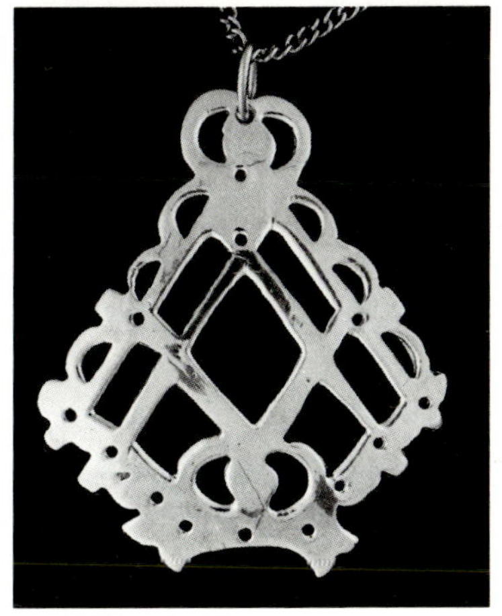

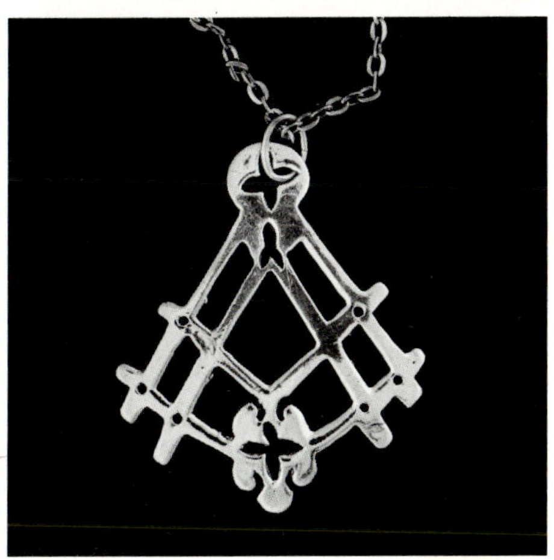

193/Ear-Wheel Pendant (modern)
MARK: Three cattails
MAKER: Anthony Green (Caledonia, Ont.)
SIZE: 6.2 cm diam.
COLL.: NMM (III-I-1535)

194/Turtle Pendant (modern)
MARK: Eel
MAKER: Arthur Powless (Ohsweken, Ont.)
SIZE: 4.0 cm h. × 2.7 cm w.
COLL.: NMM (III-I-1533)

195/Beaver Earrings (modern)
MARK: Canoe
MAKER: Elwood Green (Caledonia, Ont.)
SIZE: 4 cm l.
COLL.: NMM (NL-C-Z-F-24)

196/Turtle Stickpin (modern)
MARK: Canoe
MAKER: Elwood Green (Caledonia, Ont.)
SIZE: 8.0 cm l. × 1.3 cm w.
COLL.: NMM (NL-C-Z-F-25)

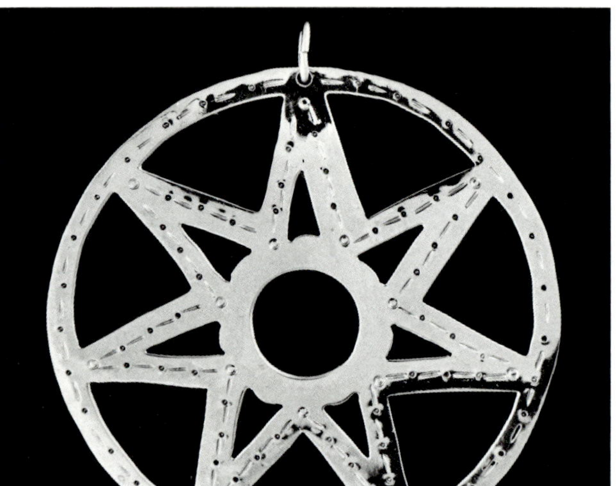

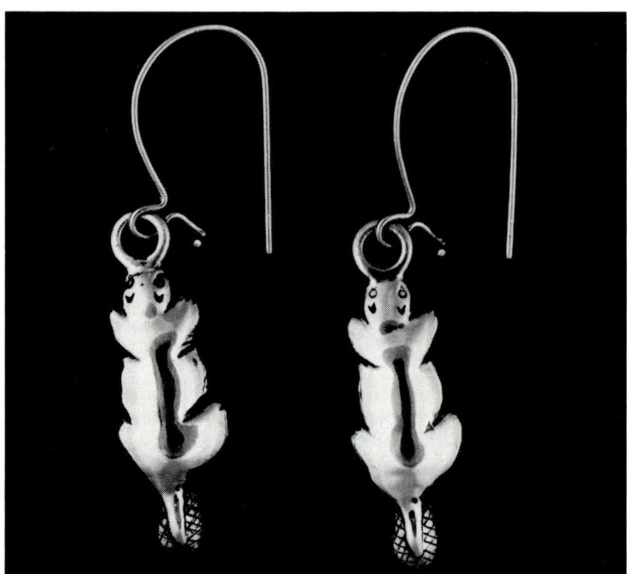

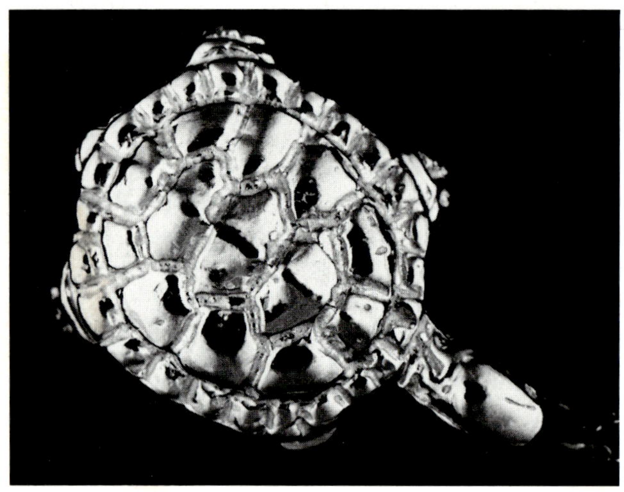

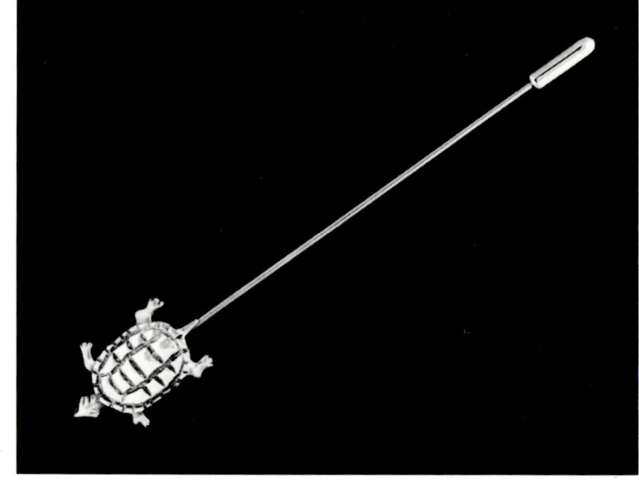

197/"Kissing Otters" Ring (modern)
MARK: Canoe
MAKER: Elwood Green (Caledonia, Ont.)
SIZE: Boss, 2.0 cm h. × 1.5 cm w.
COLL.: NMM (NL-C-Z-F-26)

198/Beaver Ring (modern)
MARK: Canoe
MAKER: Elwood Green (Caledonia, Ont.)
SIZE: Boss, 2 cm diam.
COLL.: NMM (NL-C-Z-F-27)

199/Silver Cornhusk Doll (modern)
MARK: Eel
MAKER: Arthur Powless (Ohsweken, Ont.)
SIZE: 5.5 cm h. × 4.0 cm w.
COLL.: NMM (NL-C-Z-F-28)

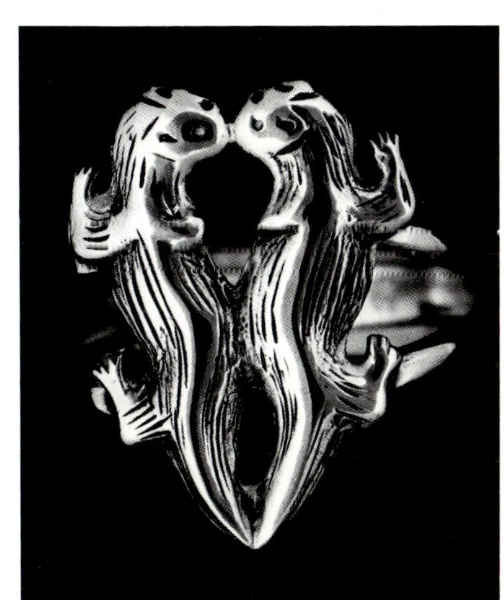

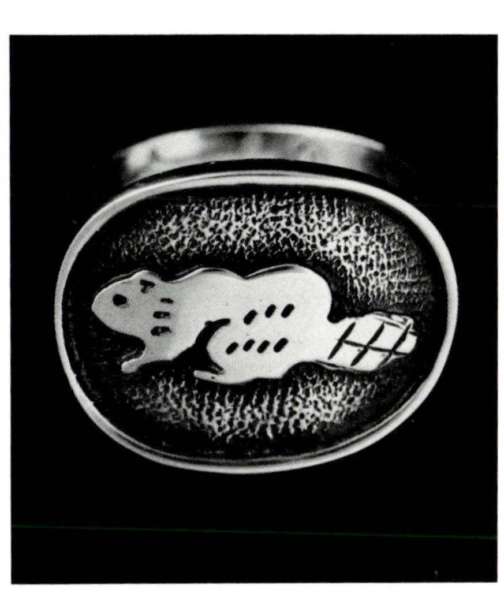

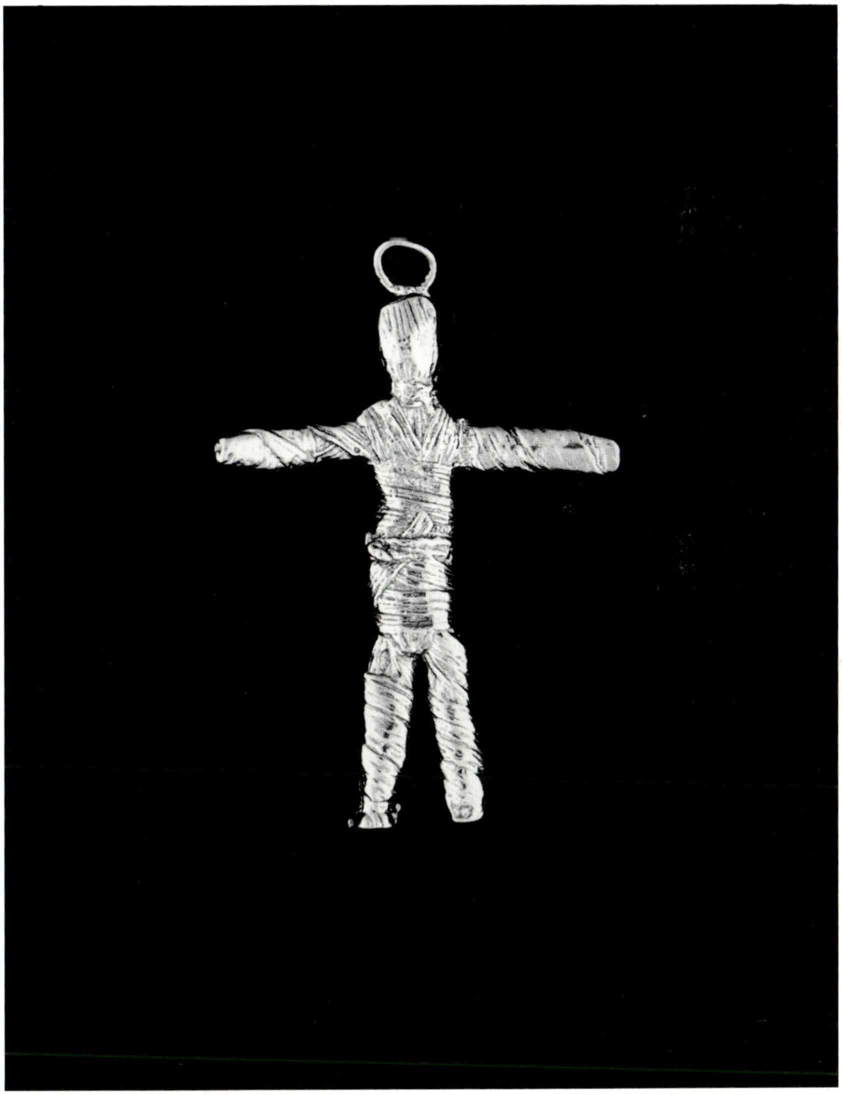

200/Weeping-Heart Pendant (modern)
MARK: Eel
MAKER: Arthur Powless (Ohsweken, Ont.)
SIZE: 3 cm h. × 2 cm w.
COLL.: NMM (NL-C-Z-F-29)

201/Star Brooch (modern)
MARK: Eel
MAKER: Arthur Powless (Ohsweken, Ont.)
SIZE: 7.5 cm diam.
COLL.: NMM (NL-C-Z-F-32)

202/Round "Four Winds" Pendant (modern)
MARK: Eel
MAKER: Arthur Powless (Ohsweken, Ont.)
SIZE: 2.7 cm diam.
COLL.: NMM (NL-C-Z-F-14)

203/Crescent Gorget (modern)
MARK: Canoe
MAKER: Elwood Green (Caledonia, Ont.)
SIZE: 11 cm w. × 3 cm h.
COLL.: NMM (NL-C-Z-F-33)

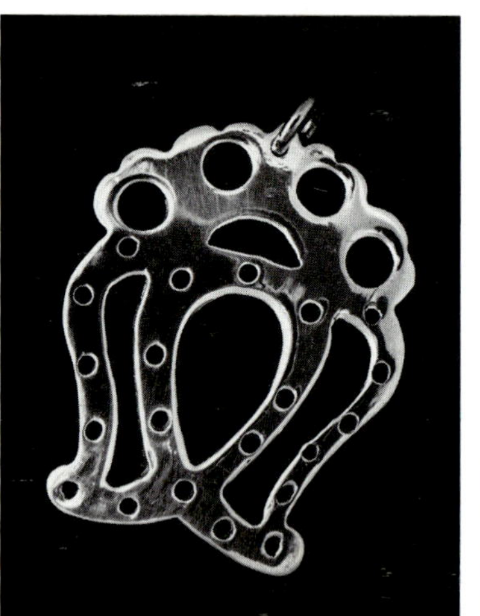

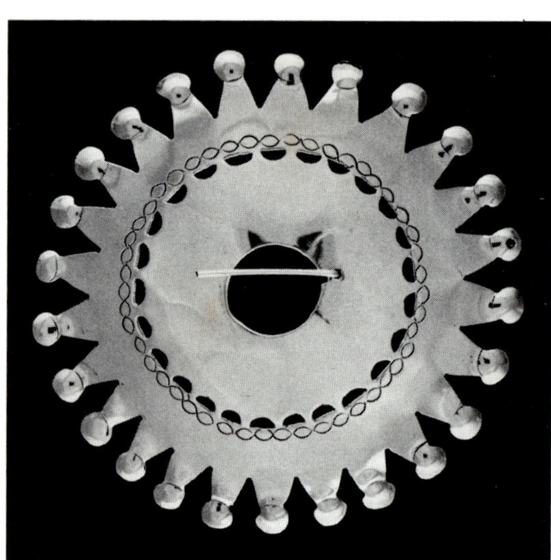

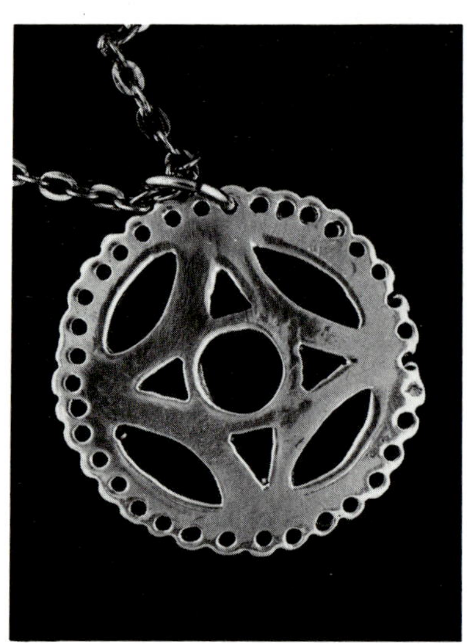

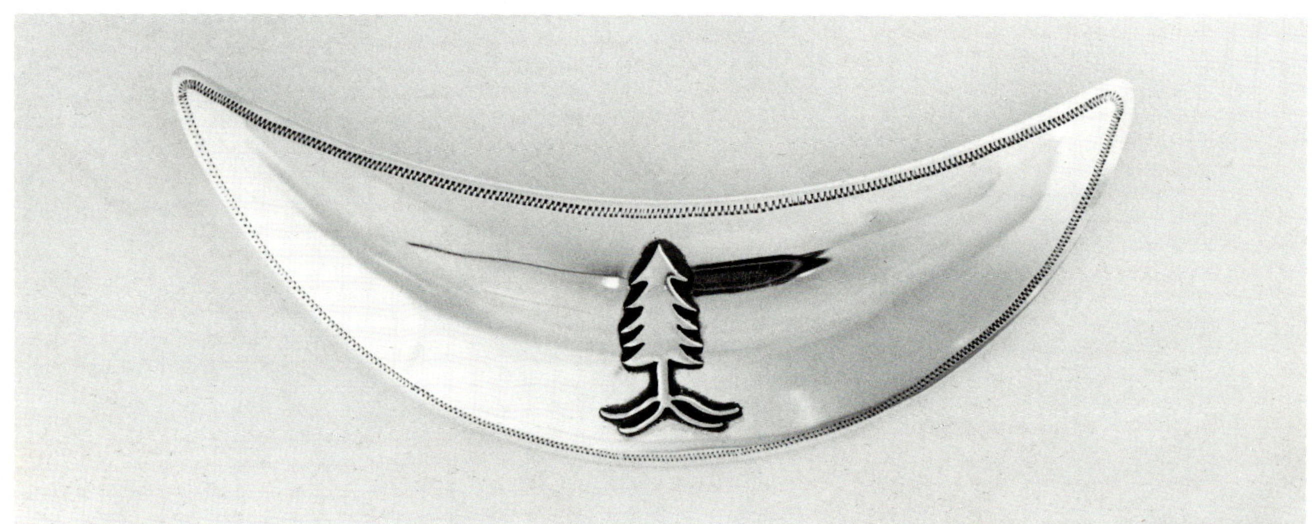

204/Star Brooch
(modern)
MARK: Canoe
MAKER: Elwood Green
(Caledonia, Ont.)
SIZE: 4.5 cm diam.
COLL.: NMM (NL-C-Z-F-34)

205/Brooch with Leaf Motif
(modern)
MARK: Canoe
MAKER: Elwood Green
(Caledonia, Ont.)
SIZE: 6 cm diam.
COLL.: NMM (NL-C-Z-F-35)

206/Round Brooch
(modern)
MARK: Canoe
MAKER: Elwood Green
(Caledonia, Ont.)
SIZE: 3.5 cm diam.
COLL.: NMM (NL-C-Z-F-36)

207/Clan Pendant
(modern)
MARK: Eel
MAKER: Arthur Powless
(Ohsweken, Ont.)
SIZE: 6.2 cm diam.
COLL.: NMM (NL-C-Z-F-31)

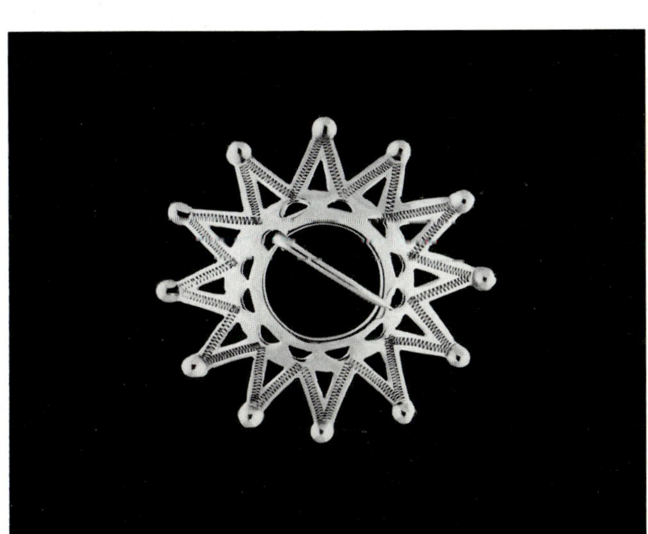

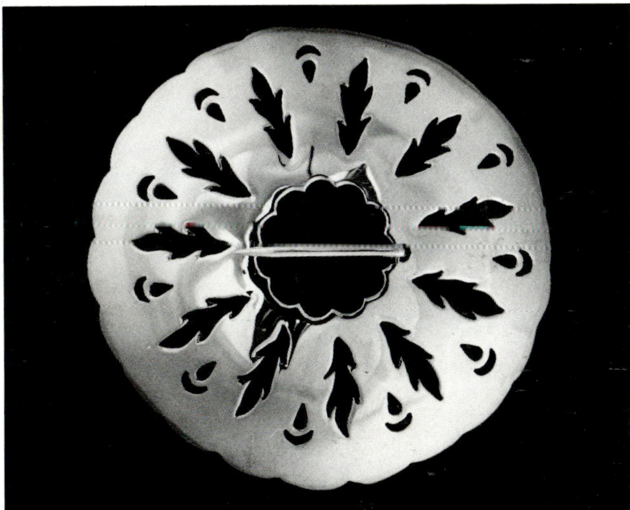

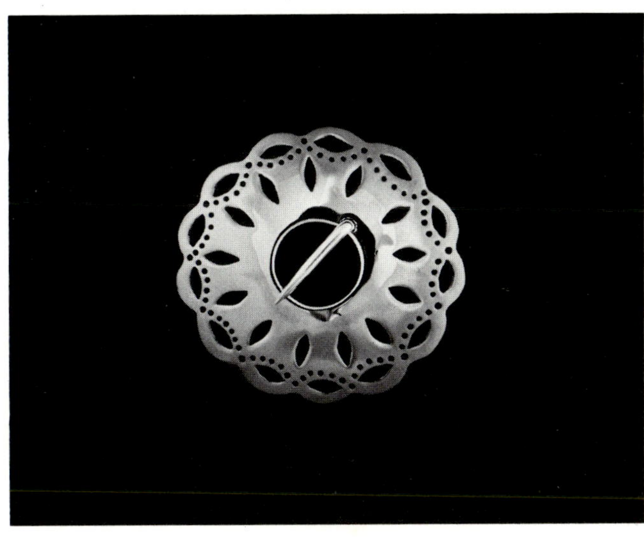

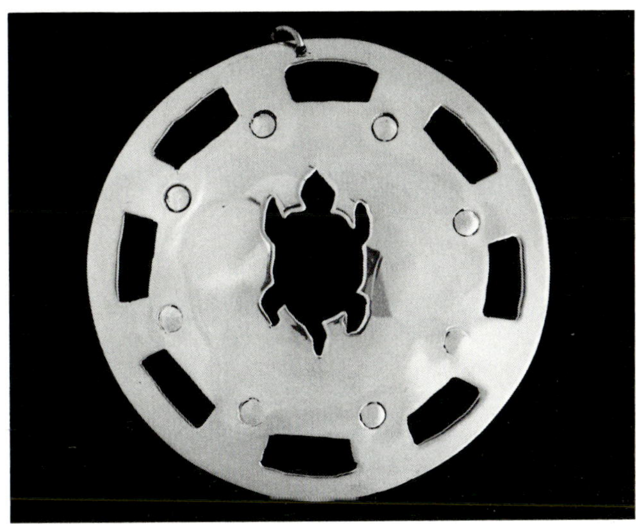

208/Double-Heart Brooch with Bird Heads (modern)
MARK: 3 cattails
MAKER: Anthony Green (Caledonia, Ont.)
SIZE: 5 cm h. × 4 cm w.
COLL.: NMM (NL-C-Z-F-17)

209/Double-Heart Pendant (modern)
MARK: Eel
MAKER: Arthur Powless (Ohsweken, Ont.)
SIZE: 3.0 cm h. × 3.2 cm w.
COLL.: NMM (NL-C-Z-F-30)

210/Double-Heart Pendant with Bird Heads (modern)
MARK: AG
MAKER: Anthony Green (Caledonia, Ont.)
SIZE: 8 cm h. × 6 cm w.
COLL.: NMM (III-I-1534)

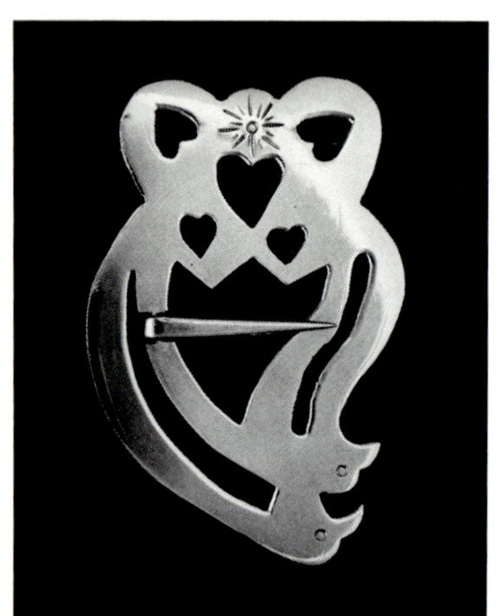

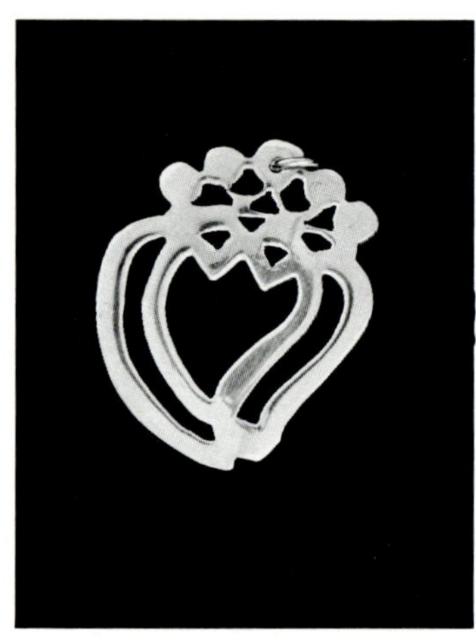

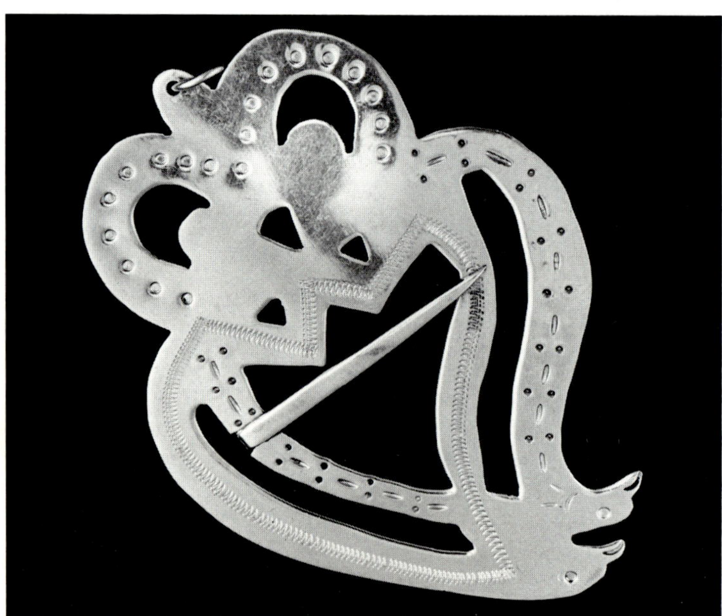

BIBLIOGRAPHY

Published source materials for a study of fur trade silver in North America are rare. Moreover, those that exist are not readily available in most library collections.

Before the first studies of Indian trade silver were published in the 1930s and 40s, little was known of the origin or significance of the artifacts, and early theories attributed all silver manufacture to the Iroquois and other Indians, and dated them to the early eighteenth century. The publications of Marius Barbeau, a National Museum of Canada anthropologist, and Ramsay Traquair, a specialist in Quebec silversmithing, were the first to suggest the European origins of the silver. Since then, several other articles and books have appeared, although the body of literature is not large. The following selection includes the most important publications on the subject to date.

Alberts, Robert C.
"Trade Silver and Indian Silver Work in the Great Lakes Region". *Wisconsin Archeologist,* vol. 34, no. 1, pp. 1–121.

Barbeau, Marius
"Indian Silversmiths on the Pacific Coast". *Proceedings and Transactions of the Royal Society of Canada,* ser. 3, vol. 33, sec. 2 (1939), pp. 23–8.

"Indian Trade Silver". *Proceedings and Transactions of the Royal Society of Canada,* ser. 3, vol. 34, sec. 2 (1940) pp. 27–41.

"Old Canadian Silver". *Canadian Geographical Journal,* vol. 22, no. 3 (Mar. 1941), pp. 150–62.

Harrington, M.R.
"Iroquois Silverwork". *Anthropological Papers of the American Museum of Natural History,* vol. 1, pt. 6 (1908), pp. 351–69, pls. 23–9.

Jester, Margo
"Peace Medals". *American Indian Tradition,* vol. 7, no. 5 (1961), pp. 149–57.

McLachlan, R.W.
"Medals Awarded to Canadian Indians". *Canadian Antiquarian and Numismatic Journal,* ser. 3, vol. 2, no. 1 (Jan. 1899), pp. 1–14; no. 2 (Apr. 1899), pp. 93–6.

Parker, Arthur C.
"The Origins of Iroquois Silversmithing". *American Anthropologist,* n.s., vol. 12, no. 3 (July–Sept. 1910), pp. 349–57.

Traquair, Ramsay
"Montreal and the Indian Trade Silver". *Canadian Historical Review,* vol. 19, no. 1 (Mar. 1938), pp. 1–8.

The Old Silver of Quebec. Published under the auspices of the Art Association of Montreal. Toronto: Macmillan, 1940.

Woodward, Arthur
"Highlights on Indian Trade Silver". *The Magazine Antiques,* vol. 47, no. 6 (June 1945), pp. 328–31.

"Indian Use of the Silver Gorget". *Indian Notes,* vol. 3, no. 4 (Oct. 1926), pp. 232–49.

To understand the significance of trade silver in the context of the fur trade and the culture of North American Indians, several interpretive works would be helpful. The following books and articles contribute to a wider general knowledge of the period, although they rarely deal directly with the use of silver in trade.

Bolus, Malvina
"Four Kings Came to Dinner with Their Honours", *The Beaver,* Outfit 304:2 (Autumn 1973), pp. 4–11.

Jacobs, Wilbur R.
Wilderness Politics and Indian Gifts: The Northern Colonial Frontier, 1748–63. Lincoln: University of Nebraska Press, 1966. Previously published as *Diplomacy and Indian Gifts.* Stanford, Calif.: Stanford University Press, 1950.

Johnson, William
The Papers of Sir William Johnson. 14 vols. Albany, N.Y.: University of the State of New York, 1921–65.

Meyer, David
"The Red Deer River Grave: an Historical Burial". *Napao,* vol. 4, no. 1 (July 1973), pp. 2–28.

Quimby, George Irving
Indian Culture and European Trade Goods. Madison: University of Wisconsin Press, 1966.

Rotstein, Abraham
"Trade and Politics: an Institutional Approach". *Western Canadian Journal of Anthropology,* vol. 3, no. 1 (1972), pp. 1–28.

Saum, Lewis O.
The Fur Trader and the Indian. Seattle: University of Washington Press, 1965.

Washburn, Wilcomb E.
"Symbol, Utility, and Aesthetics in the Indian Fur Trade". In *Aspects of the Fur Trade: Selected Papers of the 1965 North American Fur Trade Conference.* St. Paul: Minnesota Historical Society, 1967, pp. 50–4; also published in *Minnesota History,* vol. 40, no. 4 (Winter 1966), pp. 198–202.

Washburn, Wilcomb E., ed.
The Indian and the White Man. Documents in American Civilization Series. New York: New York University Press; Garden City, N.Y.: Anchor Books, 1964.

In recent years, several important publications have appeared on the subject of the Canadian silversmith and his role in Canadian history. These are helpful in providing a better understanding of the silversmiths' backgrounds and the scope of their professional work, as well as an appreciation of the significance of silver itself in early North America.

Langdon, John E.
Canadian Silversmiths 1700–1900. Toronto: Stinehour Press, 1966.

Guide to Marks on Early Canadian Silver, 18th and 19th Centuries. Toronto: Ryerson Press, 1968.

"Silversmithing in Canada during the French Colonial Period". In *Winterthur Conference Report, 14th, 1968: Spanish, French and English Traditions in the Colonial Silver of North America.* Winterthur, Del.: Henry Francis du Pont Winterthur Museum, 1969, pp. 47–64.

Massicotte, E. Z.
"L'argentier Huguet-Latour". *Bulletin des Recherches historiques,* vol. 46, no. 9 (Sept. 1940), pp. 284–7.

Piers, Harry
Master Goldsmiths and Silversmiths of Nova Scotia and Their Marks. Halifax: Antiquarian Club, 1948.

Trudel, Jean
Silver in New France. Ottawa: National Gallery of Canada, 1974.

ILLUSTRATION CREDITS

ESSAY SECTION

1 Re-strike of the original copper plate engraved in 1770. Courtesy New York Historical Society.

2 Lithograph, 1825, after a painting by Edward Chatfield. Photograph courtesy Public Archives of Canada, Ottawa (C-38948).

3 Coll.: National Museum of Man, Ottawa. Photograph by Richard Garner.

4 Courtesy Public Archives of Canada, National Medal Collection, Ottawa. Photograph by Richard Garner.

5 Courtesy State Historical Society of Wisconsin, Madison.

6 *Left:* courtesy American Numismatic Society, New York. *Right:* courtesy Public Archives of Canada, National Medal Collection, Ottawa. Photographs by Richard Garner.

7 Courtesy Library of Congress, Washington, D.C.

8 Courtesy Public Archives of Canada, National Medal Collection, Ottawa. Photograph by Richard Garner.

9 From a daguerreotype taken in 1836. Courtesy Public Archives of Canada, National Medal Collection, Ottawa (C-8543).

10 *Top:* courtesy Public Archives of Canada, National Medal Collection, Ottawa. *Bottom:* courtesy American Numismatic Society, New York. Photograph by Richard Garner.

11 Courtesy Museum of the American Indian, Heye Foundation, New York. Photograph by Richard Garner.

12 *Top and bottom:* collection of National Museum of Man, Ottawa. *Centre:* courtesy Museum of the American Indian, Heye Foundation, New York. Photographs by Richard Garner.

13 Courtesy Museum of the American Indian, Heye Foundation, New York. Photograph by Richard Garner.

14 Reprinted, by permission of the author, from John E. Langdon, *Canadian Silversmiths, 1700–1900* (Toronto, 1966), pl. 3.

15 Photographs by Richard Garner.

16 Reproduced from the J.B. Blondeau Account Book, 1777–89, fol. 80. Courtesy McCord Museum, Montreal.

17 Coll.: National Museum of Man, Ottawa. Photograph by Richard Garner.

18 National Museums of Canada, Ottawa.

19 Illustration by Rogers for G.D. Warburton, *The Conquest of Canada,* 2d ed. (London, 1850), vol. 2, pt. 2, after p. 446. Photograph courtesy Public Archives of Canada, Ottawa (C-16859).

20 Extracted from *The Papers of Sir William Johnson,* vol. 2 (Albany, N.Y.: University of the State of New York, 1922), pp. 990–91.

21 Coll.: National Museum of Man, Ottawa. Photograph by Richard Garner.

22 Illustration for Peter Jones, *History of the Ojibway Indians* (London, 1861), facing p. 95.

23 Courtesy Royal Ontario Museum, Toronto.

24 *Centre:* courtesy National Gallery of Canada, Henry Birks Collection of Canadian Silver, Ottawa. *Clockwise from top left:* collection of National Museum of Man, Ottawa *(first two)*; courtesy Museum of the American Indian, Heye Foundation, New York *(next three)*; collection of National Museum of Man, Ottawa. Photograph by Richard Garner.

25 *Left and top:* collection of National Museum of Man, Ottawa. *Right:* courtesy Museum of the American Indian, Heye Foundation, New York. *Bottom:* courtesy Ottawa Masonic Corporation, Ottawa. Photograph by Richard Garner.

26 Courtesy Cable G. Ball, Tippecanoe County Historical Association, Lafayette, Ind.

27 Oil on paper by Paul Kane, 1846. Courtesy Stark Museum of Art, Orange, Texas.

28 Etching by Mrs. John Graves Simcoe. Courtesy Archives of Ontario, Toronto.

29 Oil on canvas by George Catlin, 1830–39. Courtesy National Collection of Fine Arts, Smithsonian Institution, Washington, D.C.

30 Lithograph by J.O. Lewis, c. 1835. Courtesy Amon Carter Museum, Fort Worth, Texas.

31 Coll.: National Museum of Man, Ottawa. Photograph by Richard Garner.

32 *Two crosses at left:* collection of National Museum of Man, Ottawa. *Large cross:* courtesy McCord Museum, Montreal. *Earrings:* courtesy University of Saskatchewan, Saskatoon. Photograph by Richard Garner.

33 Courtesy Museum of the American Indian, Heye Foundation, New York. Photograph by Richard Garner.

34 *Gorget:* courtesy McCord Museum, Montreal. *Cross:* courtesy Museum of the American Indian, Heye Foundation, New York. Photographs by Richard Garner.

35 Courtesy Museum of the American Indian, Heye Foundation, New York.

36 Courtesy Museum of the American Indian, Heye Foundation, New York.

37 Coll.: National Museum of Man, Ottawa. Photograph by Richard Garner.

38 Coll.: National Museum of Man, Ottawa. Photograph by Richard Garner.

39 Coll.: National Museum of Man, Ottawa. Photographs by Richard Garner.

CATALOGUE SECTION

All photographs by Richard Garner except for numbers 6, 98 and 99, which were obtained from the National Museum of Antiquities of Scotland, Edinburgh.

COLOUR PLATES

I *Commemoration of the Reception of Robert Symes as Honorary Chief of the Huron Tribes at Lorette,* oil on canvas, 1838–9. Courtesy Château Ramezay, Montreal.

II Watercolour, 1827. Courtesy Thomas Gilcrease Institute of American History and Art, Tulsa, Okla.

III *Captain W. Andrew Bulger Saying Farewell at Fort MacKay, Prairie du Chien, Wisconsin, 1815,* ink and watercolour, c. 1823. Courtesy Amon Carter Museum, Fort Worth, Texas.

IV Photograph by Richard Garner.

V Coll.: National Museum of Man, Ottawa. Photograph by Richard Garner.

VI Oil on paper, c. 1840. Courtesy Château Ramezay, Montreal.

VII *Two Ottawa Chiefs, Who with Others Lately Came Down from Michillimachinac, Lake Huron, to Have a Talk with Their Great Father, the King, or His Representative,* by Sir Joshua Jebb, watercolour, 1813–20. Courtesy Peabody Museum of Archaeology and Ethnology, Harvard University, Cambridge, Mass.

VIII *Pocahantas and Son*, by an unknown artist. Courtesy Mrs. Sylvia Stevenson, Edinburgh. (Pocahantas is unlikely to have posed for this portrait as she lived a century before trade silver was prevalent in North America.)

IX *Mani-Tow-Wa-Bay (He-Devil), Ojibway Chief*, oil on paper, 1846. Courtesy Glenbow Museum, Calgary.

X *Portrait of Joseph Brant*, by George Romney, oil on canvas, c. 1776. Courtesy National Gallery of Canada, Ottawa.

XI *Ju-Ah-Kis-Gaw (Ojibwa Woman with Child in Cradle)*, oil on canvas, 1834. Courtesy National Collection of Fine Arts, Smithsonian Insitution, Washington, D.C.

XII National Film Board, Ottawa.

Index

The artifacts in the exhibition have not been indexed.

Numbers in italics refer to illustration captions.